THE RELIGIOUS
RIGHT

A Reference Handbook

THE RELIGIOUS
RIGHT

A Reference Handbook

Glenn H. Utter
and
John W. Storey

CONTEMPORARY
WORLD ISSUES

ABC-CLIO

Santa Barbara, California
Denver, Colorado
Oxford, England

Copyright © 1995 by Glenn H. Utter and John W. Storey

All rights reserved. No part of this publication may be reproduced, stored in a retrieval system, or transmitted, in any form or by any means, electronic, mechanical, photocopying, recording, or otherwise, except for the inclusion of brief quotations in a review, without prior permission in writing from the publishers.

Library of Congress Cataloging-in-Publication Data

Utter, Glenn H.
   The religious right : a reference handbook / Glenn H. Utter and John W. Storey.
      p.   cm.—(Contemporary world issues)
   Includes bibliographical references and index.
      1. Conservatism—Religious aspects—Christianity—History—20th century.   2. Conservatism—Religious aspects—Christianity— History—20th century—Study and teaching.   3. Christianity and politics—History—20th century.   4. Christianity and politics— History —20th century—Study and teaching.   5. United States— Politics and government—20th century.   6. United States—Politics and government—20th century—Study and teaching.
      7. Evangelicalism—United States—History—20th century.   8. United States—Church history—20th century.   9. United States—Church history—20th century—Study and teaching. [1. Evangelicalism— United States—History—20th—Study and teaching.]   I. Storey, John W.   II. Title.   III. Series.
BR526.S76   1995
277.3′0825—dc20   95-44344
                                                                   CIP

ISBN 0-87436-778-6

0   01 00 99 98 97 96 95   10 9 8 7 6 5 4 3 2 1

ABC-CLIO, Inc.
130 Cremona Drive, P.O. Box 1911
Santa Barbara, California 93116-1911

This book is printed on acid-free paper ∞.

Manufactured in the United States of America

For our parents

Contents

Preface

In 1930 the eminent philosopher Ludwig Wittgenstein remarked in a foreword that he would like to say, "This book is written to the glory of God." But he thought better of it, fearing that readers of the time would misunderstand his intent, that he had written not out of pride and vanity but good will. A reference to the glory of God at one time would have been appropriate, perhaps even expected. That Wittgenstein thought the purpose of his expression would be lost on a large portion of the population of the 1930s attested to the trend toward secularization, a trend that disturbs many Americans today, large majorities of whom have consistently expressed a belief in God. In weighing the potential for success of the contemporary religious right, the ongoing effects of secularization must be kept in mind.

Terms such as "religious right" and "Christian right" are difficult to pin down largely because they encompass groups of considerable diversity, ranging from mainline and evangelical Protestants to conservative Jews and Catholics. Religious right has generally been the expression of choice for the authors, as it is somewhat more inclusive than Christian right. This latter phrase makes it impossible to include Jews, for instance, some of whom have identified with Christian conservatives on various issues. Another problem arises with regard to "evangelical." Specifically, who are the evangelicals, and are they all on the political right? To answer the second half of the question first: no, evangelicals are to be found on both sides of the political spectrum. The Sojourners offer a case in point. Theological conservatism notwithstanding, this group is on the left with regard to matters such as poverty and nuclear disarmament. It looks at issues from the vantage point of those at the bottom of society. African American evangelicals likewise often join the left in debates over civil rights and other concerns.

"Evangelical" is almost as elusive a term as religious right. Theologically, an evangelical is one who claims a personal relationship with Jesus based upon a "born again" experience, accepts the authority of the Bible in matters of faith and practice, and spreads the gospel through evangelism. Since the early 1800s most American Protestants, save Episcopalians, have been evangelicals. Historically, the term is derived from the Greek *evangelion*, meaning "good news," and it was applied in the sixteenth century to Lutherans in Germany; in the eighteenth century to those Anglicans who introduced hymn singing, Sunday schools, and missionary societies; in the late nineteenth and early twentieth centuries to those American Protestants who were dubbed fundamentalists; in the early twentieth century to Pentecostals in America; and since the 1940s to conservative American Protestants who wish to be differentiated from fundamentalists. In this last sense, the difference is more a matter of temperament than theology. Jerry Falwell is a fundamentalist; Billy Graham is an evangelical. Although in this book we frequently use evangelical as a catchall for all conservative Protestants, we just as frequently distinguish between mainline bodies, such as Presbyterians, Methodists, Episcopalians, and Disciples of Christ, and evangelical groups, such as Southern Baptists, Assemblies of God, Missouri Synod Lutherans, and Churches of Christ.

Individuals such as J. Gresham Machen and Cyrus Scofield have been included in this study because they provide continuity, showing that various facets of the contemporary religious right have roots in the nineteenth century. The premillennialism of Jerry Falwell can be seen in John Nelson Darby, for instance, and Francis Schaeffer's repudiation of secular humanism bears similarities to Machen's earlier condemnation of liberalism. Otherwise, this study deals only with individuals and organizations on the religious right since World War II that have endeavored to influence public policy through the political process. Thus, we treat the religious right as an essentially political movement that courts voters for "moral" candidates, lobbies Congress on everything from public school prayer to abortion, and joins religious conservatives in judicial proceedings involving home schooling, sex education, and textbooks. Accordingly, the focus is upon people such as Billy James Hargis, who fashioned the Christian Crusade, and Pat Robertson, founder of the Christian Coalition.

Alexis de Tocqueville, that observant Frenchman who traveled America during the presidency of Andrew Jackson, was impressed by this country's separation of church and state. Indeed, he noted that the American clergy prided itself on aloofness from politics. This stance was wise, he thought, for in nations such as his own, where the flag and the cross were allies, there was no way to criticize the state without rebuking the church. Americans, by contrast, could indulge in bitter political debates without trampling religious institutions. Of course, Tocqueville was not altogether correct. The great political controversies in this country, from slavery to abortion, have always involved fundamental moral considerations. And the churches have readily joined the fray, fighting and dividing over these concerns. Still, Tocqueville's observation seems basically sound. When religion identifies itself intimately with a political cause, and then wraps that cause in the flag and anoints it with God, the opposition has little recourse but to attack both its political and religious adversaries. Over time, both the religious left and right have invoked God's blessing in behalf of political objectives and in so doing have at times shown a certain self-righteous arrogance; but the contemporary religious right has carried the identification of God and Caesar to a new level through its "moral" report cards, which on the basis of voting records designate politicians as basically godly or ungodly. Most significantly, perhaps, these report cards disclose the intimacy between the current religious right and conservative Republicans. Among other things, this study helps to elucidate this development.

The authors are indebted to numerous individuals, and it is a pleasure to acknowledge them. Three of our colleagues at Lamar University, Professors James Vanderleeuw, Department of Political Science, Larry Osborne, Department of Computer Science, and James Love, Department of Sociology, Social Work and Criminal Justice, were particularly helpful. Vanderleeuw reviewed the sta-

tistical data, and Osborne and Love assisted with computer re-
sources. Bob Persons, research analyst, Roper Center for Public
Opinion Research, provided invaluable information, while Patty
Cargill and Karen Wright, members of Bethlehem Lutheran
Church in Beaumont, Texas, volunteered useful insights. Yolanda
Shaw, the History Department secretary, typed much of the manu-
script, JoAnn Borel, a history graduate student, researched the
Christian Coalition, and Mark Asteris, media services coordinator,
Gray Library, Lamar University, furnished information on video
materials. The authors, of course, accept full responsibility for any
errors of judgment or fact.

Introduction

1

Thomas Jefferson's famous metaphor to the contrary notwithstanding, there has never been an absolute wall between church and state in American society. Ever since the Puritans came ashore in the early 1600s, religious leaders have often sought to influence public policy on a variety of social issues, and political leaders of all persuasions have just as readily appealed to the divine. A generation before the Civil War, for instance, the churches had already clashed and divided over slavery; in the late nineteenth and early twentieth centuries the social gospel inspired many churchgoers to pursue legislative remedies to urban industrial ills; the adoption of the Eighteenth Amendment on prohibition in 1919 was a crowning achievement for the religious establishment; and today many religious bodies maintain lobbyists in the nation's capital to sway politicians on everything from prayer in public schools to racial justice.

To many religious leaders, political activism in no way violates the separation of church and state, for in their view religion has a responsibility to address vital issues. Likewise, public officials have often invoked the authority of religion, hinting that a divine force directed American history. Both Abraham Lincoln in his second inaugural and John F. Kennedy in his 1961 address, for instance, used a religious framework to explain national purpose. In 1949 Harry Truman described the Cold War as a contest between the powers of light and darkness, and in 1953 "God's Float" led Dwight D. Eisenhower's inaugural parade. Further blurring the line between church and state has been the tendency of many Americans to shroud their history in religious symbolism, with George Washington likened to Moses and July 4 and December 25 both serving as occasions for nationalistic and religious exaltation.

There is no denying the religiosity of the American public. Alexis de Tocqueville, that discerning Frenchman who crisscrossed the nation from New York to New Orleans in 1831, was struck by this phenomenon. There was "no country in the world," he observed, "where the Christian religion retains a greater influence over the souls of men than in America." Tocqueville's observation has a contemporary ring, for recent surveys suggest that America is perhaps the most religious of the modern western nations. Current surveys show that 96 percent of all adult Americans believe in God, 70 percent belong to a church or synagogue, 40 percent actually attend church weekly, 59 percent believe religion is an important aspect of daily life, and 65 percent consider religion the answer to many of the nation's present ills. These numbers augur well for calls to political action rooted in religious principles, as shown only a generation or so ago by the "religious left." In pursuit of racial justice, for instance, the National Council of Churches pricked the nation's conscience in the 1950s and 1960s. This coalition of religious groups, along with Presidents Kennedy and Lyndon B. Johnson, challenged Americans to live up to the egalitarian ideals of their faith. Accordingly, the council brought the power of religion to bear on the civil rights legislation of the 1960s.[1]

Given this country's longstanding interaction between religion and politics, why has the religious right attracted such attention since World War II? Why have Jerry Falwell and the Moral Majority and Pat Robertson and the Christian Coalition aroused such alarm in some quarters? What is so different about the religious right? In terms of fundamental theological concerns, there is nothing particularly new. Contemporary Christians on the right are no less disturbed by higher criticism of the Bible and Darwinian evolution than their conservative forebears of the late nineteenth and early twentieth centuries, as attested to by persistent efforts over the last decade or so to have "creation science" accorded equal time with Darwinism in public-school classrooms.

It is not theology so much as active involvement in the political process that separates the contemporary religious right from conservative religious forces of the pre–World War II era. Believing that Armageddon was nigh, conservative Christians, especially those of a fundamentalist and evangelical variety, have traditionally concentrated more on redeeming sinners and preparing themselves for the imminent return of Jesus than on active political involvement. The Joneses of South Carolina—Bob, Sr., Bob, Jr., and Bob III, leaders of the fundamentalist Bob Jones University in Greenville, South Carolina—still reflect this viewpoint, and so did Falwell until the 1970s. Agitated by the political activism of the religious left in behalf of civil rights reforms, the future leader of the Moral Majority informed his Lynchburg, Virginia, congregation in 1965 that God had given no command to engage "in marches, demonstrations, or any other [political] actions." He added that preachers were "not called to be politicians but soul winners." But Falwell underwent a dramatic metamorphosis. At a special bicentennial service on July 4, 1976, the Virginian fused a nationalistic love of country with an intense religious zeal. "The idea that religion and politics don't mix was invented by the Devil to keep Christians from running their own country," asserted Falwell. "If [there is] any place in the world we need Christianity," he continued, "it's in Washington. And that's why preachers long since need to get over that intimidation forced upon us by liberals, that if we mention anything about politics, we are degrading our ministry."[2]

Falwell's political awakening, as well as that of multitudes of other Americans on the religious right, can be understood only in terms of foreign and domestic developments since World War II. To people on the religious, as well as political, right, the years since 1945 have been fraught with peril. Abroad, the communists appeared to be winning the Cold War, as exemplified by the triumph of Mao Tse-tung in China, the failure to achieve victory in Korea, the costly quagmire in Vietnam, the continuing presence of Fidel Castro in Cuba, the "giveaway" of the Panama Canal, and leftist successes in Central America. And at home "socialist" governmental programs (the religious right tends to equate liberalism with socialism and socialism with communism), the teaching of evolution in the public schools, a soaring divorce rate, Supreme Court decisions banning organized prayer in the public schools, growing numbers of abortions, urban violence and crime, the Equal Rights Amendment (ERA), the assertiveness of the "gay" community, "smutty" television programs, and the AIDS epidemic confirmed the religious right's belief that cherished moral values were in decline.

Uniting the voices of the religious right in the late 1940s was an intense fear of communism. Indeed, a symbiosis swiftly emerged between the religious and political right. Politicians such as Senator Joseph McCarthy of Wisconsin drew support from the religious right, for instance, while otherwise obscure preachers such as Carl McIntire gained national prominence through close association with the political right. Thus, in defense of God and country, preachers and politicians of the right embraced in a righteous crusade to save America. McIntire was typical. Now in his late 80s, this autocratic and self-righteous Presbyterian has become an elder statesman of sorts for a certain segment of the religious right. Fiercely independent, he forged his own denomination in 1937, the Bible Presbyterian Church, and through the weekly columns of the *Christian Beacon* kept his followers advised on matters of God and Caesar. By the 1950s he had established a network of educational institutions, such as the Faith Theological Seminary in Philadelphia, and had begun to broadcast his messages for religious and political redemption on a regular program titled *The Twentieth-Century Reformation Hour.* Basically, McIntire told Americans that national well-being hinged upon a return to "old-time" Christian values, values upon which the nation presumably had been founded. Accomplishing this goal would not be easy, however, because of the communist conspiracy. According to McIntire, the major Protestant bodies all harbored communists, the National Council of Churches was nothing but a communist front, and the Revised Standard Version of the Bible was communist-inspired. At the height of his influence in the early 1960s, McIntire's call for national salvation, as heard daily on his radio program, was carried by at least 200 stations.[3]

By 1960 the religious right had become more crowded as additional crusaders joined the cause, notably the trio of Edgar C. Bundy, Frederick Schwarz, and Billy James Hargis. Bundy, an ordained Southern Baptist minister without a congregation, took charge of the Church League of America in 1956. This ultraconservative agency, which Bundy moved from Chicago to Wheaton, Illinois, labored to awaken Protestant ministers to the reality of the communist conspiracy. Schwarz, an Australian physician and lay preacher who had come to the United States initially at the request of McIntire, launched the Christian Anti-Communism Crusade in 1952. His prominence was enhanced considerably by Billy Graham, who arranged for him to address a group of congressmen on communism in 1957. Schwarz repeatedly told American audiences that the communist method of conquest was infiltration, a process he believed already far advanced in the halls of academe, the press corps, and the State Department. More zealous perhaps than the other two, Hargis, a Disciples of Christ minister, began the Christian Echoes National Ministry, better known as the Christian Crusade, in 1951. Although closely associated in the mid-1950s with McIntire's organizations, Hargis increasingly went his own way. From radio in the 1960s he moved to television in the early 1970s with smoothly packaged programs carried, at one stage, by 146 stations. In 1973 he founded American Christian College.[4]

These ministers often enjoyed cordial ties to secular counterparts, thereby fuzzing the line in the public's mind between the religious and secular right. Such was the case of Robert Welch, who founded the John Birch Society in 1958. Welch was a well-educated, widely traveled, and successful businessman who had become disillusioned with politics after running unsuccessfully for lieutenant-governor of Massachusetts and supporting the failed presidential candidacy of Senator Robert A. Taft of Ohio in 1952. In 1956 he retired from business and became an anticommunist warrior. Welch was not a minister, but the John Birch Society was named for "a young fundamentalist Baptist preacher from Macon, Georgia," who allegedly had been murdered by Chinese Communists after World War II. And ministers on the right certainly saw an ally in Welch and his organization. McIntire called the society "a good patriotic American organization," and Hargis referred to Welch as "a great American patriot." Such admiration was not surprising, for Welch and the preachers had much in common.[5]

The early ministers of the religious right, as well as Welch, were as one not only in their intense anticommunism, but also in their conspiratorial view of history. The "paranoid style in American politics" was historian Richard Hofstadter's description of the tendency to see conspiracy as the causal force in American history. Certainly men such as McIntire, Hargis, and Welch were nothing if not suspicious of those with whom they disagreed. They took for granted that their adversaries were pawns of Satan and thus parties to a sinister conspiracy in which outward acts concealed darker intentions. Within this context, for instance, Supreme Court decisions regarding prayer in the public schools were just one aspect of a broader communist conspiracy to destroy the Christian moorings upon which the Founding Fathers supposedly had planted the nation. More an article of faith than the product of empirical observation, such a view of history was unaffected by evidence. Hargis, for example, considers that the recent collapse of communism in central and eastern Europe fooled everyone but him. While the American news media *"looks the other way,"* he asserted in August 1994, communism "is making a dramatic, secret comeback. . . . There is a Red threat and it is alive and thriving."[6] Time has changed nothing for Hargis. The conspiracy is ongoing, protected by the silence of the liberal media.

Preachers such as McIntire and Hargis have remained active, but they have been forced into the background by the easing of the anticommunist hysteria that fueled their rise in the 1950s. For all but the most devout true believers, it is difficult to sustain a belief in a communist conspiracy in light of the removal of the Berlin Wall, the unification of Germany, and the fall of the Soviet Union. Consequently, the resurgence of the new religious right in the 1970s was led by a group of electronic preachers—Robertson, president of the Christian Broadcasting Network (CBN) and host of *The 700 Club*; James Robison, a Texas Southern Baptist; and Falwell, leader of the Moral Majority. Preachers such as these still employed apocalyptic imagery in discussing the global struggle—liberty against atheistic communism, light against darkness—but the constant emphasis upon communist conspiracy ebbed. Instead of communism, "secular humanism" unified these newer leaders of the religious right. Many religious conservatives thought that secular humanists, who supposedly were entrenched in the courts, media, and schools, systematically undermined the supernaturalism of Judeo-Christianity. Robertson was typical. In 1986 he rebuked the "small elite of lawyers, judges, and educators" who had "taken the Holy Bible from our young and replaced it with the thoughts of Charles Darwin, Karl Marx, Sigmund Freud, and John Dewey."[7]

Like "modernism" of an earlier era, secular humanism quickly became an evangelical catchall for every imaginable "sin," from violence in the streets to the lack of discipline in the public schools. To combat these ills, however, the more recent religious right has been much readier to join the political fray than its counterpart of the 1950s. Whereas McIntire and Hargis often spoke to political issues and frequently endorsed specific bills, such as those seeking to "restore" prayer in the public schools, Falwell and Robertson have been far more inclined to instruct their followers on issues, conduct voter-registration drives, engage in legislative lobbying, and target specific politicians for defeat.

By the mid-1970s the social concerns that brought predominantly white groups together on the religious right generally fell into one of three categories—educational, family, or moral. As evidenced by the Supreme Court's 1962–1963 school prayer decisions, the growing trend toward secularization in the public schools not only alarmed many conservative Christians, but also prompted some of them to seek private schooling for their children. Just as many Catholics had insulated themselves within a system of parochial schools in the nineteenth century, some Protestant evangelicals sought to do the same in the twentieth century. Robertson voiced the mood when he wrote in 1980: "Christians must educate their youth in new schools which teach biblical principles and a biblical life-style in which the Lordship of Jesus Christ is acknowledged in every facet of their lives."[8] Of course, a logical consequence of the private school movement was support for tuition tax credits, and therein lay the possibility of cooperation between Protestant evangelicals and Catholics.

Another area of likely agreement among people of differing faiths was the family. Of special concern were the ERA and the Supreme Court's 1973 decision on abortion. Paradoxically, many conservatives affirmed their support of women while simultaneously denouncing the ERA. They asserted that they did not oppose equality of treatment for women, but rather any fundamental restructuring of the family allegedly at odds with the Bible. Consequently, religious conservatives opposed the ERA, convinced it would alter scripturally rooted male-female roles and even legitimize homosexuality. Robertson spoke for many others when he asserted that the proposed amendment would protect "homosexuals, lesbians, sadomasochists, and . . . anyone else who engaged in any other sexual practice whether or not that practice was prohibited by the Bible, religious dogma, existing federal or state law."[9] As for abortion, the position of many evangelical Protestants and Catholics was essentially the same—except when the mother's life was endangered, the rights of the fetus were paramount. The moral concerns of the religious right revolved around drug abuse, pornography, and television programs and movies.

With its constant barrage of nudity, profanity, and violence, television was a frequent target. Donald E. Wildmon, a Methodist minister from Tupelo, Mississippi, believed the industry undermined "family" values, and in the mid-1970s he launched a movement to purify the airwaves.[10]

The outcome of the 1976 presidential race brought hope to many religious conservatives, for Jimmy Carter was an acknowledged "born-again" Southern Baptist from the Deep South, a Georgian with whom many on the religious right could easily identify. Moreover, by focusing national attention on and enhancing the stature of evangelicals, Carter's victory emboldened many on the religious right increasingly to measure public issues against biblical standards of morality. As a result, matters of moral concern to Christian conservatives became politicized. In turn, Christian conservatives increasingly entered the political fray not only to protect their way of life, but also to "restore" the nation to its moral roots. Ironically, President Carter himself soon incurred the wrath of his religious kinfolk. They were dismayed by his endorsement of the ERA, his failure to prevent federally subsidized abortions, his refusal to promote legislation allowing voluntary prayer in the public schools, and the suggestion in 1978 of his commissioner to the Internal Revenue Service that Christian schools should be taxed. A common assessment was that of Tim LaHaye, a Californian and one of the religious right's more prominent voices. "Between 1976 and 1980," he wrote in 1981, "I watched a professing Christian become president of the United States and then surround himself with a host of humanistic cabinet ministers" who "nearly destroyed our nation."[11]

LaHaye's frustration was matched by that of Falwell. By the late 1970s the articulate Virginia pastor had become an institution of sorts. His Thomas Road Church, an independent Baptist congregation, numbered approximately 15,000, his Sunday services, *The Old-Time Gospel Hour*, entered millions of homes via radio and television, and his capacity for fundraising was already well established. The disenchantment of people such as LaHaye and Falwell with the Carter administration coincided with the appearance of several conservative lobbyists, men who saw in disaffected religious conservatives a reservoir of potential voters for conservative political causes. The key figures were Howard Phillips, leader of the right-wing lobbying group Conservative Caucus; Edward A. McAteer, a marketing specialist from Colgate-Palmolive Company and a Southern Baptist layman; Robert Billings, head of the National Christian Action Coalition; Richard Viguerie, a direct-mail expert who began the *Conservative Digest;* and Paul Weyrich, a Catholic who had organized the Committee for the Survival of a Free Congress in 1974. Credit goes primarily to Billings and McAteer for bringing Falwell and Weyrich together, thereby wedding secular and religious conservatives.[12]

Whether secular conservatives such as Weyrich subsequently dominated and used religious conservatives such as Falwell is debatable. The director of the People for the American Way, a liberal lobby, insisted that the political right actually created the religious right.[13] This assertion is clearly inaccurate. The religious right had been around for a long time, and the relationship that evolved between it and the political right in the late 1970s was symbiotic. The politically savvy Weyrich coined the term "moral majority" and brought organizational talent to the movement, while Falwell added righteous indignation and promised voters for the cause. Together, Weyrich, Falwell, and others forged the Moral Majority, Inc., in 1979 and set out to rescue America from secular humanism. Popular perception to the contrary notwithstanding, the Moral Majority endeavored from the outset to draw support from conservative Catholics, Jews, and Mormons. Indeed, Falwell's willingness to broaden the organization's base sometimes offended his Christian fundamentalist allies.

The Moral Majority was only one of three conservative religious institutions created in 1979. The other two were the Christian Voice and the Religious Roundtable. A California-based organization that by 1980 claimed the support of 37,000 pastors from 45 denominations and a membership of 187,000,[14] the Christian Voice assumed the task of evaluating the morality of public officials. To do this, it developed a morality scale based on 14 key issues. A politician whose position coincided with that of the Christian Voice was deemed "moral." Disturbed and angered by societal changes involving the family, women, sex, divorce, homosexuality, and television programming, the Christian Voice was against abortion, racial quotas, forced busing, the Department of Education, gay rights, SALT II, pornography, drugs, higher taxes, and sex education without parental consent. It was for the "restoration" of prayer in the public schools, free enterprise, the defense of Taiwan, and a balanced federal budget. Republicans usually came closer to meeting the Christian Voice's standard of Christian morality than Democrats. But when convicted Abscam defendants scored higher on the Christian Voice's morality scale than congressional proponents of alleviating world hunger and poverty, it seemed that the moral report cards had more to do with "correct" political behavior than morality.[15]

The Religious Roundtable, McAteer's principal organizational contribution to the religious right, attempted to connect prominent figures from the political and religious right. In August 1980 it sponsored the National Affairs Briefing in Dallas, Texas. Nonpartisan billing to the contrary, this was a Protestant fundamentalist and conservative Republican affair. The Southern Baptist patriarch W. A. Criswell, the longtime pastor of the First Baptist Church, Dallas, attended, as did Ronald Reagan, the only presidential candidate present. This meeting attracted national attention, not all positive. The stridency of some of the speakers and the hints of anti-Semitism bothered many Americans.

Although the Moral Majority shared the field with other organizations on the religious right in 1979–1980, it soon became the primary focus of national attention. With the presidential race of 1980 looming, the Moral Majority hastily established local chapters in 47 states, conducted voter registration drives and educational seminars for religious conservatives, and targeted several prominent politicians for defeat. Although it claimed to be nonpartisan, the Moral Majority invariably opposed liberal Democrats in 1980, such as Senators George McGovern of South Dakota, Frank Church of Idaho, Alan Cranston of California, John Culver of Iowa, and Birch Bayh of Indiana. And Falwell's eagerness to discredit President Carter prompted him, just weeks before the election, to fabricate an unflattering story about homosexuals on the president's staff. The minister later confessed his lie, but he remained undaunted.[16] The Moral Majority tended to equate morality with a narrow set of political options and was clearly more comfortable with conservative Republicans.

The results of the 1980 elections thrilled the religious right, although analysts disagreed sharply over the causes for the defeat of incumbents Carter, McGovern, Church, and Bayh. To be sure, Falwell, as well as Weyrich, Phillips, McAteer, and Viguerie, claimed considerable responsibility. As Viguerie put it, "the white followers of the TV evangelical preachers gave Ronald Reagan two-thirds of his 10-point margin in the election." But other postelection observers were far more skeptical, suggesting that Falwell and his followers merely rode, but did not create, the anti-administration sentiment so evident in the election. Bayh agreed, explaining his loss more in terms of high interest and unemployment rates than the religious right. According to this analysis, President Reagan was not especially beholden to religious conservatives. Accordingly, he did not appoint a representative of the Moral Majority to a major administration post and disregarded Falwell's objections to the appointment of Sandra Day O'Connor to the Supreme Court. With an eye toward the midterm congressional elections, however, Reagan did seek to soothe the religious right by choosing Billings for an important post in the Department of Education, appointing C. Everett Koop, an evangelical opponent of abortion, as surgeon general, taking a stronger stand against abortion, and endorsing a constitutional amendment allowing organized prayer in the public schools.[17]

Probably never as influential as either its followers or detractors supposed, the force of the Moral Majority definitely ebbed as the 1980s progressed. The group was assailed from within and without. Falwell and Weyrich had faced a dilemma from the beginning. How could the Moral Majority expand its base by appealing to moderate religious conservatives without alienating its staunchly fundamentalist core? The difficulty was apparent by the early 1980s. As Falwell eased toward the evangelical center, territory long occupied by Billy Graham, he quickly aroused suspicion. By softening somewhat his opposition to abortion, allowing that it was permissible if the mother's life was endangered, endorsing equal rights for women, once the ERA had become "a dead issue," and distancing himself from the unabashedly anti-Catholic Bob Jones, Jr., Falwell gained few converts from the evangelical mainstream and angered many on the fundamentalist right. Jones, for instance, called the Moral Majority the instrument of Satan and Falwell "the most dangerous man in America as far as Biblical Christianity is concerned." Such outbursts supported the assessment of Graham, who doubted that Falwell could move with his constituency into the evangelical mainstream.[18]

Many critics outside the religious fold were just as bitingly critical as Jones. To rouse Americans to the allegedly intolerant and dangerous views of the Moral Majority, several former senators who had been defeated in 1980 took to the stump in 1981–1982. McGovern, for instance, organized Americans for Common Sense to counter Falwell's group. And Senator Barry Goldwater of Arizona, the elder statesman of Republican conservatism, castigated the Virginian for his ideological rigidity. Goldwater's rebuke had been sparked by Falwell's opposition to the Supreme Court nomination of O'Connor. Meanwhile, John Buchanan, director of People for the American Way, loudly observed that the Christian Voice's "morality report cards" consistently gave low marks to African American, Jewish, and female lawmakers. Coincidentally, Buchanan had been one of the lawmakers the Moral Majority opposed in 1980. Although he was an ordained Southern Baptist minister and a Republican congressman from Alabama, his vote to extend the time allowed for passage of the ERA had angered Falwell. Buchanan subsequently lost in the GOP primary.[19] The distinguished historian Henry Steele Commager offered a critique of Falwell and the religious right at the Conference on Church and State at Baylor University in Waco, Texas, in 1982. He charged that the likes of "Oral Roberts and Jerry Falwell and their camp followers" concerned "themselves not with public sin but with private vice, or what they conclude is vice—especially the sins of the flesh and of infidelity, which they interpret by their own standards." While wringing their hands over "personal sin," in other words, they have little if anything to say about "social sins." According to Commager: "They have much to say about the wickedness of limiting posterity, whether by birth control or abortion, but very little if anything to say about the kind of world children will be born into or about the systematic destruction of a rightful inheritance of natural resources."[20]

As Falwell discovered, political activism by one side invariably generated counterattacks by the other side. After all, the religious right itself had been to some extent a response to the activism of the religious left in the 1950s and 1960s. The result for Falwell and the Moral Majority was a negative public perception. A Gallup Poll in late 1981 disclosed that over half the people who were aware of the Moral Majority viewed it unfavorably, and the response to Falwell personally was equally critical.[21] The consequence of Falwell's growing unpopularity was that many conservative politicians refused to be identified with the Moral Majority in the elections of 1982, 1984, and 1986. With his influence apparently waning, Falwell changed the name of the Moral Majority to Liberty Federation in January 1986 and thereafter lowered his political profile. "I've redirected my priorities," he later explained, "and have no intention of working as hard in the political arena as I have in the past."[22]

If Falwell had expected calm to accompany his political retreat, he was sorely disappointed. With glaring evidence of material excess and sexual misbehavior, the PTL and Jimmy Swaggart scandals unfolded in 1987–1988. Stunned, the faithful retaliated against all the major televangelists by withholding contributions and voicing disapproval. A Gallup Poll in 1987 showed that 62 percent of the American public now viewed Falwell unfavorably, a negative rating surpassed only by Oral Roberts, 72 percent, and Jim Bakker, 77 percent. Twenty-four percent of those polled even found fault with Graham. By mid-1988 the PTL was ruined, Swaggart was disgraced, Robertson's presidential foray was a shambles, and Falwell faced financial disaster.[23] In 1989 the Moral Majority was dissolved.

The Moral Majority collapsed, but the religious right survived. Indeed, it became more aggressive, particularly at the local and state levels, under the leadership of Robertson. Never close, the relationship between Falwell and Robertson sheds some light on the religious right itself. Contrary to popular assumption, the religious right has never been particularly cohesive. People on the religious right, while sharing some of the same social concerns, often follow different drummers. Robertson, for instance, after initially agreeing in 1979 to serve as a director of McAteer's Religious Roundtable, soon recoiled from active involvement in any of the new organizations of the religious right. His explanation was vintage evangelical conservatism. Christians should concentrate on winning souls, he said, instead of votes. Later, in the fall 1980, he remarked that critics had found "an easy target" in the religious right "because the conservative Evangelicals involved in politics—Christian Voice, Moral Majority, and Religious Roundtable—have been, at times, unsophisticated, simplistic and inept."[24] As for Falwell, his professed friendship for Robertson did not translate into support of the latter's bid for the presidency. "I personally wish," Falwell said in 1987, "that no minister would ever run for . . . political office."[25] George Bush, not Robertson, was Falwell's choice to succeed President Reagan in 1988. As exemplified by Falwell and Robertson, the religious right was a union of kindred spirits in which there were many fissures.

Robertson's withdrawal from religious right organizations in 1980 in no way diminished his support of conservative social causes. On the contrary, he maintained close ties to prominent figures on the religious and secular right, such as Weyrich and Senator Jesse Helms of North Carolina, and gave conservative commentators easy access to *The 700 Club*. He also began building a political apparatus of his own. In 1981 Robertson founded the Freedom Council, an organization designed to educate Christians on political issues, followed in 1982 by the National Legal

Foundation, which offered legal assistance to religious causes. And in 1985–1986 he presided over the Council on National Policy, a conservative group that was periodically briefed on issues by figures such as Senator Helms and Secretary of Education William Bennett.

By 1987 the successful televangelist clearly had his sights set on the presidency, apparently convinced he could overcome an unfavorable Gallup Poll rating of 50 percent. But amid the lingering PTL and Swaggart scandals, as well as serious reservations among many Americans about electing a charismatic preacher to the presidency, the effort foundered. Robertson's political ambition had exceeded his grasp.[26] Columnist William F. Buckley offered an assessment, writing in 1987 that while Robertson said all the things conservatives wanted to hear, Americans nonetheless were overwhelmingly unprepared "to believe that any minister is, ultimately, a serious candidate."[27]

Following the presidential debacle, Robertson regrouped. In 1989 he started the Christian Coalition and named the youthful Ralph Reed its executive secretary. This organization differed in at least one significant way from the Moral Majority. Whereas Falwell's group operated largely from the top down, seeking to achieve its ends by swaying politicians in the nation's capital, Robertson's coalition was a grass-roots effort to influence policies at the local and state levels. By 1994 the movement claimed almost 1,500,000 members, and its effect on local school board and state races was apparent from coast to coast. Indeed, Christian conservatives had gained control of Republican Party leadership in Texas, Virginia, Oregon, Washington, Iowa, South Carolina, and Minnesota, and comprised substantial voting blocs in New York, California, and practically all the southern states.

Obviously at home within the Republican Party, evangelicals had displaced mainline Protestants as the largest single constituency in the party of Lincoln by the early 1990s. And their impact was apparent in one of the more closely watched races of 1994. In Virginia Republican Oliver North, the darling of the religious right, eventually lost a bitterly fought contest to the Democratic incumbent, Senator Charles Robb. This race disclosed not only the religious right's control of the Republican apparatus in Virginia, but also its willingness to overlook the "sins" of the candidate who supported its political agenda.

School board elections, meanwhile, because they traditionally attract only a small percentage of the electorate, enhance the chance of any well-organized and determined group to obtain control. And Christian conservatives, sharing with multitudes of other Americans the current frustration with the public schools over everything from low scores on achievement tests to controversial textbooks to violence in the hallways, have been quick to seize the opportunity. A study in 1993 estimated that of the nation's 95,000 school board members 7,153 were conservative Christians.[28] Texas was one of the major battlefields in the 1994 fall elections. With 60,000 members and 136 chapters in the Lone Star State, the Christian Coalition had its eyes on the state's 15-member Board of Education. To avoid jeopardizing its non-profit status, the Christian Coalition endorsed no candidate by name, but rather encouraged its membership to support "conservatives." This approach left no doubt as to the anointed candidate in six of the districts. Republicans subsequently won three of those races, giving candidates beholden to the religious right an eight-to-seven majority on the Texas board.[29]

The political activism of Falwell and Robertson raises anew the issue of religion and politics. Preachers certainly have the right to run for office, and organized religion is entitled to bring pressure to bear on matters of public concern. That is exactly what the religious left did in the 1950s and 1960s, and so also the religious right in the 1970s and 1980s. The dispute arises over the arrogation of God by one side to support a specific set of political objectives, thereby implying that the other side is ungodly and irreligious. Admittedly a biased observer, John Buchanan suggests that "the fatal flaw of the religious Right is to baptize the mentality of the John Birch Society."[30] This assurance of God's support perhaps accounts for the religious right's propensity for harsh, judgmental rhetoric, such as Robertson's outburst in Iowa in 1992: "The feminist agenda is not about equal rights for women," he asserted. "It is about a socialist, anti-family political movement that encourages women to leave their husbands, kill their children, practice witchcraft, destroy capitalism and become lesbians."[31] Certainly people who supported the "feminist agenda" would be likely to interpret Robertson's speech as inflammatory.

The religious right was especially active in the 1994 elections. The Christian Coalition alone distributed about 33 million voter guides and manned a vast network of telephone banks shortly before the November balloting. Exhilarated by the subsequent results, Louis Sheldon, leader of the Traditional Values Coalition, expressed the mood of fellow religionists. "The election of 1980 with Ronald Reagan was great," said he, but after the 1994 outcome "it's like we've died and gone to heaven."[32] Whether the Republican landslide was due more to the failure of Democratic leadership, the pervasive frustration of the general populace, or the political activism of the religious right is uncertain. Nevertheless, the Christian Coalition's Reed promptly claimed considerable credit for the religious right in the high-profile Republican victories of Steven Stockman over House veteran Jack Brooks of Texas, Rick Santorum over incumbent Senator Harris Wofford of Pennsylvania, and George W. Bush over Governor Ann Richards of Texas. Of course, religious conservatives also suffered several setbacks, most notably North in Virginia.[33]

Perhaps the only certainty of the 1994 elections is that they aligned Congress more closely with the country's present mood of conservatism, a mood not only apparent before the election but also hospitable to many of the religious right's objectives. Television, for instance, long the bête noire of the religious right, has recently treated religious subjects more sympathetically, as seen in such programs as *Picket Fences, L.A. Law, Northern Exposure,* and *Christy.* And a special commentator on religion has joined Peter Jennings on ABC's evening news. This change in programming was noticed by L. Brent Bozell, chairman of the conservative Media Research Center, who exclaimed that "something's happening out there."[34]

Another issue dear to religious conservatives, a constitutional amendment on prayer in the public schools, appears closer to reality now than in 1980. Laws in Georgia, Virginia, Maryland, Mississippi, Tennessee, and Alabama already allow for a moment of silence, and similar legislation is pending in Florida, Oklahoma, Pennsylvania, and South Carolina. "We need a moral guidepost for our children," argues Jay Sekulow, chief counsel for Robertson's American Center for Law and Justice, and this momentum for prayer "is coming from the soul of America." One Georgia teacher has already been fired for ignoring "the soul of America."[35] And therein lies the concern. Those outside the politically assertive religious right may well wonder how tolerant it will be toward Americans who do not subscribe to its view of "traditional values."

This decrease in tolerance in turn raises questions about the likelihood of the religious right extending much beyond its white Protestant base, despite some efforts by Falwell, Reed, and others. To be sure, a mutual concern over such family-related issues as abortion, sex, education in the schools, and the proposed Equal Rights Amendment (ERA) has enabled some Protestant fundamentalists and conservative Jews, Mormons, and Catholics to ignore theological differences and join hands in the quest for "family values." Phyllis Schlafly and Don Feder are illustrative. Stung by the ERA, which was approved by Congress in 1972 but never ratified by the required three-fourths of the state legislatures, and the Supreme Court's decision on abortion in 1973, Schlafly, a Roman Catholic, started the Eagle Forum in 1975. This organization spearheaded the drive to kill the ERA, and in so doing drew the support of Falwell. More recently, Feder, an Orthodox Jew and a columnist for the *Boston Herald*, sided with Robertson on abortion and homosexuality. Speaking to Christian conservatives, he told a radio audience in 1994 that "there are religious Jews out there who share your values, who are as troubled as you about the direction this nation is moving in." Secular liberals who wanted to purge the public square of all vestiges of religion were more alarming to Feder than Christian conservatives who promoted biblically rooted moral absolutes.[36]

The capacity of people as diverse as Schlafly, Feder, and Falwell to rise above theological differences in pursuit of common social values surely encourages political strategists who see a pool of religious conservative voters for Republican causes. But is such cooperation sustainable? Can strongly felt doctrinal differences be set aside so easily in behalf of political objectives? Some evidence suggests that the religious right's umbrella is unlikely to extend far beyond its white Protestant base. Numerous Jewish leaders took exception to Feder, for instance, asserting that he was not in the mainstream of Judaism. Saul Rosenthal, a regional director of the Anti-Defamation League (ADL) in Denver, Colorado, added that if "fundamentalist Christians" and "fundamentalist Jews" succeeded with regard to abortion, homosexuality, school prayer, and tuition vouchers, many Jews, along with Muslims, Buddhists, Hindus, Sikhs, and others, would be ostracized.[37] Similarly, a 1994 ADL report, "The Religious Right: The Assault on Tolerance and Pluralism in America," castigated Robertson and the Christian Coalition for insensitivity. The report accused the Coalition of being "exclusionist," of indulging in a "rhetoric of fear" for political purposes, and of resorting to a political style "reminiscent . . . [of] Joseph McCarthy in the 1950s." Robertson's book, *The New World Order* (1991), was particularly offensive because of its alleged anti-Semitism.[38]

Tensions have also surfaced between Protestant fundamentalists and Catholics, ironically over a statement intended to promote harmony. In 1994 several prominent Catholics and Protestants, including Southern Baptists Larry Lewis and Richard Land, signed a document entitled *Evangelicals and Catholics Together: The Christian Mission in the Third Millennium*. Lewis, president of the Southern Baptist Convention's Home Mission Board, and Land, executive director of the body's Christian Life Commission, saw this as a move to "consolidate the influence of evangelicals and Catholics in addressing moral issues." Nevertheless, sharp protests from many rank-and-file Baptists prompted Lewis and Land recently to withdraw their signatures. In this case, ancient theological differences frustrated efforts at cooperation on common moral goals.[39]

Another barrier to the religious right's ecumenical efforts has been race. Although African American Christians, especially those in the South, shared Falwell's theological conservatism, they never joined the Moral Majority in sizeable numbers. The same is true of the Christian Coalition. A plausible explanation is that many religiously conservative whites have all too frequently opposed political and social initiatives beneficial to minorities. The close association between the religious right and Senator Jesse Helms, a North Carolina Republican, illustrates the problem. It would be difficult for many blacks to feel comfortable in a movement that welcomes a politician who has always objected to civil rights legislation and now criticizes federal programs to assist the poor. As noted by a political scientist at Texas Southern University, a historically black institution in Houston, Texas: "Some of us wonder, do they [the religious right] simply want to stop the clock, . . . [or] turn it back?"[40] Overtures by Reed and others notwithstanding, the "ecumenism" of the religious right appears unlikely to reach far beyond white Protestants and their social concerns.

Notes

1. See Sanford Kessler, *Tocqueville's Civil Religion, American Christianity and the Prospects for Freedom* (Albany: State University of New York Press, 1994), p. 12; Alexis de Tocqueville, *Democracy in America*, 12th ed., vol. 1 (New York: Vintage, 1945), p. 314; "Emerging Trends," Princeton Religious Research Center, December 1992, p. 1, April 1993, pp. 3–4, January 1994, pp. 1–3, March 1994, pp. 1–2; James F. Findlay, Jr., *Church People in the Struggle* (New York: Oxford University Press, 1993), pp. 3–75; and John W. Storey, "Religious Fundamentalism and Politics of the Far Right," in

Conflict and Change, America 1939 to Present (St. Louis: River City, 1983), pp. 65–76.

2. Richard V. Pierard, "Religion and the New Right in Contemporary American Politics," in *Religion and Politics* (Waco, TX: Baylor University Press, 1983), p. 64.

3. Storey, "Religious Fundamentalism," pp. 67–68.

4. Ibid,. pp. 68–72.

5. Ibid., p. 72.

6. Richard Hofstadter, *The Paranoid Style in American Politics and Other Essays* (New York: Vintage, 1966), pp. 3–40; and Billy James Hargis, *Christian Crusade Newspaper*, 42 (August 1994), p. 1.

7. See David Edwin Harrell, Jr., *Pat Robertson, A Personal, Religious and Political Portrait* (New York: Harper and Row, 1987), p. 212.

8. Ibid., p. 207.

9. Ibid., p. 205.

10. Storey, "Religious Fundamentalism," p. 75.

11. Harrell, *Pat Robertson*, pp. 184–185.

12. See *Newsweek*, September 15, 1980, pp. 28–36.

13. Harrell, *Pat Robertson*, p. 185.

14. *Houston Chronicle*, July 8, 1980, sec. 4, p. 28.

15. See Pierard, "Religion and the New Right," p. 63. See also *Christian Century*, April 16, 1980, pp. 444–446, June 18–25, 1980, p. 687, and October 8, 1980, p. 940.

16. *Newsweek*, September 15, 1980, p. 32.

17. See Pierard, "Religion and the New Right," pp. 67–68, 71.

18. Walter H. Capps, *The New Religious Right: Piety, Partiotism, and Politics* (Columbia: University of South Carolina Press, 1990), p. 99; and *Newsweek*, April 26, 1982, pp. 89–91.

19. *US News & World Report*, June 21, 1982, pp. 43–44. See also *Newsweek*, September 15, 1980, p. 32.

20. Henry Steele Commager, "Religion and Politics in American History," in *Religion and Politics* (Waco, TX: Baylor University Press, 1983), pp. 53–54.

21. *US News & World Report*, June 21, 1982, pp. 43–44; *Newsweek*, June 13, 1981, p. 2A, and August 21, 1981, p. 143.

22. *Houston Chronicle*, April 5, 1987, sec. 1, p. 7.

23. *Newsweek*, July 13, 1987, p. 52, and July 11, 1988, pp. 26–28.

24. Harrell, *Pat Robertston*, pp. 187–188.

25. *Houston Chronicle,* April 5, 1987, sec. 1, p. 7.

26. See Harrell, *Pat Robertson,* pp. 80 81, 188, 207, 214–215; and *Newsweek,* July 13, 1987, p. 52.

27. Harrell, *Pat Robertson,* p. 226.

28. *Houston Chronicle,* September 4, 1994, pp. 20–21A.

29. Ibid., p. 21A. See also November 10, 1994, pp. 25, 27, 30A.

30. Harrell, *Pat Robertson,* p. 218.

31. *Houston Chronicle,* September 4, 1991, p. 21A.

32. Ibid., November 10, 1994, p. 26A.

33. Ibid.

34. Ibid,. June 4, 1994, sec. E, p. 1.

35. *Newsweek,* October 3, 1994, p. 48.

36. *Dallas Morning News,* February 18, 1995, p. 1G.

37. Ibid., p. 4G.

38. *Houston Chronicle,* April 4, 1995, p. 4A; and *Baptists Today* (Decatur, GA), April 6, 1995, p. 19.

39. *The Religion and Society Report* (Mt. Morris, IL), 12 (April 1995), pp. 1–3; *Baptists Today,* March 23, 1995, p. 5, and April 12, 1995, pp. 3–4.

40. *Houston Chronicle,* December 12, 1994, p. 6A.

Chronology 2

1835–1836   *Life of Jesus* by the German theologian David Friedrick Strauss not only creates a sensation in Europe, but also comes to symbolize the kind of biblical scholarship that will appall American religious conservatives in the latter nineteenth century. Relying upon the "myth theory," Strauss argues that Jesus represented not a divine intervention in history, but rather a psychological projection of the beliefs of people at a particular moment. Such an interpretation offends many religious conservatives.

1843   William Miller, a New York farmer and Baptist preacher, predicts that Jesus will return to earth on March 21. After Jesus fails to appear, Miller adjusts his calculations, which are based primarily on the prophecies of Daniel, and announces the return will occur on October 22, 1844.

1859   Charles Darwin's *Origin of Species* sets forth a theory of evolution based upon natural selection. To the religious community, the implications of Darwin are astonishing. In one fell swoop the British naturalist replaces purpose, direction, and spirit with a random, nondirected, and thoroughly materialistic explanation of existence. Although many Christians seek to reconcile their faith with the new science, just as many recoil and prepare for battle against the new ideas.

1871   James Freeman Clarke's widely read *Ten Great Religions* disturbs many Christian conservatives, for it suggests that Christianity is just one of many important religions and that many things thought to be unique to Judeo-Christianity, such as floods, crucifixions, resurrections, and virgin births, are actually common to other religions.

1874   Francis L. Patton of McCormick Theological Seminary, a Presbyterian institution in Chicago, charges the pastor of the Fourth Presbyterian Church in Chicago, David Swing, with heresy—with violating the Westminster Confession of Faith (1646), a creedal statement to which most Presbyterians subscribe. Although acquitted by the local presbytery, Swing nonetheless resigns and establishes an independent congregation.

               In *Outline of Cosmic Philosophy*, John Fiske, a popular philosopher and historian associated for a while with Harvard University, seeks to resolve the conflict between religion and Darwin by simply asserting that evolution is God's way of doing things.

1876   Religious conservatives led primarily by Presbyterians launch the Niagara Bible Conferences. Influenced greatly by John Nelson Darby (1800–1882), an Anglican minister who helped establish the Plymouth Brethren movement in Great Britain, these conferences, which will occur annually for about a quarter century, concentrate on biblical prophecy.

Darby's sway is readily apparent in the widespread acceptance by many who attend these meetings of dispensational premillennialism, the twofold belief that history is divided into seven distinct dispensations and that Christ's return will inaugurate a thousand-year reign of earthly righteousness.

1878   Professor Alexander Winchell of Vanderbilt University is censured by the General Conference of the Southern Methodist Church for contradicting the Genesis account of creation. When the professor refuses to resign, the Methodist school eliminates his position.

1879   Southern Baptist Theological Seminary in Louisville, Kentucky, forces one of its professors, Crawford H. Toy, to resign for questioning the absolute authority of the Bible.

1882   Professor Ezra P. Gould is fired from Newton Theological Seminary, a Baptist institution in Massachusetts, for heretical teachings. At issue is the question of biblical infallibility.

1886   The uncle of Woodrow Wilson, Professor James Woodrow of Columbia Theological Seminary, a Presbyterian institution in South Carolina, is fired as a result of an address in which he argues that Darwinian evolution and religion are reconcilable.

    To educate students in an institution untainted by modernist sentiments, the world-renowned evangelist Dwight L. Moody establishes the Moody Bible Institute in Chicago. Its curriculum is steeped in missions, evangelism, and Bible prophecy. The school becomes the prototype for countless other "Bible institutes" across the nation.

1891   Professor Charles A. Briggs of Union Theological Seminary (New York) faces heresy charges because of his rejection of the theory of "verbal inspiration" of the Bible. Although Union Seminary, a Presbyte-

1891 (*cont.*)	rian school, stands behind him, Briggs resolves the problem for the Presbyterians by becoming an Episcopalian.
1892	Professor Henry Preserved Smith of Lane Theological Seminary, a Presbyterian school in Cincinnati, Ohio, is convicted of heresy by the Presbytery of Cincinnati. As with Professor Charles A. Briggs, whom Smith had defended, the Lane professor is at odds with denominational conservatives on the issue of biblical inspiration. Smith subsequently obtains a librarian's position at Union Seminary and becomes a Congregationalist.
1895	The Niagara Bible Conference enunciates the five "essentials" of Christianity, essentials that will guide fundamentalists from this point forward—the inerrancy of the Bible, the deity and virgin birth of Jesus, the substitutionary atonement, the bodily resurrection of Jesus, and the second coming.
1896	The founding president of Cornell University, Andrew Dickinson White, writes *A History of the Warfare of Science with Theology*. At sharp variance with the fundamentalists, who fear science, White argues that religion has retarded scientific thought.
1909	An annotated edition of the scriptures, *The Scofield Reference Bible*, perhaps the most influential source of dispensational premillennial ideas in the twentieth century, is prepared by Cyrus I. Scofield (1843–1912), a lawyer-turned-preacher who pastored the First Congregational Church, Dallas, Texas, from 1882 to 1895 and again from 1902 to 1907. Scofield's commentaries subsequently become "the Bible" for many fundamentalists.
1910–1915	*The Fundamentals: A Testimony to the Truth*, a set of twelve pamphlets each about 125 pages long, is published over a five-year period at the expense of two wealthy Presbyterian laymen from California. Distributed free to ministers, seminary professors,

theology students, Sunday school directors, and YMCA leaders throughout the country, these booklets, each written by a prominent religious conservative, not only reaffirm the "essentials" of the Niagara Bible Conference of 1895, but also denounce evolution, higher criticism, Catholicism, Mormonism, Jehovah's Witnesses, Christian Science, Spiritualism, and much more.

1919   In an effort to give direction to their crusade against modernism, some 6,000 like-minded believers, spurred on by William Bell Riley, pastor of the First Baptist Church, Minneapolis, from 1897 to 1942, gather in Philadelphia and create the World's Christian Fundamentals Association. This organization, which includes the country's most prominent fundamentalists, leads the charge in favor of antievolution laws and against John T. Scopes for teaching evolution in Tennessee.

Ratification of the Eighteenth Amendment, which ushers in national prohibition, is viewed with justifiable pride by many church people, for they, working closely with the Anti-Saloon League and other agencies, contributed measurably to the amendment's success.

1920   Curtis Lee Laws, the editor of *The Watchman-Examiner*, a Northern Baptist paper, coins the term "fundamentalist," asserting that such a Christian is one willing to battle for the fundamentals of the faith.

1922   President Frank L. McVey of the University of Kentucky urges the people of his state to oppose the antievolution bill being debated by the state legislature. McVey's courageous stand contributes to the bill's subsequent defeat in Kentucky.

1923   The Oklahoma legislature passes the nation's first antievolution law, followed a short time later by Florida, the adopted home of William Jennings

1923 (*cont.*)	Bryan, who crusades tirelessly for antievolution laws.
1924	Reflecting liberal sentiment within Presbyterianism, the Auburn Affirmation rejects such basic fundamentals as inerrancy of the Bible, the virgin birth, substitutionary atonement, and bodily resurrection of Jesus, and the reality of biblical miracles. Appalled by this statement, J. Gresham Machen rallies the denomination's conservative forces.
1925	The Tennessee legislature enacts a measure making it illegal to teach evolution in the public schools. A few months later John Thomas Scopes, a young teacher in Dayton, is brought to trial for violating the new statute. The resulting "monkey affair" attracts national attention, for it pits two prominent figures against one another. The American Civil Liberties Union retains the famous Chicago criminal attorney Clarence Darrow for the defense, and the World's Christian Fundamentals Association brings in the former secretary of state and frequent presidential contender William Jennings Bryan for the prosecution. Inasmuch as Scopes is convicted and the antievolution law upheld, the fundamentalists prevail at Dayton. Nevertheless, many Americans are appalled by the whole spectacle and question the wisdom of state-mandated "solutions" to moral and religious questions. The World's Christian Fundamentals Association declines rather abruptly after the trial.
	Upon Bryan's death, which occurs just days after the conclusion of the Scopes trial, Paul W. Rood, a California evangelist, organizes the Bryan Bible League in Turlock, California. Fiercely opposed to the theory of biological evolution, Rood and the Bryan Bible League spearhead the failed attempt to enact an antievolution law on the West Coast.
1926	The Mississippi legislature passes an antievolution law.

Bob Jones, Sr., founds his college in College Point, Florida. This fundamentalist school is unaffiliated with any religious denomination.

1928   Arkansas, which is the only state to put the matter to a popular referendum, outlaws the teaching of evolution by a vote of almost two to one. Although this is the last of five southern states to pass such legislation, the same objective is achieved throughout the country, North and South, by applying pressure at the local level, notably on school boards.

1929   J. Gresham Machen abandons Princeton Theological Seminary because of its liberal teachings and founds his own Westminster Theological Seminary in Philadelphia.

1933   Thirty-four American humanists, including educator John Dewey, sign *The Humanist Manifesto*, which fundamentalists will later point to as "the Bible" of secular humanism.

1936   The liberal wing of the Presbyterian Church defrocks J. Gresham Machen, who promptly establishes the Presbyterian Church of America.

1941   To counter the Federal (later National) Council of Churches, Carl McIntire founds the American Council of Christian Churches. Made in the image of its creator, this fundamentalist organization is rigidly separatist, admitting to membership only those who share its narrow theology and who eschew association with nonbelievers.

Under the auspices of the Moody Bible Institute, five evangelical scientists journey to Chicago to discuss formation of a creationist society. The result is the American Scientific Affiliation, whose growing membership is dominated by Mennonites, Baptists, and Presbyterians in the middle Atlantic and midwestern states. Tension soon emerges within the organization between strict biblical literalists and

1941
(*cont.*)

evangelical scientists inclined toward a more meta-phorical view of Genesis.

1942

The National Association of Evangelicals, which welcomes both individuals and denominations into its membership, is established as a fundamentalist alternative to the Federal Council of Churches. It soon becomes an alternative for many conservative Christians who are uncomfortable with the rigid dogmatism of fundamentalists such as Carl Mc-Intire and Bob Jones.

1947

Radio evangelist Charles Fuller establishes Fuller Theological Seminary in Pasadena, California. This institution becomes identified with a more moder-ate, less separatist variety of fundamentalism. In the tradition of John Nelson Darby and C. I. Scofield, Fuller is a dispensationalist.

Bob Jones University moves to its present site in Greenville, South Carolina.

1951

With headquarters in Cincinnati, Ohio, Circuit Rid-ers, Inc., is organized to combat socialism and/or communism and all other forms of alleged anti-American teachings in the Methodist Church. Actu-ally, Myers Lowman, founder of this group, scrutinizes virtually all the major religious bodies in America and identifies sizeable numbers in each as either communist or procommunist. He considers approximately one-third of the scholars who col-laborated on the Revised Standard Version of the Bible to be pro-communist.

Another crusading anticommunist, Billy James Har-gis, incorporates the Christian Echoes National Min-istry, better known as the Christian Crusade.

1953

At the behest of Carl McIntire, Billy James Hargis takes charge of a Bible Balloons project to float por-tions of the Bible into eastern European communist countries in gas-filled balloons. On May 7 some 10,000 balloons are set aloft from West Germany.

1954   The phrase "under God" is added to the pledge of allegiance to the flag. This kind of government support for religion appeals to many religious conservatives.

Bernard Ramm, a Baptist theologian and philosopher of science, publishes *The Christian View of Science and Scripture,* which provides theological support for a more progressive approach to creationism, an approach more in harmony with conventional geology regarding the age of the earth and humankind.

1956   "In God We Trust," which was inscribed on American currency the previous year, becomes the national motto. Coming at the height of Cold War tensions, this and other gestures of government support for religion appeal to many Americans.

1958   A group named for "a young fundamentalist Baptist preacher from Macon, Georgia," who allegedly was murdered by Chinese Communists after World War II, the John Birch Society is launched by Robert Welch. This organization and its leader enjoy cordial relations with such figures on the religious right as Carl McIntire and Billy James Hargis.

1960   Pat Robertson launches the Christian Broadcasting Network (CBN).

1962   In *Engel v. Vitale,* popularly known as the School Prayer decision, the Supreme Court declares it unconstitutional to recite a brief, nondenominational prayer that was composed by the New York State Board of Regents. The prayer declares simply: "Almighty God, we acknowledge our dependence upon Thee, and we beg Thy blessing upon us, our parents, our teachers and our Country." But to the Supreme Court, this public encouragement of reli-

1962
(*cont.*)

gion violates the establishment clause of the First Amendment. The decision ignites a furor.

Disturbed by the content of many public school textbooks, Mrs. Norma Gabler of Longview, Texas, makes her first trip to the state capital to protest to the Texas Education Agency. The teaching of evolution, as well as anything else contrary to Mrs. Gabler's religious and patriotic views, offends the Texas housewife. Along with her husband, Mel, she devotes herself hereafter to scrutinizing the state's adoption of textbooks.

1963

The Supreme Court's decision in *Abingdon v. Schempp* involves two cases of required Bible reading in the public schools of Pennsylvania and Maryland. Mindful of the public outcry against its decision of the previous year, the Court takes pains in this case to explain the government's position of neutrality in matters of religion. Taking into account both the establishment and free exercise clauses of the First Amendment, the justices declare that statutes that either advance or inhibit religious expression violate the Constitution. On this basis, the Court rules against the states of Pennsylvania and Maryland. The Maryland case is all the more appalling to many religious conservatives because it has been brought by atheist Madalyn Murray.

Although the public reaction in 1963 is somewhat more restrained than it was to the decision of the previous year, many Americans are nonetheless angered. Hence, almost immediately several congressmen and senators seek to amend the Constitution, notably Representative Frank J. Becker of New York and Senator Everett Dirkson of Illinois. These efforts are unsuccessful.

Henry M. Morris, a Southern Baptist engineer known primarily for efforts to reconcile science and biblical literalism, joins several like-minded creationists in founding the Creation Research Society in

Midland, Michigan. Although the society initially is dominated by Missouri Synod Lutherans and Baptists, it also draws some support from Seventh-Day Adventists, Reformed Presbyterians, Reformed Christians, and Brethren. Morris and his group object vigorously to the "creeping evolutionism" of the older and more "liberal" creationist society, the American Scientific Affiliation.

1965   Rousas John Rushdoony, a California evangelist, founds the Chalcedon ministries and initiates an effort to "reconstruct" society in accordance with God's laws, a society comparable to that of the seventeenth-century Puritans. Although these reconstructionists discard premillennial and dispensational eschatology, they stand with religious fundamentalists against "secular humanism," abortion, higher taxes, and bigger government. Evangelist Pat Robertson has spoken highly of Rushdoony. Although opposed to abortion, the reconstructionists do not advocate civil disobedience.

1969   Conservatives and fundamentalists among the Missouri Synod Lutherans elect J. A. O. Preus as president and embark upon a campaign to purify both the Synod and Concordia Seminary in Saint Louis. Committed to biblical inerrancy, conservative Lutherans rail against the "evils" of Darwin, Marx, and Freud.

1970   Tim LaHaye and Henry Morris establish the Christian Heritage College in San Diego, California. Their objective is to offer a liberal arts education in full accord with the Bible. The advancement of scientific creationism is a special concern, and so Morris launches the Institute for Creation Research, which in turn spearheads several efforts to find the remains of Noah's Ark.

With funds from the National Science Foundation, Jerome Bruner of Harvard University develops a new social science curriculum for the nation's fifth-

1970 (*cont.*)	and sixth-graders. Entitled *Man: A Course of Study*, the new textbooks arouse the ire of many religious conservatives because of their emphasis upon cultural relativity and de-emphasis of religion. The resulting controversy not only shelves the books and threatens the National Science Foundation itself, but also shows the ability of the religious right to mobilize its forces for a national campaign.
1971	In *Lemon v. Kurtzman* the Supreme Court sets forth criteria for determining whether a statute violates either the free exercise or establishment clauses of the First Amendment. The statute must have a secular legislative purpose; its principal effect must neither promote nor retard religion; and it must avoid excessive government entanglements with religion. Laws transgressing any one of the criteria are unconstitutional.
1973	By a margin of seven to two, the Supreme Court in *Roe v. Wade* holds that laws restricting abortion during the first six months of pregnancy are unconstitutional. No decision of the Supreme Court since the prayer cases of the early 1960s so angers the religious right. Along with "restoring" prayer in the public schools, organizations on the religious right are as one in their resolve to restrict abortions. Indeed, opposition to abortion enables many religious and political, Protestant and Catholic conservatives to overlook their differences and to cooperate in support of a common objective.
	Mel Gabler takes early retirement from Exxon Pipeline and joins his wife Norma in a full-time crusade to purge public school textbooks in Texas of unsatisfactory material. To accomplish this goal, they found Educational Research Analysts. The Gablers believe that too many textbooks undermine both Judeo-Christian values and pride in America.
1976	Jimmy Carter, a "born again" Southern Baptist layman, is elected president. Because of Carter's reli-

gious persuasion, the media suddenly show considerable interest in evangelicals and fundamentalists. Ironically, many on the religious right, initially hopeful because of Carter's victory, are soon disappointed.

1977
The National Federation for Decency, better known as the Coalition for Better Television, is organized by Donald Wildmon of Tupelo, Mississippi. Working closely with other religious right groups, particularly the Moral Majority, the coalition endeavors to make the air waves "safe" for family viewing.

1978
Jerome Kurtz, President Jimmy Carter's internal revenue commissioner, announces plans to withdraw tax exemptions from private, including church, schools that were established presumably to avoid court-ordered public school desegregation. This decision infuriates many figures on the religious right who see it as another example of government hostility toward religion.

1979
With the help of Paul Weyrich, a conservative political strategist who coins the term "moral majority," Howard Phillips, leader of the Conservative Caucus, and Edward McAteer, a marketing specialist for Colgate-Palmolive Company, Jerry Falwell establishes the Moral Majority, Inc. The purpose is to give political expression to Americans on the religious right, Americans who feel their sentiments have been ignored too long. With the 1980 presidential race on the horizon, the Moral Majority embarks upon a crusade to destroy "secular humanism" and to restore the nation's religious heritage.

The Religious Roundtable is organized under the leadership of Edward McAteer. This organization labors to bring the religious and political right together.

Headquartered in Pasadena, California, the Christian Voice identifies fourteen specific issues by

1979
(*cont.*)

which to assess the Christian morality of politicians. The organization opposes higher taxes, sex education without parental consent, forced busing, abortion, racial quotas, homosexual rights, the Department of Education, the Salt II arms agreement with the Soviet Union, drugs, and pornography. It favors free enterprise, prayer in the public schools, and a balanced federal budget.

Led by Texans Paul Pressler of Houston and Paige Patterson of Dallas, Southern Baptist fundamentalists elect one of their own president of the Southern Baptist Convention and set out to purge the denomination's schools and agencies of "liberals." By controlling the presidency and the vast appointive power that goes with that office, the fundamentalists hope to gain control of the denomination's numerous committees and boards.

1980

Sponsored by Edward McAteer's Religious Roundtable, the National Affairs Briefing at the Reunion Arena in Dallas brings together prominent figures from the religious and political right. Presidential candidate Ronald Reagan attends.

In *Stone v. Graham* the Supreme Court declares unconstitutional a Kentucky law requiring the posting of the Ten Commandments in each public elementary and secondary classroom. In the eyes of the Court, the purpose of the statute is clearly religious, for the first five commandments prescribe religious, not secular, duties.

Jerry Falwell's pamphlet, *Armageddon and the Coming War with Russia,* voices the belief, so typical of many figures on the religious right, that a Russian invasion of Israel will precipitate a nuclear war, the battle of Armageddon, in which the world will be destroyed. Echoing the sentiment, Pat Robertson goes so far as to suggest in his *700 Club Newsletter* that the titanic battle will occur by fall 1982.

Ronald Reagan is elected president with the strong support of religious right organizations, such as Jerry Falwell's Moral Majority.

1981   Jerry Falwell advises "every good Christian" to oppose President Reagan's nomination of Sandra Day O'Connor to the Supreme Court because of the abortion issue. This prompts the Republican Party's elder statesman, Senator Barry Goldwater of Arizona, to retort that "every good Christian" should give the Virginia pastor a kick in the pants.

1982   President Ronald Reagan, in obvious deference to the religious right, becomes the first incumbent president to endorse a school prayer amendment. President Reagan informs Congress that the time has come to "allow prayer back in our schools."

Louis Sheldon founds the Traditional Values Coalition, a California-based organization, and aggressively seeks the defeat of politicians at odds with his "traditional values." Sheldon opposes abortion, condom distribution and sex education in the public schools, and gays in the military; he favors prayer in public schools.

An antiabortion amendment fails to receive congressional approval after serious consideration.

1983   In *Bob Jones University v. United States* the Supreme Court strips the fundamentalist school of its tax-exempt status because of its racial practices. Convinced that the Bible prohibits interracial dating and marriage, Bob Jones University excluded African Americans until 1971, at which time blacks who were married within their race were admitted. Applications from unmarried blacks were not accepted until 1975, at which time the university prohibited interracial dating and marriage among its students. This rule leads eventually to the loss of the school's tax-exempt status.

1984   On March 5 Senate Majority Leader Howard H. Baker, Jr., opens the debate on President Reagan's proposed school prayer amendment. For two weeks the Senate grapples with the proposal. Senator Jesse Helms, a Republican from North Carolina, favors the proposal, while Senators Lowell Weicker and John Danforth, also Republicans, lead the opposition. When the vote is taken on March 20, a majority, 56 to 44, supports the amendment. Lacking the required two-thirds majority, however, the president's amendment fails. A defiant Senator Helms vows the fight has only begun.

During the course of debate several senators on each side of the issue indicate support for "equal access" legislation, a measure guaranteeing equal access to public school facilities for voluntary religious activities. In August Congress passes the Equal Access Act.

The Evangelical Voter, an analysis by Stuart Rothenberg and Frank Newport, challenges the assumption that evangelicals constitute a monolithic bloc of Christian voters. According to this study, income, race, education, and occupation seem to influence voting patterns more than religious beliefs. Moreover, evangelicals are more likely to be Democrats than Republicans, and they embrace diverse viewpoints. This report raises questions about the efficacy of mobilizing Christian conservatives for political purposes.

Reflecting the growing tie between the religious right and the Republican Party, televangelists Jerry Falwell and Pat Robertson appear on the podium at the National Republican Convention.

1985   In *Wallace v. Jaffree* the Supreme Court strikes down a 1981 Alabama law which allows school children a moment of silence "for meditation or voluntary prayer." The justices rule that Alabama lawmakers had violated the establishment clause of the First Amendment.

1987   In *Edwards v. Aguillard* the Supreme Court rules against Louisiana's Balanced Treatment for Creation-Science and Evolution-Science in Public School Instruction Act. This measure made it illegal to teach Darwinian evolution in Louisiana's public schools unless allowance had been made for the teaching of "creation science." According to the court, the Louisiana law promotes neither academic freedom nor scientific knowledge.

On March 4 Judge W. Brevard Hand of the United States District Court of the Southern District of Alabama in Mobile bans 31 textbooks from the public schools of Alabama on the basis that they illegally teach the "religion of secular humanism," thus violating the establishment clause of the First Amendment. Agreeing that secular humanism is a religion, many conservative Christians hail Judge Hand's ruling, which is reversed by the 11th U.S. Circuit Court of Appeals in August.

Televangelist Jim Bakker, founder of the PTL ("Praise the Lord" or "People that Love") Club, is accused of adultery and financial wrongdoing. Jerry Falwell, momentarily given control of Bakker's empire, soon becomes embroiled in a nasty struggle to retain PTL.

The Southern Baptist Convention faces another battle between the fundamentalist forces and the more moderate wing of the organization. Despite the efforts of a peace committee to resolve the conflict, the conservatives score another victory, electing inerrantist Adrian Rogers to the presidency of the convention. Later in the year, however, the conservatives lose the fight for control of Mercer University and several state governing boards.

1987
(*cont.*)

Reflecting growing conservative control, the Southern Baptist Convention's Public Affairs Committee votes by a narrow seven-to-five margin to support the U.S. Supreme Court nomination of Judge Robert Bork, whose positions on pornography, homosexuality, and the role of religion in American history strike a responsive chord within the convention.

The National Conference of Catholic Bishops voices concern over the influence of Protestant fundamentalism on certain Catholics, notably Hispanics. Protestant theologian Carl F. H. Henry quickly retorts that the bishops are still waging war against the Reformation. This mild exchange highlights the problem facing conservative Catholics and Protestants who attempt to rise above theological differences in behalf of common social and political objectives.

In the case of *Mozert v. Hawkins County Board of Education,* a three-judge appeals court panel unanimously overturns an earlier ruling of U.S. District Court Judge Thomas G. Hull, who had allowed the children of Christian fundamentalists to take reading classes at home in lieu of reading public-school textbooks offensive to their beliefs. The books in question supposedly contained passages on witchcraft, astrology, pacifism, and feminism. To many conservative Christians, this decision is just another example of discrimination against fundamentalists.

1988

Although ultimately unsuccessful, Pat Robertson mounts a campaign for the presidency and early in the year outpolls Vice-President George Bush in the Iowa caucuses. Fissures on the religious right soon surface, as many of the other right-wing evangelists support alternative candidates.

Jimmy Swaggart, the enormously successful Pentecostal from Baton Rouge, Louisiana, is engulfed in a sex scandal that undermines his ministry. This scandal, along with the PTL disgrace, has a damaging impact on televangelism in general. Donations fall sharply, forcing severe cutbacks in numerous ministries. For instance, Swaggart's college collapses and Falwell's faces bankruptcy.

Operation Rescue, one of the more aggressive anti-abortion groups, emerges into national prominence by the usage of civil disobedience against abortion clinics. This group not only pickets, but also attempts to block women from entering clinics. As a result of protests at the Democratic National Convention, demonstrators from Operation Rescue clog Atlanta's jails. Although religious fundamentalists applaud the objective, not all support the group's militant tactics. Christian reconstructionists, for instance, oppose such militancy.

The release of Martin Scorsese's film, *The Last Temptation of Christ,* angers the religious right. Pat Robertson denounces the movie, and Donald Wildmon runs counteradvertisements on 700 Christian radio stations and mails out over two million letters. Conservative columnist Pat Buchanan encourages the attack.

1989   The Christian Coalition, with headquarters in Chesapeake, Virginia, is organized in the wake of Pat Robertson's failed presidential bid in 1988. Describing itself as pro-family, this organization opposes abortion, pornography, condom distribution, waiting periods for handgun purchases, and tax and welfare programs that allegedly discriminate against mothers who stay home with their children. By keeping a "scorecard" on each member of Congress, this organization keeps local constituents informed on how their representatives and senators vote on "family" and "moral" issues.

1990   In *Board of Education of Westside Community School District v. Mergens,* the Supreme Court upholds the Equal Access Act, thereby ensuring religious groups

1990
(*cont.*)
the same access as secular groups to public school facilities.

In an effort to head off a possible fundamentalist takeover, Baylor University in Waco, Texas, the largest Southern Baptist university in the world, declares its independence of the Baptist General Convention of Texas. Angry fundamentalists call the move "an act of piracy," but Baylor leaders respond that they are saving the school from the fundamentalist-moderate controversy that currently engulfs the Southern Baptist Convention.

1991
Paul Weyrich's National Empowerment Television (NET) hits the airwaves. Its purpose is not only to make the public aware of what is wrong with the government, but also to offer prescriptions for change. Viewer call-ins consume much of the new network's air time.

1992
The growing influence of the religious right within the Republican Party is evident at the national convention in Houston, Texas, where the party's platform embraces the "pro-family" positions of the Christian right, most notably on abortion.

1993
Pat Robertson asserts that "there is no such thing [as separation of church and state] in the Constitution. It's a lie of the left, and we're not going to take it anymore."

1994
Dr. Jacob A. O. (Jack) Preus, the former president of the Lutheran Church–Missouri Synod who has led the attack against the denomination's liberals, dies in August in Burnsville, Minnesota.

Condemning President Bill Clinton's "liberal agenda," Pat Robertson's Christian Coalition mounts a vigorous attack on the president and the Democratic Party. The objective is to "reclaim America" by defeating liberal Democrats in the November congressional elections.

Former Marine lieutenant-colonel Oliver North, who attracts national attention because of his role in the Iran-Contra scandal, wins the Republican Party's nomination for the U.S. Senate from Virginia. A born-again Christian who appeals openly to the religious right, North has the endorsement of Pat Robertson. North eventually loses the bitterly fought race to the Democratic incumbent, Charles Robb.

The growing political influence of the religious right at the state level is apparent not only in Virginia, but also in Texas, Oklahoma, and South Carolina. In Texas, for instance, religious conservatives obtain a majority on the state's Education Board; in Oklahoma, a traditionally Democratic stronghold, Republicans, with the help of Christian conservatives, capture the statehouse and seize a 7-to-1 majority in the congressional delegation; and in South Carolina, a Southern Baptist fundamentalist, David Beasley, defeats a popular Democrat in the gubernatorial race.

The Anti-Defamation League releases a report entitled *The Religious Right: The Assault on Tolerance and Pluralism in America,* which accuses evangelical and fundamentalist Christian leaders of playing upon fear and hatred in pursuit of political power. The report singles out the Christian Coalition, calling it exclusionist, hostile toward Jews, and a threat to American democracy, pluralism, and religious freedom. Pat Robertson replies that the report is filled with half-truths and fabrications "reminiscent of the political style practiced by Joseph McCarthy in the 1950s." This war of words illustrates the difficulty of sustained cooperation between conservative Jews and Christians in the quest for certain objectives of the religious right.

L. Brent Bozell, chairman of the conservative Media Research Center, notes that such television programs as *Picket Fences, L.A. Law, Northern Exposure,*

1994
(*cont.*)

and *Christy* have begun to treat religious figures and subjects with more sensitivity.

Several prominent Roman Catholics and evangelical Protestants issue *Evangelicals and Catholics Together: The Christian Mission in the Third Millennium*. This cautious statement of cooperation between groups that in the past have quarrelled bitterly over matters of doctrine dismays many evangelical Christians. Although conservative Protestants and Catholics often share common positions on abortion and school prayer, ancient theological differences continue to hamper political cooperation.

Candidates beholden to the religious right score major victories in the November elections, as the Republicans obtain a majority in the House of Representatives for the first time in 40 years and also regain control of the Senate. The religious right is quick to claim credit for the Republican landslide. A jubilant Ralph Reed of the Christian Coalition proclaims that the election results put "to rest once and for all the myth" that religious conservatives "are a liability rather than an asset in the Republican Party."

1995

More than 30 Jewish and conservative Christian leaders hold a five-hour meeting in Washington, D.C., in an effort to stem the angry rhetoric prompted by last year's Anti-Defamation League report on the Christian right. In essence, the two sides agree to disagree without rancor. Jerry Falwell describes the gathering as positive, and Ralph Reed hopes to avoid such hostility in the future, but Abraham Foxman of the Anti-Defamation League declares that "the report stands." Foxman acknowledges that the report has caused Christian conservatives "pain," but hastily adds that Jews are also pained by the seeming anti-Semitism of some of Pat Robertson's remarks and the religious right's constant reference to the United States as a "Christian" nation.

Encouraged by the recent national elections, leaders of eight conservative and evangelical Christian groups prepare a constitutional amendment that would allow student-led prayers in public schools. Asked about school prayer on *This Week with David Brinkley,* a weekly ABC television program, House Speaker Newt Gingrich, Republican of Georgia, replies that a religious freedom bill of some sort, one that would go beyond merely school prayer, probably would come before the House after the Easter recess.

Two prominent Southern Baptist leaders, Larry Lewis, president of the Southern Baptist Home Mission Board, and Richard Land, executive director of the convention's Christian Life Commission, come under attack for signing *Evangelicals and Catholics Together.* Critics contend the document is heretical, making too many concessions to Catholic doctrine, while defenders counter that theological differences should not deter evangelicals and Catholics from working together on such issues as abortion and school prayer. Nevertheless, Lewis and Land remove their signatures from the controversial document, evidence that the road to political cooperation between religious conservatives on various cultural concerns is fraught with theological land mines.

Christian Coalition director Ralph Reed outlines his organization's "Contract with the American Family." Consisting of ten proposals, the contract calls for more restrictions on abortion; school vouchers; a religious equality amendment; the elimination of funding for the National Endowment for the Arts, the National Endowment for the Humanities, and the Corporation for Public Broadcasting; reduced funding for the Legal Services Corporation; the dismantling of the Department of Education; and the end of federal involvement in welfare. Republicans Newt Gingrich, Phil Gramm, and Bob Dole applaud the contract, but several religious leaders voice concern. Rabbi David Saperstein of the Union of Ameri-

1995
(*cont.*)

can Hebrew Congregations, for instance, fears the contract "will divide the nation along religious lines."

In a 5-4 decision, *Rosenberger v. Rector & Visitors of University of Virginia,* the Supreme Court rules that the University of Virginia, a state school, violated the free speech of Christian students in 1992 by refusing monetary assistance for *Wide Awake,* a Christian magazine. This decision is of enormous significance for issues related to church and state.

Speaking from convention headquarters in Nashville, Tennessee, Jim Henry, president of the Southern Baptist Convention, and Richard Land, head of the convention's Christian Life Commission, declare their opposition to President Bill Clinton's nomination of Henry Foster as U.S. surgeon general. The two Baptist leaders object to Foster's stand on abortion. This opposition brings a stern rebuke on *NBC Nightly News* from journalist and fellow Baptist Bill Moyers, who asserts that the Southern Baptist Convention has been "captured by a political posse allied with the Republican Party." Concludes Moyers: "The irony is that Henry Foster, M.D., himself a Baptist, has been a life-long crusader against teenage pregnancy and probably more successful at preaching abstinence than a dozen doctors of theology. But when God becomes partisan, religion becomes unforgiving and all subtlety excommunicated."

Biographical Sketches

3

Most of the individuals covered here have risen to prominence since World War II. Intellectually and theologically, however, much of the contemporary religious right is rooted in the late nineteenth and early twentieth centuries. To provide some sense of continuity, therefore, several figures from the earlier era, such as John Nelson Darby and J. Gresham Machen, have been included. Other individuals, such as Robert Welch and Paul Weyrich, more political conservatives than fundamentalist Christians, have been included because their goals have much in common with those of the religious right. Inasmuch as people on the religious right are often associated with organizations, and in fact organizations often have been built around particular personalities, readers should consult Chapter 5 with these biographies.

Robert J. Billings (1926–)

A major supporter of Christian schools, Robert Billings was a member of the Department of Education during President Ronald Reagan's administration. He graduated from Bob Jones University and served as a high school principal, but left that position because of what he considered excessive government interference and the dominance of humanist values in public education. He and his wife began establishing Christian schools across the nation. He also served as president of Hyles-Anderson College. In 1976 he ran an unsuccessful campaign for Congress. Billings founded the National Christian Action Coalition in 1978, a successor to Christian School Action. One of the coalition's major goals was to oppose government involvement in Christian schools. Consequently, Billings directed the effort against the Internal Revenue Service when that agency in 1978 sought to deny tax exemption to Christian schools for alleged racial discrimination. In 1979 he helped to persuade Jerry Falwell to form Moral Majority and assisted in rallying support for Falwell among influential people on the religious right. He became that organization's first executive director.

Billings left the Moral Majority in 1980 to serve as a religious adviser in Ronald Reagan's campaign for the presidency. After Reagan became president, Billings was named the director of regional offices in the Department of Education. In this post he played a major role in fending off Internal Revenue Service proposals to tax religious schools. Even so, in 1983 the Supreme Court reversed the Reagan administration's decision to grant tax-exempt status to Billings's alma mater, Bob Jones University. Like other leaders of the religious right in 1988, Billings supported a Republican candidate for president, backing Senator Robert Dole's unsuccessful attempt to gain the nomination. Billings has been quoted as saying that people do not wish to think for themselves, but desire leadership and want to be told what to think by those who are more closely involved with politics.

William Jennings Bryan (1860–1924)

William Jennings Bryan's influence on the development of the religious right stems largely from his participation as a prosecutor in the 1925 Scopes trial in which John T. Scopes was charged with violating a state law forbidding the teaching of evolution in the public schools of Tennessee. At issue in this trial was the conflict between a literal interpretation of the Bible and scientific explanations of natural events, a conflict in which fundamentalists disclosed deep suspicions toward a modern society seemingly at odds with their religious beliefs. Despite his association with fundamentalist opposition to evolution theory, Bryan's political life involved the pursuit of objectives that cannot readily be associated with a religious right ideology, then or now.

Bryan, a native of southern Illinois, graduated as class valedictorian from Illinois College in 1881. He entered Union Law School in Chicago and received his degree in 1883. He moved to Lincoln, Nebraska, in 1887, immediately became active in politics, and was elected to the U.S. House of Representatives in 1890. In 1896 he captured the Democratic Party's nomination for the presidency. The American people rejected him at the polls in 1896, again in 1900, and yet again in 1908, giving Bryan the dubious distinction of having been defeated in three presidential elections. After Woodrow Wilson was elected president in 1912, he chose Bryan as his secretary of state. Bryan attempted to maintain a basically pacifist stance and opposed American involvement in World War I. Wilson's policy of "neutrality," which in fact favored Great Britain and France, led Bryan to resign his position in the Wilson cabinet.

Unlike many fundamentalists, Bryan did not find premillennialism an attractive doctrine. He supported many progressive policies and causes: women's suffrage, direct popular election of the president, a national minimum wage, direct election of U.S. senators, a graduated income tax, and the use of government to control the power of corporations. On other issues, such as prohibition and Sabbatarianism, Bryan took more conservative positions closer to the hearts of fundamentalists.

Bryan opposed the teaching of evolution, an issue to which he devoted increasing attention as his influence in politics faltered. He argued that state legislatures had the right to restrict the teaching of evolution, at least to the extent that such instruction must label evolution as a mere hypothesis or "guess" as to the origin of humankind. Evolution was not only a poorly founded conjecture, but also represented a serious threat to society. Acceptance of the social Darwinian view of the survival of the fittest, which to Bryan was the essence of evolution, would weaken God's presence in people's lives. He regarded the teaching of evolution to be an issue best decided democratically: the people have the right to control their own schools and can do so through the institutions of representative democracy. This view gained new popularity in some state legislatures in the 1980s.

Bryan was ill equipped to criticize the theory of evolution and a scientific method about which he knew virtually nothing. He had generally limited his reading to the Bible and such other sources as the classics and the writings of Thomas Jefferson. Except for the daily newspaper, he inquired little into developments of the modern world. Although the World's Christian Fundamentals Association had asked him to prosecute Scopes, prominent fundamentalists left him to face the crafty Clarence Darrow alone. Bryan and Darrow, Scopes's defense attorney, confronted each other directly at the 1925 trial. When he unwisely agreed to be cross-examined by Darrow, Bryan's ignorance of the theory he so strongly criticized became apparent. Perhaps of greatest dismay to fundamentalists, Darrow elicited from Bryan a willingness to compromise a literal interpretation of the Bible. Due to Bryan's nationally reported humiliation, the jury's guilty verdict against Scopes was a pyrrhic victory. Bryan died within a week of the trial's conclusion.

Edgar C. Bundy (1915–)

During the 1950s and 1960s Edgar Bundy, executive director of the Church League of America, played a leading role in the anticommunist movement. After receiving a B.A. from Wheaton College in 1938, he enlisted in the army in 1941 and served for six years, ultimately reaching the rank of major. In 1942, still in the army, he became an ordained Southern Baptist minister. After World War II Bundy served as chief of research and analysis in the Intelligence Section of the Alaskan Air Command. He left the military in 1948 to become the city editor of the Wheaton, Illinois, *Daily Journal.* The following year the Senate Appropriations Committee invited him to testify on the communist threat in the Far East. Numerous invitations to speak at meetings of various political and patriotic groups soon followed, and for a time he worked with Carl McIntire in public relations and as a researcher.

Bundy became active in the Illinois American Legion, playing a role in condemning the *Girl Scout Handbook* for containing "un-American" material and writing a resolution for the Legion's 1955 national convention declaring the United Nations Educational, Scientific, and Cultural Organization subversive. In 1956 the Church League of America named him its executive director. He edited the organization's *News and Views,* which became an important source of information on anticommunism for the religious right. Bundy recorded lectures with titles such as "The Perils of the Social Gospel" and "The Perversion of the Bible" for usage by organizations in countersubversion seminars. His book *Collectiv-*

ism in the Churches (1958) described the way in which various elements in American society, including those supporting the social gospel, were subverting American liberty.

Charles E. Coughlin (1891–1979)

The controversial "radio priest" of the 1930s and precursor of contemporary televangelism, Charles Coughlin had an estimated radio audience of 40 million listeners during the height of his fame. If not a major player, he was a considerable irritant in American politics of the 1930s. Coughlin studied theology at St. Michael's College at the University of Toronto and, after teaching at Assumption College in Windsor, Ontario, for six years, entered the diocese of Detroit in 1923. Possessing a rich baritone voice, Coughlin early on made occasional radio broadcasts. In 1925 he was appointed priest in a parish in Royal Oak, a suburb of Detroit. Coughlin began a radio program in order to raise funds to remedy the financial problems of the parish. By 1930 broadcasts from his church, the Shrine of the Little Flower, were carried over several Columbia Broadcasting System stations. After CBS dropped his program, Coughlin established his own network that ultimately included 26 independent stations. With the start of the Great Depression, he focused on the international monetary crisis and assailed those groups, particularly the big banks, allegedly responsible for America's economic plight. Although initially a Roosevelt supporter, Coughlin soon became a severe critic of New Deal policies and a fierce opponent of communism.

In the mid-1930s Coughlin entered more directly into politics. In 1935 persistent rumors circulated that he and Governor Huey Long of Louisiana were gravitating toward one another, and in 1936 he supported third-party candidate William Lemke for the presidency. That same year Coughlin founded the National Union for Social Justice and the magazine *Social Justice*. The magazine became controversial for publishing such things as the discredited *Protocols of the Elders of Zion*, which prompted charges of anti-Semitism. Partially due to his opposition to American involvement in World War II, Coughlin came under federal grand jury investigation. In 1942 he ceased publication of his magazine and ended his radio program after it came increasingly under review by church authorities. Although Coughlin occasionally wrote about political issues, he remained out of the public limelight, devoting his energies to priestly duties in his Detroit parish until his retirement in 1966.

John Nelson Darby (1800–1882)

This Anglican minister, who left the Church of Ireland to become a leader of the Plymouth Brethren, found in post–Civil War America fertile soil for his dispensational premillennial beliefs. Between 1859 and 1877 he toured this country at least six times, winning numerous converts to his views, particularly among Baptists and Presbyterians. Through the likes of James Brooks, Cyrus Scofield, and J. Frank Norris, Darby's influence on American fundamentalism has been substantial. Born in London, Darby was educated at Trinity College, opened a law practice in Ireland, became a minister upon conversion to Christianity, soon declared Anglicanism bankrupt, and joined the Brethren in 1828 because of their simple ways, congregational autonomy, and adherence to scripture. When the Brethren split in the 1840s, Darby became the leader of the more rigid faction, called the Darbyites.

For the most part, Darby's dispensational premillennialism was rather conventional. He divided history into distinct epochs, or dispensations, each of which differed with regard to God's plan of redemption. The crucifixion and the Jewish rejection of Jesus marked the end of one dispensation and opened another, the church age. This era in turn would end with the Rapture, followed swiftly by the seven-year reign of the Antichrist, a period of Tribulation during which Jews would be horribly persecuted. The eventual defeat of the Antichrist at the Battle of Armageddon and the triumphal return of Christ would initiate the millennium. The most distinctive aspect of Darby's thought centered on the reestablishment of a Jewish nation. Indeed, Darby's end-of-time scenario was tied closely to the fate of the Jews, a surviving remnant of whom supposedly would come to recognize Jesus as the long-awaited Messiah.

Several factors account for the acceptance of Darbyism in this country. First, Darby vigorously defended and zealously promoted his variant of dispensational premillennialism. Second, in an age when Darwinism and liberal theology undermined confidence in the scriptures, Darby's emphasis upon biblical authority and literalism appealed to many conservatives. And, third, the Niagara Bible Conferences initiated by Brooks, the success of the Scofield Reference Bible, and the prominence of Norris among fundamentalists ensured a wide audience.

James C. Dobson (1936–)

A psychologist and former professor of pediatrics at the University of Southern California School of Medicine, James Dobson heads Focus on the Family, an organization concerned with social issues affecting the "traditional" family structure. He hosts a 30-minute weekday radio program that provides advice on a variety of problems people face in contemporary family life. Dobson emphasizes traditional Christian values, although, unlike other radio evangelists, he does not present an explicitly Christian message and seldom refers directly to biblical texts. His book on child rearing, *Dare To Discipline,* became a popular evangelical alternative on the subject. Dobson's radio program is heard on 1,450 stations in the United States and other countries. He has a large staff, including several licensed family counselors who deal with emergency situations and other trained staff members who deal with less urgent cases. The total staff of Focus on the Family, which is headquartered in Colorado Springs, Colorado, is estimated at 700.

Although Dobson has refused to endorse political candidates, he has become involved in national politics when issues affecting the family have arisen. He was selected to attend a White House Conference on the Family during President Jimmy Carter's administration, and he served on six government panels during President Ronald Reagan's administration, the most notable of which was the Commission on Pornography headed by Attorney General Edwin Meese. In 1988 Dobson's organization began sponsoring the Family Research Council, a Washington-based organization. After the difficulties religious right leaders experienced during the late 1980s, Dobson was mentioned as the most promising leader of the Christian right for the 1990s. However, Dobson has been unwilling to accept such a designation, perhaps demonstrating a cautious attitude toward overt political involvement.

Colonel V. Doner (1949–)

Colonel Doner, presently head of Christian Action Council in Santa Rosa, California, was one of the co-founders of Christian Voice, a religious right organization that became active in national politics in the 1980s. Doner and his colleagues in Christian Voice claimed that, through their campaign activities, they were responsible for defeating President Jimmy Carter and 30 incumbent congressmen in the 1980 election. Christian Voice published moral report cards on congressional Democrats and ran controversial campaign ads, including one that identified President Carter with the homosexual rights movement. Doner was noted for his combative style in his appearances on such television programs as *60 Minutes* and *Phil Donahue.*

In his book *The Samaritan Strategy* (1989), Doner pondered the political activities of the religious right movement of the 1980s. He described the movement's association with the Republican Party and revealed the extent of Republican financial support in 1984 in establishing the American Coalition for Traditional Values. Doner claimed that by 1986 Republican leaders had begun to fear the expanding influence of the Christian right and therefore halted financial assistance. Doner left Washington in 1986, having decided that the religious right had failed to achieve its objectives. After leaving Washington, Doner, reflecting on past political involvement, concluded that the religious right neglected to demonstrate sufficient concern for those in need, such as the homeless and abused children. Altering strategy, Doner began to seek contacts with more liberal evangelical Christians to try to work together in achieving common service goals. He claimed that Christians will merit the opportunity for leadership in their communities by caring for those in need.

Jerry Falwell (1932–)

The religious right's most prominent spokesman by the early 1980s, Jerry Falwell demonstrated that fundamentalist Christians could be effectively involved in the political process. Raised among rowdy bootleggers in the hill country of central Virginia, his formative years gave no hint of his later religious stature. After becoming a Christian in 1952, he attended Bible Baptist College in Missouri. Four years later he returned home to Lynchburg, established an independent Baptist church in a vacant bottling plant, promptly took to the airwaves with a 30-minute radio program, and within six months aired his first telecast. The smoothly articulate pastor quickly became an institution. From only 35 members in 1956, his Thomas Road congregation numbered almost 20,000 by the early 1980s and his Sunday service, *The Old-Time Gospel Hour,* was carried to an estimated 21 million faithful listeners via 681 radio and television stations. Falwell's fundraising capacity was impressive. By 1980 he was generating about one million dollars per week, enough to sustain a college, Liberty Baptist, with approximately 3,000 students, a home for alcoholics, a children's day school, a seminary, 62 assistant pastors, and 1,300 employees.

As noteworthy as these church-related achievements were, Falwell was becoming better known to the American public primarily because of his venture into politics. Assisted by such conservative political strategists as Paul Weyrich, Howard Phillips, and Edward A. McAteer, the popular video preacher launched Moral Majority, Inc., in 1979. The purpose was to give political voice to a growing tide of disenchanted Christian fundamentalists, who, like Falwell himself, had traditionally abstained from the political process. By the late 1970s Falwell was convinced that America's moral decline, as presumably exemplified in Supreme Court decisions on prayer in the public schools and abortion, the pervasiveness of "smutty" television, the assertiveness of the gay community, and the push for the Equal Rights Amendment, could be reversed only by vigorous political activism from the religious right. Ironically, it was disappointment with another "born-again" Christian, President Jimmy Carter, a Southern Baptist layman, that prompted Falwell to political action.

The extent to which Moral Majority contributed to the success of conservative Republicans in the 1980s is open to debate, but there is no denying the organization's efforts. It hastily established local chapters in all the states, conducted voter registration campaigns and educational seminars, and targeted liberal Democrats for defeat. Claims of nonpartisanship notwithstanding, Moral Majority clearly was more at ease with a conservative Republican agenda. The organization was never very successful in attracting nonfundamentalists, and so in an effort to broaden its support, Falwell renamed it Liberty Federation in 1987. That same year Falwell's ministries, like those of many other televangelists, suffered serious economic losses in the wake of the PTL scandal. A Gallup Poll disclosed that 62 percent of the American public viewed the preacher unfavorably. Consequently, in 1989 Falwell dissolved Moral Majority, assumed a lower profile, and devoted more attention to this local congregation and college.

William ("Billy") Franklin Graham (1918–)

Although less active politically than other key figures on the religious right, Billy Graham can be credited with practicing a biblically based and passionate style of evangelism that set the standard for many others. He helped to make evangelical Christianity acceptable once again to the general American public. Graham attended Bob Jones University in 1936 and Florida Bible Institute from 1937 to 1940, where he was ordained a Southern Baptist minister in 1939, and he graduated from Wheaton College in 1943. He assumed the pastorate at the First Baptist Church in Western Springs, Illinois, in 1943 and the following year became a preacher for the Youth for Christ organization. From 1947 to 1952 Graham served as president of Northwestern Schools in Minneapolis, Minnesota. During the early postwar years he began holding highly successful crusades, and in 1950 he formed the Billy Graham Evangelistic Association to help coordinate his activities. In 1952 Graham resigned from Northwestern Schools and moved to Montreat, North Carolina. In 1955, believing that the journal *Christian Century* was too liberal, he assisted in establishing the more conservative *Christianity Today.*

In 1952 President-elect Dwight Eisenhower asked for Graham's advice about an inaugural prayer, and thus began the evangelist's long association with national political figures. He gave the opening prayer at President Lyndon Johnson's 1965 inauguration and led President Richard Nixon's Sunday worship services at the White House. Not surprisingly, Graham became known as the "friend to presidents." After Nixon's resignation under the shadow of the Watergate scandal, Graham showed less enthusiasm for such political associations.

In the 1950s and 1960s Graham, in accord with other religious right leaders, was a strong anticommunist. During the American involvement in Vietnam, he was an uncritical supporter of government policy. On other public policy issues, Graham took conservative stands, such as opposing the school prayer ban and criticizing the Supreme Court for being too lenient with criminals. Although he emphasizes a decidedly conservative theology and focuses primarily on the need for personal conversion, Graham has been willing to express his concern for social justice. This willingness first became apparent in the early 1950s when he ended segregated seating at his crusades. In the 1980s he unexpectedly began to raise questions about the dangers of the arms race. Although some elements of the religious right have criticized Graham's more moderate, essentially nonpolitical evangelism, attitude surveys over the years indicate he has consistently remained one of the more esteemed Americans.

Robert Grant (1936–)

One of the leading figures in the religious right during the 1980s, Grant was one of the founders of Christian Voice in 1978 and of the American Freedom Coalition (AFC) in 1987. He remains president of AFC. He graduated from Wheaton College and Fuller Theological Seminary and was the founding dean of the California Graduate School of Theology. In 1975 he established American Christian Cause, a California organization that opposed gay rights and pornography. Christian Voice, originally named Citizens United in 1976 and briefly called American Christians United, became well known for constructing moral report cards that rated congressional and presidential candidates on a variety of issues, including foreign policy. For instance, Grant and his organization considered support for the Reagan administration's Strategic Defense Initiative, known as "Star Wars," to be pro-biblical. He also agreed with attempts of the Reagan administration to provide aid to the Nicaraguan contras.

After the poor showing of his candidates in the 1986 congressional elections, Grant decided that Christians must cooperate with other groups, including non-Christians, to achieve common objectives. The religious right had become fragmented, having failed to build an effective coalition. Grant became one of the founders of the American Freedom Coalition and assumed the title of president. In establishing the new organization, he reportedly accepted financial assistance from Sun Myung Moon's Unification Church. In addition, a number of administrative officers were said to be members of the Unification Church. Grant stated that he did not agree with the Unification Church's theology and claimed that no one religious group dominated AFC. In order to achieve a just cause, Grant concluded, sometimes money had to be accepted from those who have it and are willing to contribute.

Billy James Hargis (1925–)

In the depths of the Cold War in the 1950s, Billy James Hargis represented the propensity of evangelists on the religious right to combine a fundamentalist Christian message with extreme patriotism and anticommunism. In 1943 Hargis began his studies for the ministry at Ozark Bible College in Bentonville, Arkansas, but remained there only a year. He ultimately received a Bachelor of Arts degree from Pikes Peak Bible Seminary in 1957 and a Bachelor of Theology degree from Burton College in Colorado Springs, Colorado, in 1958. He was awarded an honorary Doctor of Laws degree from Bob Jones University in 1961. Hargis founded the Christian Crusade organization to save America from communism. To this day each issue of his *Christian Crusade Newspaper* contains the quote "All I want to do is preach Jesus and save America." He gained notoriety in 1953 by participating with Carl McIntire in the Bible Balloon project, a plan to float balloons carrying Bible messages to Iron Curtain countries. In the early 1960s Hargis became more actively involved in politics, urging his followers to work for conservatives in election campaigns. During the tumultuous times of the late 1960s and early 1970s, Hargis identified campus radicals, antiwar protesters, and advocates of black power with communism and a general decline of moral values in America.

In 1974 Hargis announced that, due to health problems, he was giving up much of his work in the Christian Crusade and was resigning as president of the American Christian College in Tulsa, which had been founded just five years earlier. He also intended to stop his tours of the country and cease his weekly syndicated television programs. A strong opponent of sexual transgressions, Hargis in 1976 found himself accused of sexual misconduct by one female and three male students at his college. He emphatically denied the charges. The accusations came on the heels of Hargis's final separation from the American Christian College. Since then, Hargis has maintained his Christian Crusade ministry in Neosho, Missouri, and conducts yearly Bible conferences that include a good deal of political commentary. More recent issues of *Christian Crusade Newspaper* continue to warn against the dangers of communism and celebrate conservative Republican victories in the 1994 congressional elections. However, Hargis has never regained his earlier fame and influence.

Gary Jarmin (1949–)

As one of the religious right's more active leaders during the 1980s, Gary Jarmin played a key role as a legislative lobbyist. In the late 1980s he was instrumental in refocusing part of the movement away from explicitly Christian lobbying efforts in Washington and toward a more secular, grass-roots orientation. Jarmin was the legislative director of Christian Voice and the administrator of the organization's Moral Government Fund, a political action committee that made donations to congressional campaigns in the 1980s. Christian Voice began the controversial practice of issuing moral ratings of congressional and state officials. The organization grew out of anti–gay rights and antipornography campaigns in California in the late 1970s. Jarmin became field director for American Coalition for Traditional Values in 1984 and also became the political director for American Freedom Coalition when the new organization was established in 1987. A major objective for AFC, Jarmin believed, was the building of local organizations, called precinct councils, to concentrate on local issues. Among the reasons for the new emphasis were an increasing awareness of social needs and a growing desire to avoid theological divisions, along with the emerging realization that increased religious toleration was necessary in order to build alliances with other organizations that shared the AFC's goals.

The general ineffectiveness of the religious right in the 1986 congressional elections convinced Jarmin and others that Christians by themselves could not alter the political mood of the country. Others on the religious right were troubled with Jarmin's apparent willingness to accept support from, and work with, representatives of Reverend Sun Myung Moon's Unification Church. In the mid-1980s Jarmin characterized the Republican Party as an instrument to be used to achieve the objectives of the Christian right. As Reagan's presidency drew to a close, Jarmin noted that the Christian right had not achieved all that it had sought, but that involvement with the administration had provided valuable experience in government and politics.

Bob Jones, Sr. (1883–1968)

No family perhaps has been more vigorous in the battle against modernism than that of Bob Jones, Sr. And perhaps there has been no family trio more alike in fundamentalist temperament and theology than Jones, Sr., Bob Jones, Jr. (1911–), and Bob Jones III (1939–). An Alabama native, Jones, Sr., was converted in a Methodist church at age 11, preached his first revival at 12, had a brush-arbor church with 54 members at 13, was a licensed minister at 15, became a circuit rider at 16, and was orphaned at 17. Although an eager student, Jones enjoyed limited opportunities for schooling. In December 1900 he enrolled at Southern University in Greensboro, Alabama, but left after two years to become a full-time evangelist. An effective pulpiteer, many observers compared him to Billy Sunday. Although best known in the South, he preached in much of the North, from Illinois to New York.

Jones, Sr., accepted the Bible literally, as do his son and grandson, and any deviation from this narrow approach was heresy. Accordingly, he abandoned Methodism, convinced the denomination had embraced modernism, and devoted himself to fundamentalist causes. He was active in the World's Christian Fundamentals Association, founded in 1919; he served on the Moody Bible Institute's continuing education faculty; and in 1926 he established his own college, Bob Jones University, which has been located in Greenville, South Carolina, since 1947. The presidency of the school has passed from father to son to grandson.

Despite many interests in common with other religious fundamentalists, the Joneses represent a separatist variety of fundamentalism. They will therefore have nothing to do with either unbelievers or those who associate with unbelievers. In the 1950s and 1960s, for instance, they denounced Billy Graham for allowing nonfundamentalists to participate in his local crusades and for not directing converts to fundamentalist congregations. Likewise, in the 1980s they scorned Jerry Falwell for allowing Catholics and other "infidels" into the Moral Majority. Carl McIntire was the kind of fundamentalist most admired by the Joneses, and, like McIntire, the Joneses have been unwilling to play down theological differences for the sake of political cooperation.

Beverly LaHaye (1930–)

Wife of religious right leader Tim LaHaye, Beverly LaHaye has played a major role in organizing conservative Christian women in support of the religious right's political agenda. LaHaye, whose father died when she was young, grew up in Missouri and Michigan during the Great Depression. With her husband, she first gained national attention in the 1970s by offering seminars that advocated greater sexual gratification for Christian married couples. She and her husband Tim published *The Act of Marriage: The Beauty of Sexual Love,* which within a few years had sold more than one million copies. The book is essentially a sex manual for Christians. She began her own ministry in the late 1970s, publishing such books as *The Spirit-Controlled Woman* (1976) and *How To Develop Your Child's Temperament* (1977). Although LaHaye regards women as individuals in their own right who should engage actively in politics, she advises them to remain subordinate to their husbands and to household duties.

In 1979 she formed Concerned Women for America (CWA) with only nine members. By 1987 she claimed a membership of more than 500,000 women organized into 1,800 local chapters. In 1985 LaHaye moved with her husband to Washington, D.C., where she established the new national office of CWA. In 1987 she was given life tenure as president of the organization. LaHaye has gained a well-deserved reputation for effective political advocacy on behalf of conservative Christian causes. In September 1987 she testified in favor of Robert Bork, President Ronald Reagan's unsuccessful nominee to the Supreme Court. LaHaye has concentrated her efforts as much on local as on national issues. For instance, CWA was given credit in 1986 for the defeat of an Equal Rights Amendment to the Vermont state constitution.

Tim LaHaye (1926–)

Tim LaHaye first gained national prominence for his Family Life Seminars and workshops on Christian marriage, which he conducted with his wife, Beverly. The LaHayes co-authored *The Act of Marriage: The Beauty of Sexual Love,* in which they claimed Christians can experience great sexual enjoyment. LaHaye attended Western Conservative Baptist Seminary and in 1956 moved to San Diego, California, to become the pastor of the Scott Memorial Baptist Church. His book *The Battle for the Mind* (1980) focused on "secular humanism" as a major threat to Christianity. He defined humanism as a religion that places sole confidence in human beings and acknowledges no need for God. In *The Coming Peace in the Middle East* (1984), LaHaye identified philosophies and philosophers he considered harmful to humankind.

One of the founders of Moral Majority, he started a branch of that organization, Californians for Biblical Morality, in 1980. That same year he created the Council for National Policy, a coalition of religious right leaders. In 1983 LaHaye established the American Coalition for Traditional Values (ACTV), which conducted a voter registration campaign for the 1984 election. After the election, LaHaye announced that the organization had registered two million voters, although other sources claimed a much lower number. One of LaHaye's objectives was to acquire more government appointments for born-again Christians in President Ronald

Reagan's second administration. LaHaye moved ACTV headquarters to Washington, D.C., in 1985, and in January 1986 reports surfaced that he had received financial support for ACTV from a representative of Sun Myung Moon's Unification Church. The following year LaHaye became an honorary national co-chairman of U.S. Representative Jack Kemp's campaign for the presidency, but resigned when news reports disclosed statements in his published works critical of Roman Catholics and Jews. In the 1994 elections, LaHaye was actively involved in a nationwide voter drive to get conservative Christians to the polls.

Hal Lindsey (1930–)

The most successful spinner in recent years of apocalyptic scenarios, Hal Lindsey has fueled the Christian right's belief that Armageddon is nigh. The Houston, Texas, native attended the University of Houston for two years, but dropped out, served a stint in the Coast Guard, and later worked as a tugboat captain on the Mississippi River. An avowed agnostic, he was converted as a result of reading a Gideon New Testament and soon thereafter was absorbed by the biblical prophecies of Ezekiel and Revelation. From 1958 to 1962 he attended Dallas Theological Seminary, earning a masters degree in theology. The next ten years he spent with the Campus Crusade for Christ, speaking to audiences throughout the United States and in Mexico and Canada.

In 1970 Lindsey published *The Late Great Planet Earth.* The astonishing success of this work, which reportedly sold 20 million copies in 52 languages worldwide and was made into a movie in 1978, demonstrated the appetite for the visionary genre, and Lindsey capitalized on the hunger. He churned out in rapid succession a string of apocalyptic thrillers, including *Satan Is Alive and Well* (1972), *The Terminal Generation* (1976), and *The 1980s: Countdown to Armageddon* (1980). Typical of this kind of literature, which tends to flourish during eras of national and international stress, Lindsey's works saw in current events a fulfillment of biblical prophecies about the end of time. The restoration of Israel in 1948, along with Israel's control of Jerusalem in 1967, convinced Lindsey that the "terminal generation" was at hand, although he wisely avoided precise dates. And until the 1980s, when he espoused a strong military to resist communism abroad and endorsed capitalist values to counter socialist tendencies at home, he had also generally avoided indentification with a specific political agenda.

Lindsey obviously was at ease with the religious right, and figures on the religious right, such as Pat Robertson and Jerry Falwell, were just as happy with his vision of doom, evidence of which they, too, saw in American society. Lindsey continues to present his interpretations of biblical prophecy in published works and in the broadcast media.

J. Gresham Machen (1881–1937)

This strong-willed Presbyterian professor who was schooled at Johns Hopkins University, Princeton Theological Seminary, and in Germany could be regarded as the theological and ideological grandfather of contemporary fundamentalists. As a teacher at Princeton Seminary from 1906 to 1929, he raised issues that still excite the religious right, from biblical inerrancy to open hostility toward all forms of liberalism. Typical of his unbridled attack upon modernism was *Christianity and Liberalism* (1923), a work in which he asserted that it was impossible to be a Christian and a liberal at the same time.

Increasingly intolerant of the more liberal sentiments of other denominational and seminary leaders, a disgruntled Machen left Princeton and founded Westminster Theological Seminary in Philadelphia in 1929. Continuing his attack, Machen now accused the denomination's missionaries of doctrinal infidelity. Eventually defrocked in 1936 over this dispute, he promptly established the rival Presbyterian Church of America. Even this new group was soon torn by schism, giving substance to the claim that if Machen had lived long enough, he ultimately would have been the denomination's only member. Machen's student, Carl McIntire, would go on to influence the direction of the religious right in post–World War II America.

Clarence E. Manion (1896–1979)

After leaving a 25-year career in academics, Clarence Manion established the Manion Forum of the Air, a popular political broadcast in the 1950s and 1960s. A Roman Catholic, Manion received a B.A. in 1915 from St. Mary's College in St. Mary, Kentucky. He attended Catholic University of America, receiving his M.A. in 1916 and M.Ph. in 1917. He went on to the University of Notre Dame, where he received his J.D. in 1922. In 1925 Manion was appointed professor of constitutional law at Notre Dame, and in 1941 he began serving as dean of the College of Law, a position he held until 1952. The following year he became head of President Dwight Eisenhower's Inter-Governmental Relations Commission.

Soon becoming dissatisfied with the Eisenhower administration, Manion resigned his position after one year to found the Manion Forum, a weekly radio series consisting of conservative commentary. First broadcast over 16 radio stations, by 1965 the Manion Forum was being carried by more than 300 radio and television stations. The program included Manion's own commentaries as well as interviews with political, educational, business, and military personalities. In the late 1950s Manion joined the John Birch Society, becoming one of its original directors. Although he supposedly did not always agree with the organization—for example, he did not support its claim that President Eisenhower was an agent of the Communist party—he refused to resign from the society. Known for his often extreme public statements, Manion demonstrated cordiality and personal warmth in his private life. He published several books, including *Let's Face It* (1956), *The Conservative American* (1964), and *Cancer in the Constitution* (1972). In addition to his own publications, Manion inspired and published Barry Goldwater's *Conscience of a Conservative* (1960), the book that helped launch Goldwater's successful bid for the Republican presidential nomination in 1964.

Edward A. McAteer (1927–)

With Paul Weyrich and Howard Phillips, Edward McAteer has worked tirelessly to involve the religious right in the political process. A marketing specialist from the Colgate-Palmolive Company, he is an active Southern Baptist layman whose pastor in Memphis, Tennessee, contributed significantly to the fundamentalist takeover of the Southern Baptist Convention. The Religious Roundtable, established in 1979 with a council of 56, the same number that signed the Declaration of Independence, was McAteer's primary organizational contribution to the religious right. And just as Weyrich worked to enlist Falwell for Moral Majority, McAteer sought just as diligently to bring James Robison to the Roundtable. Indeed, in 1979 McAteer recruited a quintet of notable fundamentalists—Robison, Falwell, Pat Robertson, James Kennedy, and Charles Stanley—to serve on the board of this new organization.

Bringing people from the religious and political right together, McAteer's group sponsored the National Affairs Briefing (NAB) in Dallas, Texas, in August 1980. Nonpartisan billing notwithstanding, this was a fundamentalist and conservative Republican affair. Of the 1980 presidential candidates, Ronald Reagan was the only one to attend the gathering. The national attention this meeting attracted was not altogether beneficial for either McAteer or the Christian right. The stridency of some of the speakers and the hints of anti-Semitism disturbed many Americans. And following McAteer's unsuccessful race for the U.S. Senate in 1984, the Roundtable's influence declined sharply. Although his support of conservative causes remained as fervent as ever, McAteer did not support Weyrich's effort to recast the Christian right's social objectives in terms of a secular "cultural revolution." He was too much of a Baptist fundamentalist to embrace a political strategy that deliberately omitted the God of Judeo-Christianity, however desirable the ends.

Carl McIntire (1906–)

A virulent anticommunist crusader, Carl McIntire reached the height of his influence during the Cold War era of the 1950s. As a student at Princeton Theological Seminary in the 1920s, he had come under the sway of fundamentalist J. Gresham Machen. Accordingly, when Machen left Princeton and founded Westminster Theological Seminary in 1929, McIntire followed. Upon graduation in 1931, the intelligent and energetic young Presbyterian became the pastor of a major fundamentalist congregation, the Collingswood, New Jersey, Presbyterian Church. Proving to be rigidly doctrinaire, autocratic, self-righteous, and intolerant of opposing views, McIntire subsequently disrupted almost every religious agency he touched.

In 1936 McIntire, along with Machen, was expelled from the Presbyterian Church (USA), and for a brief time thereafter he affiliated with Machen's Presbyterian Church of America. But the mixture of these two strong-willed Calvinists was volatile at best, and an eruption was not long in coming. In 1937 McIntire forged his own denomination, the Bible Presbyterian Church, and upon this foundation erected his own religious empire. He kept the faithful informed through the columns of the *Christian Beacon*, begun in 1936, and *The Twentieth-Century Reformation Hour*, a

30-minute radio broadcast begun in 1955, and he trained loyal disciples at his Faith Theological Seminary in Philadelphia and at colleges in Cape Canaveral, Florida, and Pasadena, California.

Unfortunately, McIntire's ability to create was matched by a proclivity for disruptive controversy. His autocratic methods and dogmatic beliefs invariably spawned dissent. In 1956 he was unceremoniously expelled from the American Council of Christian Churches, a body that he had founded in 1941, and in 1971 a bitter schism occurred at the Faith Theological Seminary. The school's president, most faculty members, and approximately half the students left in protest of McIntire's high-handed leadership and outspoken support of complete military victory in Vietnam.

Both prone to conspiratorial thinking, McIntire and Senator Joe McCarthy of Wisconsin gravitated naturally toward one another. The association was symbiotic. The cleric gave the politician a touch of divinity, and the politician enhanced the quarrelsome Presbyterian's national stature. McCarthy paid attention to McIntire, and therefore the preacher's charges of religious and political apostasy in high places received more extensive press coverage. A young minister whose own career as an anticommunist crusader received a boost from McIntire was Dr. Billy James Hargis.

Dwight Lyman Moody (1837–1899)

A noted nineteenth-century revivalist, Dwight L. Moody established the standard for highly organized evangelism campaigns in twentieth-century America. Born in Northfield, Massachusetts, Moody moved to Boston while still a teenager to become a boot and shoe salesman. While in Boston, Moody became active in the Young Men's Christian Association (YMCA) and the Congregational Church. He moved to Chicago in 1856 to continue his successful business ventures and there renewed his association with the YMCA. In 1860 he began to work exclusively for that religious organization and during the Civil War was involved in efforts to evangelize wounded soldiers.

In 1872 Moody traveled to Great Britain and began a popular revivalist campaign in Scotland, Ireland, and England, ending with a four-month stay in London in 1875. Returning to the United States, he conducted well-organized revival meetings in such large cities as Philadelphia, New York, and Boston. The popularity of these evangelistic efforts can be attributed to Moody's uncomplicated presentation of a loving and merciful God. Along with fellow evangelist Ira Sankey, Moody produced collections of gospel hymns that added to the enthusiasm of audiences at revival meetings. After another tour of Great Britain from 1881 to 1884, Moody began organizing annual student Bible conferences. He founded three schools: the Northfield Academy for Young Women in 1879, the Mount Hermon School for Young Men in 1881, and the Chicago Bible Institute for Home and Foreign Missions (now the Moody Bible Institute) in 1889. The latter schools served as a training ground for urban evangelists and as the source of inexpensive religious publications.

Moody's major accomplishment was to tailor traditional evangelical Protestantism for urban residents in a newly emerging industrial America. As a conservative evangelical, however, Moody found it difficult to deal with the conflicts beginning to arise between liberal and conservative wings of American Protestantism.

Ralph Reed (1961–)

Ralph Reed was born in Portsmouth, Virginia, only a short distance from Pat Robertson's first broadcast studio. His early years were interrupted by frequent moves. His father was a Navy doctor, and by the time Reed entered high school the family had lived in seven towns in five states. Upon graduation from high school in Toccoa, Georgia, he entered the University of Georgia. In summer 1981 a U.S. Senate internship took him to Washington, D.C., where he remained through the fall working with the National College Republicans. He returned to the University of Georgia in spring 1982, completed his degree, and then resumed his efforts in the nation's capital with the National College Republicans. With the approach of the 1984 senatorial race in North Carolina between Jim Hunt and Jesse Helms, the outspoken Republican incumbent whose political and religious conservatism made him a favorite of the religious right, Reed left Washington for Raleigh. He promptly founded Students for America and joined the fray in behalf of the North Carolina senator. Reed unquestionably loved politics; even so, he entered the graduate program at Emory University on a scholarship, obtained a Ph.D. in history in 1986, and anticipated a career in academia. Three years later he was the executive secretary of Robertson's new Christian Coalition.

Reed's fondness for conservative politics and causes was longstanding. As a child he read biographies of the presidents, as well as William L. Shirer's *The Rise and Fall of the Third Reich,* which impressed upon him the power of politics. At the University of Georgia he was a College Republican, debater, and columnist for the school paper, *Red and Black.* Reed eventually lost this journalistic position because he plagiarized a story. Always on the political right of every issue, Reed was a leader among campus conservatives by 1982. Shortly thereafter he discovered religion. This nominal Methodist smoked and drank until the early 1980s, whereupon he promptly put away cigarettes and John Barleycorn and became a born-again, charismatic Christian. God and Caesar now became allies, as Reed discovered the "true" meaning of politics. "I now realize," said the new convert, "that politics is a noble calling to serve God and my fellow man." Appropriately, his dissertation at Emory, which focused on the early history of church-related colleges, criticized some sectarian schools for sacrificing their religious heritage for endowments.

Although Reed supported Jack Kemp over Robertson in the 1988 presidential primaries, the Virginia televangelist admired the young man's organizational talent and religious commitment. When Robertson formed the Christian Coalition in 1989, Reed became its executive secretary. Despite his affable nature and disarming good looks, Reed is a shrewd political strategist. One admirer aptly described him as "the Christian Lee Atwater." He always wants to win, but he also recognizes that the road to victory takes many turns. Accordingly, Reed has sought to broaden the Christian Coalition, to make it more ecumenical. He therefore occasionally downplays such issues as abortion, homosexuality, and prayer in the schools, emphasizing instead taxes, crime, and education. Foes acknowledge that this apparent flexibility makes Reed a formidable opponent. Still, this is a risky strategy, and it remains to be seen whether the Christian Coalition can attract moderate conservatives without offending its hardcore base. Drawing a parallel from Reed's doctoral dissertation, one wonders how much of its base the coalition is willing to sacrifice for moderate votes.

Marion Gordon "Pat" Robertson (1930–)

Perhaps the religious right's most successful television entrepreneur, Pat Robertson was born and reared in Lexington, Virginia. The son of a prominent politician, Senator A. Willis Robertson, and a devoutly religious mother, the intelligent and charming Robertson seemed marked for success. A Phi Beta Kappa graduate of Washington and Lee University, he subsequently studied at the University of London, served as a noncombatant with the Marines in Korea (1951–1952), and enrolled in Yale Law School, graduating in 1955. Although reared a Baptist, the youthful Robertson was not particularly religious, as evidenced by a fondness for women, whiskey, and poker. In 1956 this all changed.

Following a religious experience that was helped along by a staunch fundamentalist whom his mother respected, Robertson entered the Biblical Seminary, later rechristened the New York Theological Seminary, in New York City. And it was here at this conservative enclave from 1956 to 1959 that he became a charismatic evangelical. In 1959 Robertson returned to Virginia, purchased a television station in Portsmouth, and launched the Christian Broadcasting Network (CBN) in January 1960. Three years later, seeking to raise funds to cover monthly costs of $7,000, he sought to enlist 700 listeners who would pay $10 per month. From this emerged The 700 Club and later *The 700 Club Program,* which deliberately copied the format of *The Johnny Carson Show.* Jim Bakker, a religious fund-raiser par excellence who later established the PTL complex at Charlotte, North Carolina, joined CBN in 1965. Bakker deserves considerable credit for the success of Robertson's telethons. By 1975 CBN had an estimated 110 million viewers, and in 1979 Robertson opened an impressive International Headquarters Building and CBN University at Virginia Beach. By 1987 his empire sprawled over 380 acres and employed over 4,000 people.

Robertson's social concerns were virtually identical to those of other figures on the religious right. He opposed abortion, homosexuality, pornography, and the Equal Rights Amendment, and he encouraged prayer in the public schools and tuition tax credits for private schooling. Failing miserably in the 1988 presidential campaign to translate television celebrity status into political success, Robertson nevertheless quickly regrouped. His pro-family, "values oriented politics" were institutionalized by the new Christian Coalition (CC), created in 1989. Heir to Jerry Falwell's Moral Majority, the CC embarked upon an aggressive grass-roots campaign to defeat politicians, from school board elections on up, whose values were not sufficiently pro-family.

James Robison (1943–)

Often billed as "God's Angry Man" because of a belligerent pulpit style and rigid dogmatism, James Robison was second in prominence only to Jerry Falwell in calling America to repentance for its "wicked" ways. Destitute and abandoned by her alcoholic husband, Robison's mother advertised him at birth in a Houston, Texas, newspaper and subsequently gave him to a Baptist minister and his wife in Pasadena, a Houston suburb. When Robison was five, his mother reclaimed him, headed to Austin, Texas, and over the next decade went through a series of marriages and divorces. At age 15 Robison returned to his foster parents in Pasadena, experienced conversion, and at age 18 resolved to become an evangelist.

Robison attended East Texas Baptist College and San Jacinto Junior College, but dropped out and embarked upon full-time evangelism in late 1963. At 6'3" and over 200 pounds, he was a commanding presence in the pulpit. In 1965 he established the James Robison Evangelistic Association and five years later aired his first 30-minute television program. By 1980, with headquarters at Hurst, near Fort Worth, Texas, he employed 150 full-time staff members, and his television show, *James Robison, A Man with a Message*, was carried by 100 stations in 28 states. Many observers saw the young evangelist as an eventual successor to Billy Graham.

Casting himself as pro-life, pro-moral, pro-family, and pro-America, Robison quickly became a major voice on the religious right. He denounced abortion, homosexuality, premarital sex, the Equal Rights Amendment, and "secular humanism" with as much passion as and much more stridency than Falwell, with whom he was closely associated in the 1980s. Along with Edward A. McAteer, he helped organize the Religious Roundtable in 1979, and in August the following year the Roundtable's National Affairs Briefing (NAB) at the Reunion Arena in Dallas brought him to the attention of a national audience. Despite its nonpartisan billing, the NAB turned into a love feast for presidential candidate Ronald Reagan. Typical of so many on the religious right in the 1980s, Robison saw in Reagan a knight to carry the banner for God and country.

Francis A. Schaeffer (1912–1984)

If J. Gresham Machen was the intellectual grandfather of contemporary fundamentalism, Francis Schaeffer certainly was the father.

These spiritual kinsmen both believed America had drifted far from its Christian moorings. For Machen, the "villain" was liberalism in the nation's churches; for Schaeffer, it was secular humanism in western culture. In 1929 Machen, certain that Princeton Theological Seminary had succumbed irretrievably to liberalism, left the Presbyterian school and established Westminster School of Theology in Philadelphia. Even this conservative haven soon proved too liberal for one of Machen's strong-willed disciples, Carl McIntire, who subsequently founded Faith Theological Seminary in Wilmington, Delaware, in 1937. Amid the controversy between these two doctrinaire Presbyterians, Schaeffer's theological pilgrimage began. He entered Machen's school in 1935, but finished with McIntire in 1937.

Schaeffer was born in Philadelphia. His working-class parents were nominal Lutherans. Set on a career in engineering, he went to Drexel Institute, but soon switched to Hampden-Sydney College, a Presbyterian institution in Virginia. From this liberal arts school he journeyed to Westminster Seminary, where Machen and McIntire already were feuding over matters of eschatalogy, Christian liberty, and denominational sectarianism. For a decade, 1937 to 1947, Schaeffer pastored in St. Louis, ministering primarily to blue-collar workers and children. Sponsored by the Independent Board of Presbyterian Missions, Schaeffer was sent to Europe in 1947, and over the next few years he traveled and preached extensively across the continent. In 1954 he bought a chalet in Huénoz, Switzerland, named it L'Abri, The Shelter, and became a guru of sorts to his neighbors, students, and spiritual travelers of all types. Joining an anti-McIntire group in founding Covenant College and Seminary and the Evangelical Presbyterian Church, he severed ties with his old mentor in 1956. Diagnosed with cancer in 1978, Schaeffer returned to the United States, where his attention turned increasingly to the debate on abortion.

Schaeffer's evangelistic endeavors had made him well known by the early 1960s. A torrent of well-received tapes, films, and books made him a household name in much of the English-speaking Christian world by the 1970s. In many of his 25 books Schaeffer gave the positions of the religious right a scholarly gloss. His *No Final Conflict* (1975) was a defense of biblical literalism. To question the historicity of Genesis, he argued, was to raise doubts about the reliability of all scripture. Originally conceived as a Christian response to *Civilization,* a popular PBS series by Kenneth Clark and Jacob Bronowski, Schaeffer's most sweeping assessment, *How Should We Then Live? The Rise and Decline of Western*

Thought and Culture (1976), dealt with the bête noire of the religious right, secular humanism. From the Greeks and Romans to the Renaissance to the Enlightenment, Schaeffer contrasted the "weaknesses" of human-centered cultures to the "strengths" of Christianity, which was rooted in God's absolute truth. The result of humanism could be seen in the ovens of Auschwitz and the abortion clinics of the United States. Tim LaHaye's popular work *The Battle for the Mind* (1980) owes much to Schaeffer's treatise. Written with C. Everett Koop, *Whatever Happened to the Human Race?* (1979) was an unsparing indictment of abortion. This cheapening of life Schaeffer attributed to the erosion of the Christian view of humanity. Intended as a guide for Christian activism, *A Christian Manifesto* (1981) called the righteous to battle. Schaeffer applauded Jerry Falwell's Moral Majority, for it had boldly entered the political arena in behalf of divine law. Other Christians should not only follow suit, but also, as a last resort, engage in civil disobedience. To Schaeffer, the use of state funds for abortion certainly justified such resistance. Significantly, Randall Terry, leader of Operation Rescue, one of the more militant antiabortion groups, readily acknowledges his debt to Schaeffer. Indeed, in Schaeffer all of the religious right had found a spokesman of intellectual vigor and sophistication.

Frederick Charles Schwarz (1913–)

A fervent anticommunist crusader, Fred Schwarz came to the United States from Australia in the early 1950s at the invitation of Carl McIntire and the American Council of Christian Churches. Schwarz received a medical degree from the University of Queensland and practiced as a psychiatrist in Sydney until 1953, when he came to the United States. He joined W. E. Pietsch, a radio evangelist, in Waterloo, Iowa, where he became one of the founders of the Christian Anti-Communism Crusade. Although initially tied to McIntire's American and International Councils of Christian Churches, Schwarz placed less emphasis on spreading a Christian message than on disseminating a doctrine of anticommunism. In 1958 Schwarz moved his organization to Long Beach, California. He ultimately deemphasized association with McIntire's two councils, did not appeal directly to Christian fundamendalists for support, and showed little concern for such fundamentalist positions as the premillennial return of Christ. Although he presented no clear theological position, Schwarz nonetheless saw conservative Christianity as the only possible alternative to communism.

In the 1950s Schwarz used the airwaves to disseminate his message, but increasingly thereafter he traveled the nation, offering "schools" on anticommunism. His presentations emphasized the nature of the world as divided into good and evil forces. In 1957 Schwarz received increased attention when he appeared before the House Un-American Activities Committee to testify as an expert on communism. His book *You Can Trust the Communists (To Be Communists)* portrayed communists as well-organized and exceptionally intelligent individuals whose behavior was very predictable once people understood their very logical, but ultimately insane, thought. He also characterized as mental illness the belief that negotiations with communists could bring peace. In the 1970s Schwarz and his organization were active in presenting an anticommunist message in many countries, including El Salvador and the Philippines. Now in his eighties, Schwarz continues to appeal for funds to operate the Christian Anti-Communism Crusade.

Cyrus Ingerson Scofield (1843–1921)

Cyrus Scofield is considered one of the more important figures to influence premillennialist thought in the twentieth century. Born in Tennessee, he fought on the Confederate side in the Civil War and subsequently set up a law practice in Kansas. Accused of stealing political contributions from a candidate for public office, he left Kansas in 1877, abandoning his wife and two children. She divorced him in 1883. Scofield moved to St. Louis, Missouri, where he was arrested and imprisoned on charges of forgery. While in prison Scofield was converted to Christianity. In 1882 he became pastor of the First Congregational Church in Dallas, Texas, where he edited the *Believer,* a monthly publication, and directed a Bible correspondence course.

In 1895 Scofield moved to Massachusetts to become a faculty member at Dwight L. Moody's Northfield Bible School and began work on a project to provide notes for the King James version of the Bible. The result was the *Scofield Reference Bible,* considered by many observers to be one of the more important popularizations of premillennial dispensationalism. The nontechnical presentation gained wide popularity among laypersons. Scofield believed anyone could interpret biblical prophecy. Formal learning and theological training were unnecessary. Sales of the reference Bible from its first publication in 1909 to 1967 are estimated at between five and ten million copies, and a revised edition published in 1967 so far has sold nearly three million copies. Some authorities have argued that the format of Scofield's Bible, in which notes are presented on the same page as the scriptural text, caused many readers to accord as much authority to the annotations as to the scriptures. In any event, many twentieth-century Bible students have embraced Scofield's scriptural notes, unaware perhaps of the author's specific interpretation.

Scofield divided history into distinguishable time periods, indicating that God's relationship with human beings progressed from one age to the next. Beginning with Innocence, the world proceded to the ages of Conscience, Human Government, Promise, Law, and Grace, the time period from Christ to the present. The final stage, the Kingdom Age, would occur after the prophesied Battle of Armageddon. Christ would govern the world as a theocracy for a thousand years, followed by the final judgment and the end of all ages. Scofield, like subsequent premillennialists, doubted the prospects for peace and human improvement before Christ's direct intervention. At the end of World War I Scofield claimed that any attempt to establish a world order would only hasten the coming of the Antichrist. Asserting that Christ and the Apostles were not reformers, Scofield argued that the church should prepare for the end of time rather than becoming involved in social reform. Only in the millennial age would humans turn away from their corrupted natures. Christ's rule would lead to the defeat of selfishness and the elimination of inequalities in worldly goods.

Contemporary writers such as Hal Lindsey reflect Scofield's influence. Scofield emphasized the importance of Israel as a nation, for instance, and declared in 1916 that Russia would invade the Holy Land in the end time. Although his contemporaries tended to hold the same view, Scofield put special emphasis on such an invasion in his Bible and elsewhere.

Robert H. W. Welch, Jr. (1899–1985)

Founder of the John Birch Society and its leader for 25 years, Robert Welch dedicated himself to fighting what he saw as a communist conspiracy to capture American government and society. He received a degree from the University of North Carolina and attended the U.S. Naval Academy and Harvard University

Law School, but failed to graduate from either. In 1921 he started a successful candy business. He left the company in 1956 and devoted himself thereafter to fighting the communist conspiracy that allegedly was enveloping America.

In 1958 Welch met with 11 other businessmen to form the John Birch Society, named for a Baptist missionary to China who had been killed by Chinese Communists at the end of World War II. Welch considered Birch to be the first casualty of World War III. The transcript of Welch's lengthy presentation at that meeting was published as *The Blue Book*. Representing the basic philosophy and objectives of the society, this book called for three things: "less government, more individual responsibility, and a better world." In *The Politician*, a biographical manuscript first published in 1958, Welch stated that communists had infiltrated the highest levels of American government. He believed Dwight Eisenhower had not only become president through communist maneuverings, but was also a knowing agent of the communist conspiracy. Welch charged other noted Americans, including Presidents Franklin Roosevelt and Harry Truman, Secretary of State John Foster Dulles, and General George C. Marshall, with varying levels of complicity in the communist plot to gain control of American government.

Although he came from a fundamentalist Baptist background, Welch did not maintain formal ties to that tradition. His beliefs were universalistic; he selected no particular brand of Christianity as the one true faith. His writings demonstrated a belief in the individualistic liberalism of the nineteenth century as well as a suspicion of democracy, which he described as demagoguery and fraud. After the mid-1960s Welch's fame declined. Maintaining his strong anticommunist stance, he once referred to President Ronald Reagan as a "lackey" of communist conspirators. Welch stepped down as president of the John Birch Society in 1983.

Paul Weyrich (1942–)

Sometimes described as the religious right's point man, Paul Weyrich not only enunciated conservative positions in the 1970s and 1980s in an extreme way, but also labored diligently to politicize the religious right. Behind his cherubic exterior lurked a pugnacious temperament. A Roman Catholic of blue-collar origins, he was born in Racine, Wisconsin. Strictly speaking, Weyrich was not a member of the religious right, but rather a shrewd political strategist who saw Protestant fundamentalists as an untapped pool of voters for conservative causes. The trick was to bring them into the political process and to unite them with conservative Roman Catholics. Weyrich saw in certain "social" issues an opportunity to achieve precisely this goal. There was little if any difference, he believed, between many Protestant fundamentalists and Catholics on such matters as abortion, prayer in the public schools, and anticommunism. Jerry Falwell and Pope John Paul II merely represented different sides of the same coin.

Out of headquarters in Washington, D.C., Weyrich operated the Committee for the Survival of a Free Congress, basically a training school for conservative political candidates. Along with Edward A. McAteer and Howard Phillips, he not only courted Falwell, but also minted the phrase "moral majority." As conceived by Weyrich, the Moral Majority was to bring religious fundamentalists of whatever stripe together for common political ends. Meanwhile, the Religious Roundtable, headed by McAteer, was seen by Weyrich as an umbrella organization designed to coordinate the political efforts of several religious right groups, including Moral Majority and Christian Voice. Weyrich more recently has attempted to unite religious and secular conservatives in the cause of "cultural conservatism," meaning basically political objectives that Christians, Jews, and even atheists can pursue without abandoning their respective theological positions.

Donald Ellis Wildmon (1938–)

Television programming has been the primary concern of this mild-mannered but determined Methodist minister from Tupelo, Mississippi. In the belief that most television programs undermined "traditional" family values, he encouraged his congregation one Sunday in December 1976 to turn off the tube for a week. Convinced by resulting coverage in the national press that he had hit upon an idea whose time had come, Wildmon promptly organized the National Federation for Decency in 1977, renamed the American Family Association in 1987. Headquartered initially in Wildmon's family dining room, the new organization boldly set out to purify the airwaves. By 1992 the American Family Association operated out of a new building, had a staff of 35, claimed to have 450,000 members in 640 chapters nationwide, and conducted state-of-the-art direct-mailing operations that raised over six million dollars annually.

Wildmon's strategy was twofold: first, to monitor network shows for sexual content, profanity, and violence; and, second, to threaten with boycotts the corporate sponsors of offensive programs. In this way he would punish not only the networks, but also the businesses that funded unacceptable shows. Accordingly, Pepsi, Dr. Pepper, Wendy's, Domino's Pizza, Ralston Purina, General Mills, Honda, Mazda, AT&T, and others have all incurred the preacher's wrath. The extent to which such pressure tactics have succeeded is debatable. If AT&T, as Wildmon believed, discontinued its advertisements on *Saturday Night Live* because of his threats, Holiday Inn, Johnson and Johnson, Waldenbooks, and others have ignored the television censor with apparent impunity. During the 1980s Wildmon, a member of the Moral Majority, worked closely with Jerry Falwell to make the airwaves "safe" for family viewing.

Survey Data and Quotations

4

A Survey of Conservative Christian Attitudes

This study focuses elsewhere primarily on the "elite" of the religious right—organizations and their leaders. If the religious right ended there, it would be of little consequence to the social and political fabric of America. Millions of ordinary Americans, however, agree with the religious right's conservative interpretation of American society and politics. This agreement not only adds significantly to the perceived moral force of the movement, but also accounts for the generous financial support of many conservative Christians. Multitudes of evangelical Christians, awakened in recent years by charismatic leaders and mobilized by grass-roots organizations, have become a force to be reckoned with on election day.

Religion and the American Population

To illuminate some of the religious attitudes of Americans, attitudes that help in understanding the appeal of the religious right, this

Table 1. Belief in God (percentage)

Don't believe	2
Don't know, no way to find out	3
Believe in higher power	10
Believe sometimes	4
Believe with doubts	16
Believe without doubts	64
Don't know	2

Source: 1994 General Social Survey. N=2992.
Note: The total percentage is 101 due to rounding.

chapter employs a data analysis of the National Opinion Research Center's 1994 General Social Survey conducted for the authors by the Roper Center for Public Opinion Research, as well as Gallup International's survey of American religious opinion.[1] Over 90 percent of Americans questioned in Gallup surveys since 1944 consistently express some belief in God.[2] Table 1 summarizes the results of the 1994 General Social Survey, in which respondents were asked to select the category, ranging from "I don't believe in God" to "I know God really exists and I have no doubts about it," that best expresses their belief about God. These results are consistent with the Gallup Polls, for if the four categories indicating some level of belief are combined, 94 percent of those surveyed express some level of belief in God or a "higher power."

Examining those interviewed in each of four geographical sections, the General Social Survey found that 50.0 percent in the Northeast, 61.7 percent in the Midwest, 72.7 percent in the South, and 53.4 percent in the West acknowledged a belief in God "without doubts" (N=1310).

The 1994 Supplement to the Princeton Religion Research Center's Religion in America study discloses additional characteristics of self-reported, born-again (or evangelical) Christians. A 1993 Gallup question asked respondents if they would describe themselves as "born-again," evangelical Christians.[3] Table 2 summarizes the results. Born-again, evangelical Christians tend to be female, older (over 50), residents of the South and the Midwest, from small towns, non-college attenders, lower income, and Protestant.

In analyzing the 1994 General Social Survey data, the authors adopt a procedure, similar to that used by Kenneth Wald in his study of religion and politics in America,[4] for dividing Protestant

Table 2. Born-Again, Evangelical Christians (percentage)

	Yes	No
National	42	54
Gender		
Male	36	60
Female	46	50
Age		
Under 30	36	59
30–49	40	57
50–64	46	49
65 & older	46	49
Region		
East	28	68
Midwest	40	56
South	58	38
West	33	62
Community		
Urban	39	56
Suburban	40	56
Small town, rural	51	45
Education		
Attended college	34	62
Did not attend	48	47
Household income		
$50,000 & over	29	68
$30,000–$49,000	40	57
$20,000–$29,999	41	56
Under $20,000	52	42
Religious Preference		
Protestant	54	42
Roman Catholic	21	75

Source: Gallup/Princeton Religion Research Center, 1994. N=722.
Note: Percentages exclude missing cases.

respondents into two categories: "evangelical Protestant" and "mainline Protestant." Respondents indicating their church affiliation as Missouri Synod Lutheran, Wisconsin Synod Lutheran, Southern Baptist, Churches of Christ, or Assemblies of God were categorized as "evangelical Protestant." Respondents stating their church membership as Congregationalist, Methodist, Episcopalian, Presbyterian, Disciples of Christ, Evangelical Lutheran Church in America, American Baptist, Unitarian, or Friends were categorized as "mainline Protestant." Black Protestant and Roman Catholic categories are not reported here because these groups are not directly relevant to the discussion of the religious right. The

Table 3. Evangelical and Mainline Protestant Church
Adherents

	Number	Percentage
Evangelical Protestant		
Assemblies of God	1,280,760	7.8
Churches of Christ	3,674,472	13.2
Lutheran—Missouri Synod	2,603,725	9.4
Southern Baptist Convention	18,940,682	68.1
Wisconsin Evangelical Lutheran	419,928	1.5
Total	27,800,417	100.0
Mainline Protestant		
Congregationalist	135,789	0.5
Methodist	11,091,032	43.0
Episcopalian	2,445,286	9.4
Presyterian	3,774,727	14.5
Disciples of Christ	1,037,757	4.0
Lutheran (ELCA)	5,226,798	20.2
American Baptist	1,873,731	7.2
Unitarian	190,193	0.7
Friends	130,484	0.5
Total	25,905,797	100.0

Source: Churches and Church Membership in the United States 1990.

number of Jewish respondents in the sample was so small that this group is also excluded from the data analysis. Table 3 presents the number of adherents (including children and regular participants in addition to church membership) to each of the Protestant denominations and the percentage each represents of the respective evangelical or mainline Protestant group.[5]

The following tables, drawn from the 1994 General Social Survey, compare the views of evangelical and mainline Protestants to those respondents who report having no religious affiliation. Table 4 presents the regional distribution of those respondents indicating an evangelical Protestant church affiliation in contrast to those who state an affiliation with non-evangelical, or "mainline," churches, and those who state no religious affiliation.

As expected, southern states have a disproportionately higher number of evangelical Protestants compared to the rest of the nation, with well over half of those so identified residing in this region. These survey results can be compared with actual church adherence in the two religious groups in the four regions, as

Table 4. Religious Preference by Region (percentage)

Region	Evangelical Protestant	Mainline Protestant	None
Northeast	2.9	19.8	16.4
Midwest	24.3	30.5	28.5
South	63.7	32.7	24.2
West	9.1	17.0	30.9
Total	100.0	100.0	100.0

Source: 1994 General Social Survey. N = 2781.

Table 5. Church Adherence by Region (percentage)

Region	Evangelical Protestant (N = 27,800,417)	Mainline Protestant (N = 25,905,797)
Northeast	4.7	19.0
Midwest	19.0	32.7
South	67.5	37.9
West	8.8	10.4
Total	100.0	100.0

Source: Churches and Church Membership in the United States 1990. N = 2829.

presented in Table 5. The table indicates a close relationship between the respondents' report of religious preference and actual percentage of church adherents.

Political Preferences

Recent campaigns and elections suggest a close relationship between the religious right and the Republican Party. The religious right provides voters for the party, while the party supports evangelicals on issues such as abortion, pornography, prayer in the schools, and "family values." Therefore, the authors expect a larger proportion of evangelicals to support the Republican Party than either mainline Protestants or non–church members. Table 6 presents a cross-tabulation of religious preference by political party identification. Given sampling error, there is no significant difference between the party loyalties of evangelicals and mainline Protestants. By contrast, non–church members are considerably

Table 6. Party Affiliation and Religious Preference (percentage)

	Evangelical Protestant	Mainline Protestant	None
Republican	38.6	36.9	17.3
Democratic	31.3	28.6	34.1
Independent	30.1	34.5	48.6
Total	100.0	100.0	100.0

Source: 1994 General Social Survey. N = 2829.

Table 7. Vote Preference for President, 1992 (percentage)

Candidate	Evangelical Protestant	Mainline Protestant	None
Clinton	34.6	38.7	53.5
Bush	50.4	40.9	19.8
Perot	15.0	20.4	26.7
Total	100.0	100.0	100.0

Source: 1994 General Social Survey. N = 1595.

less Republican and considerably more Independent than either evangelical or mainline Protestants.

Party identification in the United States, though a good indicator of voter preference, is a far from perfect predictor. Many evangelical Protestant Democrats may vote for a Republican candidate more conducive to their religious preferences. Table 7 suggests this possibility. A comparison of Tables 6 and 7 indicates that while the party identification of evangelical Protestants favors the Republican Party somewhat, presidential voter preference shows a greater level of voter support for that party from evangelical Protestants.

As Table 6 indicates, evangelicals overall may be slightly more likely to identify with one of the parties than mainline Protestants, and considerably more likely to do so than non–church members (approximately 70 percent, 66 percent, and 51 percent, respectively). However, approximately one-third of both evangelical and mainline Protestants also claim to be Independents. Therefore, neither party has an especially strong hold on either religious group.

Perhaps ideological preference rather than party identification is the factor that distinguishes evangelicals from mainline

Table 8. Religious Affilation and Ideological Preference
(percentage)

Ideology	Evangelical Protestant	Mainline Protestant	None
Liberal	16.0	22.3	44.9
Conservative	49.9	38.2	23.9
Moderate	30.6	35.8	29.0
Don't Know	3.5	3.7	2.2
Total	100.0	100.0	100.0

Source: 1994 General Social Survey. N = 2908.

Protestants. Table 8 furnishes some support for this alternative
expectation. A larger proportion of evangelical Protestants report
being conservative than do mainline Protestants (50 percent versus 38 percent). These findings are consistent with the common
understanding of the religious right. Therefore, to the extent that
evangelical Protestants become more politically active, one would
expect conservative candidates of either party to fare better than
liberal candidates. Organizations such as Pat Robertson's Christian Coalition, which distribute voter guides identifying the voting
records of congressmen and senators as well as the issue-positions
of state and local candidates for public office, obviously are attempting to sway the large conservative element among evangelical Protestants. Figure 1 provides an example of the voters' guides
distributed widely by the Christian Coalition and affiliated organizations during the 1994 general election campaign.

A much smaller proportion of non–church members report a
conservative preference than either evangelical or mainline Protestants (24 percent versus 50 percent and 38 percent, respectively).
This contrast highlights the importance of evangelical Protestant
support for conservative political causes.

Policy Preferences

In addition to ideological self-identification, opinions about specific policy issues are informative. For instance, the General Social
Survey asked whether too little money, about the right amount, or
too much money was being spent in various policy areas. Table 9
indicates the percentage of evangelical and mainline Protestants
who thought "too little" money was being devoted to these areas.

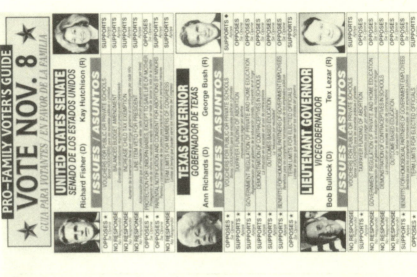

Figure 1.

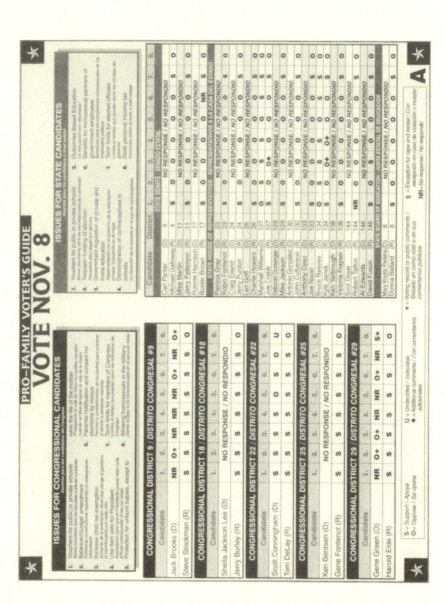

Figure 1.

Table 9. Religious Preference and the Support of Public
Spending (percentage)

Issue	Evangelical Protestant	Mainline Protestant	None
Health	58.4	57.3	63.6
Education	69.4	68.6	73.5
Cities	42.4	52.1	53.7
Environment	53.2	58.8	65.0
Welfare	10.5	7.9	17.2
Poor	53.8	50.9	59.3

Source: 1994 General Social Survey. N = 1439.

Overall, on socioeconomic issues, there is little difference between
evangelical and mainline Christians. Only slight differences were
found, and in some categories the proportion of evangelical Protestants actually exceeded that of mainline Protestants responding
"too little." The only category in which the difference between
evangelicals and mainline Protestants was pronounced regards
spending for cities, with fewer evangelicals responding "too little"
money is being spent. This probably indicates differential residence patterns for the two groups, with evangelicals more likely
to be from rural or suburban areas (see Table 2 for an indication of
the community of residence for evangelicals versus nonevangeli-
cals). A consistently larger proportion of non–church members,
however, responded that "too little" money was being spent in all
of these areas. Welfare, a major contemporary issue, represents the
least popular area for all three groups, with the highest proportion
among non–church members reaching only 17 percent.

Social and Moral Issues

Social and moral issues that leaders of the religious right have
often used in their criticisms of contemporary American society
were also surveyed. Respondents were asked, for instance, if they
thought marijuana should be made legal. The results are summarized in Table 10. The distribution follows the expected direction.
Both groups oppose legalization by large margins, but a larger
proportion of evangelicals do so. Non–church members split
roughly evenly between legalizing and not legalizing marijuana.

Respondents were asked their opinion of a married person
who has sex with someone other than his or her marriage partner.

Table 10. Religious Preference and Attitude toward Legalizing Marijuana (percentage)

	Evangelical Protestant	Mainline Protestant	None
Legalize	16.2	21.2	44.9
Don't Legalize	81.2	73.8	47.7
Don't Know	2.6	5.0	7.4
Total	100.0	100.0	100.0

Source: 1994 General Social Survey. N = 1966.

Table 11. Religious Preference and Attitude toward Extramarital Sex (percentage)

Attitude	Evangelical Protestants	Mainline Protestants	None
Always Wrong	85.3	80.4	61.6
Almost Always	11.7	11.5	18.9
Sometimes Wrong	2.1	5.3	13.0
Not Wrong	0.9	1.8	4.9
Don't Know	0.0	1.0	1.6
Total	100.0	100.0	100.0

Source: 1994 General Social Survey. N = 1947.

Table 11 provides a summary of the results. Once again, although large proportions of both evangelicals and mainline Protestants objected to extramarital sex, a larger proportion of evangelicals expressed disapproval. Combining the alternatives that such behavior is "always wrong" and "almost always wrong," 97 percent of evangelical responses fall in these two categories, compared with 92 percent of mainline Protestants. Among non–church members, on the other hand, that proportion falls to 80 percent.

Another issue of great concern to the religious right is homosexuality, particularly the assertiveness of the gay community in pursuit of homosexual rights. Figure 2 is a 1995 communication from the Traditional Values Coalition indicating this deep concern.

A General Social Survey question asked respondents if they regarded homosexuality as a matter of choice or as something that cannot be changed. Table 12 reports the responses. A much greater difference in attitudes is expressed on this issue by the two

Homosexual Invasion from Massachusetts to California

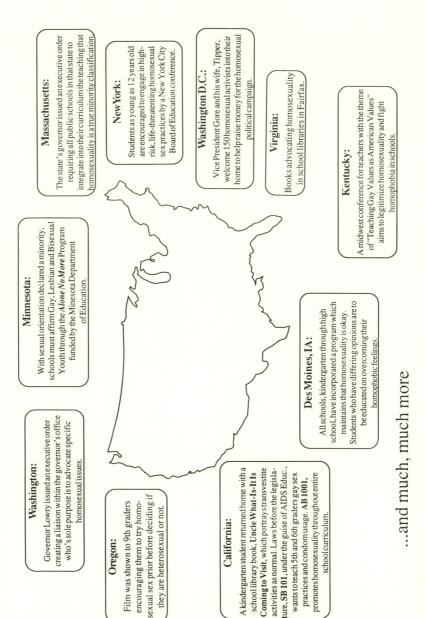

Washington:

Governor Lowry issued an executive order creating a liaison within the governor's office who's sole purpose is to advocate specific homosexual issues.

Minnesota:

With sexual orientation declared a minority, schools must affirm Gay, Lesbian and Bisexual Youth through the *Alone No More* Program funded by the Minnesota Department of Education.

Massachusetts:

The state's governor issued an executive order requiring all public schools in that state to integrate into their curriculum the teaching that homosexuality is a true minority classification.

New York:

Students as young as 12 years old are encouraged to engage in high-risk, life-threatening homosexual sex practices by a New York City Board of Education conference.

Washington D.C.:

Vice President Gore and his wife, Tipper, welcome 150 homosexual activists into their home to help praise money for the homosexual political campaign.

Virginia:

Books advocating homosexuality in school libraries in Fairfax.

Kentucky:

A midwest conference for teachers with the theme of "Teaching Gay Values as American Values" aims to legitimize homosexuality and fight homophobia in schools.

Oregon:

Film was shown to 9th graders encouraging them to try homosexual sex prior before deciding if they are heterosexual or not.

California:

A kindergarten student returned home with a school library book, **Uncle What-Is-It Is Coming to Visit**, which portrays transvestite activities as normal. Laws before the legislature, **SB 101**, under the guise of AIDS Educ., wants to teach 5th and 6th graders gay sex practices and condom usage. **AB 1001**, promotes homosexuality throughout entire school curriculum.

Des Moines, IA:

All schools, kindergarten through high school, have incorporated a program which maintains that homosexuality is okay. Students who have differing opinions are to be educated on overcoming their homophobic feelings.

...and much, much more

Figure 2.

Table 12. Religious Preference and Attitude toward Homosexuality (percentage)

	Evangelical Protestants	Mainline Protestants	None
Choice	63.2	37.7	27.0
Not a Choice	29.1	44.9	58.4
Don't Know	7.7	17.4	14.6
Total	100.0	100.0	100.0

Source: 1994 General Social Survey. N = 933.

Table 13. Do Sexual Materials Lead to a Breakdown of Morals? (percentage)

	Evangelical Protestants	Mainline Protestants	None
Yes	63.2	37.7	27.0
No	22.5	33.1	58.5
Don't Know	4.5	6.4	11.7
Total	100.0	100.0	100.0

Source: 1994 General Social Survey. N = 1002.

religious groups, with close to two-thirds of evangelical Protestants stating that homosexuality is a choice, while fewer than 40 percent of mainline Protestants hold this position. Non–church members have the lowest proportion responding that homosexuality is a choice, with only 27 percent of the group selecting this alternative.

In addition to homosexuality, the religious right expresses strong opposition to pornography. Table 13 indicates the opinions of respondents as to the relationship between pornography and the "breakdown of morals." A large majority in both groups express concern about pornography, but a larger proportion—nearly three-fourths—of evangelicals agrees that pornography is harmful to morals. By contrast, a majority of non–church members—58 percent—disagree, holding that sexual materials do not lead to a breakdown of morals. Religious right organizations have emphasized their strong opposition to both homosexuality and pornography; therefore, it is not surprising to discover that the opinions of evangelical Protestants coincide with this opposition.

Table 14. Religious Preference and Conditions under Which
an Abortion Should Be Legal (percentage)

	Evangelical Protestants	Mainline Protestants	None
Birth Defect	71.4	83.0	91.4
Unwanted	36.4	48.8	67.0
Health	87.0	89.1	94.0
Can't Afford	37.2	51.3	69.2
Rape	80.1	83.0	90.3
Not Married	34.6	49.6	63.2
Any Reason	32.9	46.6	67.0

Source: 1994 General Social Survey. N = 1947.

Abortion is perhaps the most important issue unifying religious right groups that, due to doctrinal differences, would otherwise likely have little to do with one another. A number of questions in the 1994 General Social Survey deal with the issue of abortion and the circumstances under which respondents would approve of the procedure. These circumstances include ones in which the baby may have a serious defect, the woman is married and does not want any more children, the woman's health is seriously endangered by the pregnancy, the woman cannot afford any more children, the pregnancy resulted from rape, the woman is not married and does not want to marry the man, and the woman wants an abortion for any reason at all. Table 14 indicates in each circumstance the percentage of respondents who state that an abortion should be legal. Generally, evangelicals are less likely than mainline Protestants to approve of the legal right to an abortion. The greater willingness of mainline Protestants to give weight to nonreligious factors when considering an abortion would be viewed by many on the religious right as a "humanist" perspective. In some circumstances, however, a large majority of evangelicals are willing to support this legal right. These conditions include the strong chance that there is a birth defect, that the health of the pregnant woman is seriously endangered, or that the pregnancy resulted from rape. Among those expressing no religious preference, the proportion willing to support abortion is consistently higher than for either religious group, and in no circumstance does this support fall below a majority.

If these survey results truly reflect the attitudes of most evangelicals, the more militant antiabortion groups do not represent accurately the opinions of evangelical Americans, a large majority of whom are willing to accept legal abortion in some of the circumstances already mentioned. Both religious groups, however, are much less willing to sanction legal abortions under other conditions. Just over one-third of evangelical Protestants and only a thin majority of mainline Protestants regard insufficient income a justification for an abortion, and under 50 percent of both religous groups are willing to approve of abortions if the mother does not want any more children or if the mother is not married. The complexity of opinions on this question leads to the conclusion that there is no easy solution to the abortion issue.

The religious right has made prayer in public schools one of its major causes and advocates a constitutional amendment to allow at least voluntary prayer. Table 15 summarizes the results of a question that asked respondents their opinion of the United States Supreme Court's ruling that no state or local government may require the reading of the Lord's Prayer or Bible verses in public schools. The responses suggest that conservative Christian leadership has strong backing from evangelical Protestants, nearly three-fourths of whom register disapproval. In addition, a majority of mainline Protestants also disagree with the court's decision, although the proportion of evangelicals who disapprove is much greater. Among those with no church affiliation, a majority (63 percent) support the Supreme Court decision.

Religious right leaders and organizations, by providing unambiguous positions on many social issues, may be an important influence in creating characteristically unambiguous attitudes among evangelicals. These leaders and organizations, along with conservative politicians, stand to benefit in the political arena. Therefore, it may prove informative to examine the percentage of persons surveyed who responded "Don't Know" in each of the three groups for Tables 10, 11, 12, 13, and 15. This compari-

Table 15. Supreme Court Decision on Lord's Prayer and Bible Reading (percentage)

	Evangelical Protestants	Mainline Protestants	None
Approve	24.0	37.5	63.1
Disapprove	74.2	58.0	29.4
Don't Know	1.8	4.5	7.5
Total	100.0	100.0	100.0

Source: 1994 General Social Survey. N = 1927.

Table 16. Percentage of "Don't Know" Responses

Table	Evangelical	Mainline	None
10	2.6	5.0	7.4
11	0.0	1.0	1.6
12	7.7	17.4	14.6
13	4.5	6.4	11.7
15	1.8	4.5	7.5

son is presented in Table 16. Although the differences are not always significant, evangelical Protestants consistently have the smallest percentage of "Don't Know" responses. Those expressing no religious preference have the highest percent of "Don't Know" responses to every question except one: attitude toward homosexuality (Table 11). This pattern of responses suggests that evangelical Protestants are more likely to form opinions on social issues, and, as already noted, these opinions are more likely to be conservative.

Holding an opinion on an issue does not necessarily lead to action in support of that opinion. One of the main objectives of religious right organizations has been to activate evangelical Protestants politically. Accordingly, General Social Survey reports were examined to determine the extent to which evangelicals participate in the electoral process. Assuming that over-reporting of voter turnout applies equally to each group, Evangelical voting levels (73.3 percent voting) compare favorably with mainline Protestants (72.8 percent voting). Inasmuch as evangelical Protestants traditionally have tended to remain aloof from the political arena, this finding suggests that the efforts of religious right organizations have been successful in getting growing numbers of the faithful to the polls. Interestingly, a significantly smaller proportion, 62.7 percent, of those with no religious affiliation report having voted, which is another indication that religious leaders and organizations have some impact on participation.

Potential for Success

The preceding discussion suggests that, with a few exceptions, large proportions of evangelical Protestants hold conservative views on many social and moral issues consistent with the religious right. In addition, the proportion of the American public expressing a belief in God remains high. The Religion in America study reports that majorities of Americans polled respond that they pray to God, read the Bible, and consider the Bible to be inerrant.[6] Further survey results indicate that Americans consider religion an important part of their lives. For more than 40 years the Gallup organization has asked Americans "How important would you say religion is in your own life—very important, fairly important, or not very important?"[7] The percentage of those interviewed who responded that religion is either "very" or "fairly" important remains consistently high, falling in the 85–90 percent range over the 40 years the question has been asked.

Although these findings bode well for the religious right, disclosing the possibility of directing American politics away from perceived secular trends, one should be wary of glib conclusions. Many students of the religious right seriously doubt the movement's ability to impose its influence more widely on what they perceive to be an essentially secularized American society. Some limited evidence for this reservation can be found in survey results on marital status, found in Table 17. In a fundamental area of moral life and "family values," no significant differences are evident between evangelical and mainline Protestants with regard to the percentage in each group reporting being divorced. In fact, non–church members have a divorce rate that is not markedly higher than the two religious groups.[8] Further, responses to questions dealing with abortion, summarized in Table 14, indicate the willingness of both evangelical and mainline Protestants to acknowledge situations in which abortion appears to be a reasonable alternative, despite efforts of the religious right to invoke biblical mandates against the practice.

Table 17. Marital Status and Religious Preference (percentage)

	Evangelical Protestants	Mainline Protestants	None
Married	54.5	56.7	38.7
Single	13.0	15.4	33.9
Divorced	15.7	14.5	20.8
Separated	3.5	2.3	3.7
Widowed	13.3	11.1	2.9
Total	100.0	100.0	100.0

Source: 1994 General Social Survey. N = 2919.

These observations suggest that contemporary social conditions may be deeply at odds with certain of the goals of the religious right. Social changes resulting from the improving economic status of women and advancing technology (such as the RU-486 abortion pill) make possible what previously would have been unthinkable. And such changes, when combined with the presupposed value of individual choice that underpins classical liberal ideology, permit a freedom often at odds with the "traditional values" the religious right advocates. To attempt to limit such developments can be compared with trying to put the proverbial genie back in the bottle. Nonetheless, we recognize the genuine concern of those evangelical Christians who wish to achieve what they perceive to be a better world for themselves and their children. Therefore, we expect the religious right to remain active, but not necessarily to consistently achieve major victories in the American political arena.

Quotations

The following quotations express the positions of individuals in the religious right on issues of major concern to the movement. No quotation is necessarily representative of all leaders. Quotations from analysts and critics, who offer an evaluation of the movement, are also included.

American Christian Heritage

The critical issue of our day is the relationship of Christ and His Word to our political and legal system in the United States. Who has jurisdiction over every aspect of American society, Jesus Christ or the State? Is this to be a Christian nation or a humanistic nation? The only faithful answer that a Bible-believing Christian can give is this: "Blessed is the nation whose God is the LORD" (Psalm 33:12). "For the LORD is our judge, the LORD is our lawgiver, the LORD is our king; He will save us" (Isaiah 33:22).
   Gary DeMar, *God and Government: A Biblical and Historical Study* (1982)

You find that anytime America was on its knees, both our economy and our security and our spiritual temperature rose at the same time, and whenever we got off our knees all three have deteriorated.

Robert J. Billings, *Christian Century*
(October 8, 1980)

The Constitution, as far as we're concerned, is a Christian document.

Gary Jarmin, *Christian Century*
(April 16, 1980)

Antiabortion

Beliefs have no credibility when unaccompanied by sacrifice. We must stubbornly refuse to remain silent in the face of the holocaust of God's unborn children. Not all of us in the church will be called upon by our Lord to do the same thing in the same way. All of us can, however, be supportive of sacrificial intervention that gives credibility to our words. This must involve much more than peaceful civil disobedience at abortion clinics to save the lives of unborn children. But surely it can include it.

Randy C. Alcorn, *Is Rescuing Right?* (1990)

Anticommunism

Make no mistake about it. The Communists are winning. Hitler died; Nazism died with him. Mussolini died; Fascism died with him. Tojo died; Japanese militarism died with him. Stalin is dead; COMMUNISM LIVES ON. Lenin is dead; COMMUNISM LIVES ON. Why? Because Communism is a *satanic* weapon more powerful than the atom bomb, hydrogen bomb, cobalt bomb, or all of them combined, to bring about the seven-year Tribulation Period in which the whole world will worship Satan and his son, the anti-Christ, who will be the leader of a godless world government, and his religious counter-part, the "false prophet," the false Messiah.

Billy James Hargis, *Communist America:*
Must It Be? (1986)

Material forces alone do not determine the destinies of men. The resources of an infinite God can change the balance of material assets. These resources are liberated through the prayer, the sacrifice, and the intelligent organization of people filled with the love of God. Fundamentally, the problem is a moral and spiritual one. The foundations of freedom must be girded with a moral and spiritual revival. As free men humbly seek God and present their bodies, minds and hearts to their country and the cause of all mankind, we may well believe that tyranny shall not triumph and freedom shall not perish from the earth.

> Fred Schwarz, *You Can Trust the Communists*
> *(To Be Communists)* (1960)

For not only is this loss of reinforcing faith in the cement of our morals a weakness in itself of immense significance, but like all of our weaknesses it has been pounced upon by the Communists, and used and made worse by them with great skill and determination for their own purposes. . . . The Communists are able to use this lack of moral stamina among their enemies in a thousand ways to make their own progress easier and the conquest of those enemies more rapid.

> Robert Welch, *The Blue Book of the John Birch*
> *Society* (1961)

Biblical Inerrancy

If Paul is wrong in this factual statement about Eve's coming from Adam [1 Cor. 11.8], there is no reason to have certainty in the authority of any New Testament factual statement, including the factual statement that Christ rose physically from the dead.

> Francis A. Schaeffer, *No Final Conflict: The*
> *Bible without Error in All That It Affirms*
> (1975)

Being wholly and verbally God-given, Scripture is without error or fault in all its teaching, no less in what it states about God's acts in creation, about the events of world history, and about its own literary origins under God, than in its witness to God's saving grace in individual lives. This authority of Scripture is inescapably impaired if this total divine inerrancy is in any way limited or disregarded, or made relative to a view of truth contrary to the Bible's own; and such lapses bring serious loss to both the individual and the Church.

> Chicago Statement on Biblical Inerrancy,
> Norman L. Geisler, ed., *Inerrancy* (1979)

No one, as far as I know, holds that the English translation of the Bible is absolutely infallible and inerrant. The doctrine held by many is that the Scriptures *as originally given* were absolutely infallible and inerrant, and that our English translation is a *substantially accurate* rendering of the Scriptures as originally given. We do not possess the original manuscripts of the Bible. These original manuscripts were copied many times with great care and exactness, but naturally some errors crept into the copies that were made. We now possess so many good copies that by comparing one with another, we can tell with great precision just what the original text was. Indeed, for all practical purposes the original text is now settled. There is not one important doctrine that hangs upon any doubtful reading of the text.

Reuben A. Torrey, *Difficulties and Alleged Errors and Contradictions in the Bible* (1907)

Economics and Capitalism

When men are taught that the capitalist system is rigged against them, that they have a legal and moral right to welfare payments, and that those who live well as a result of their own labor, effort, and forecasting skills are immoral and owe the bulk of their wealth to the poor, we must recognize the source of these teachings: the pits of hell.

Gary North, *The Sinai Strategy: Economics and the Ten Commandments* (1986)

The Bible promotes free enterprise. The book of Proverbs and the parables of our Lord clearly promote private property ownership and the principles of capitalism. We therefore are strong free-enterprisers.

Jerry Falwell, *Houston Chronicle* (April 5, 1987)

Work is the heart and soul, the cornerstone of Biblical charity. In fact, much of the outworking of Biblical charity is little more than a subfunction of the doctrine of work. Its operating resources are the fruit of work: the tithe, hospitality, private initiative, and voluntary relief. Its basic methodologies are rooted in the work-ethic: gleaning, training, lending, and facilitating. Its primary objectives revolve around a comprehension of the goodness of work: productivity, rehabilitation, and entrepreneurial effort.

George Grant, *Bringing in the Sheaves: Transforming Poverty into Productivity* (1988)

Education

When a student reads in a math book that there are no absolutes,
every value he's been taught is destroyed. And the next thing you
know, the student turns to crime and drugs. . . .

Crime, violence, immorality and illiteracy . . . the seeds of
decadence are being taught universally in schools.
Mel and Norma Gabler, *Texas Monthly*
(November 1982)

Evolution and Creationism

Perhaps the most difficult doctrine which evolution has yet to
reconcile to religion is the position that man, by the supposition
that he evolved into a higher organism from a man-like ape (or
ape-like man), is no more than a specialized primate. The implica-
tion, of course, is that all physical, intellectual and social traits in
man can be observed in a rudimental state in apes. While there are
some who speak of the social behavior of apes; the human-like
mannerisms of dogs; the intelligence of chimpanzees, dolphins, or
whales; true religion teaches that man is a unique being in all
creation.
Dean R. Zimmerman, *Evolution: A Golden
Calf* (1976)

Patriotism

We are not a perfect nation, but we are still a free nation because
we have the blessings of God upon us. We must continue to
follow in a path that will ensure that blessing. We must not forget
that it is God Almighty who has made and preserved us as a
nation.
Jerry Falwell, *Listen, America!* (1980)

It's sad to think of the school children of the past who cringed at
the thought of their flag touching the ground while being removed
from the school flagpole. It's grim to remember the price paid for
her raising at Iwo Jima. It's distressing to think of tears shed by

wives and mothers who have seen her draped over the coffin of a loved one. But it's a marvel that no one has figured out why she can now be publicly burned. What further sign does God need give us as proof we have been conquered?

Pastor Pete Peters, *America the Conquered* (1991)

Political Activism and Strategy

You wait until the Sunday before the election and you distribute [moral report cards] all in one day. The election is held on Tuesday. Now why do we distribute them the Sunday before? It needs to be fresh in the voter's mind. Voters do not have a particularly long retention period. Number two, it does not give the liberal candidate that we're opposing time to go run back to all the churches screaming that he's not really that way, which is what they try to do if you give them a chance. Thirdly, when that liberal National Council of Churches minister stands in front of the pulpit and denounces the report card in the church service, it's too late because you've distributed it on Sunday, the election was held on Tuesday, and the minister denounces it the next Sunday, you see.

Colonel Doner, quoted in Sara Diamond, *Spiritual Warfare: The Politics of the Christian Right* (1989)

Friends, we are in real trouble right now, and it is time to take a stand and tell the authorities: "We can not and will not obey you when it means to surrender the lordship of Christ." Then we should be ready to defend ourselves in court and go to jail if necessary for our convictions. After all, we would be in pretty good company since much of the New Testament was penned in prison!

Don Boys, *Christian Resistance: An Idea Whose Time Has Come—Again* (1985)

I realize that it is "popular" to be a born-again Christian. But for some strange reason it is "unpopular" to stand up and fight against the sins of our nation. Will you take a stand and help me Clean Up America? How would you answer these questions: Do you approve of pornographic and obscene classroom textbooks being used under the guise of sex education? Do you approve of the present laws legalizing abortion-on-demand that resulted in the murder of more than one million babies last year? Do you approve of the growing trend towards sex and violence replacing family-oriented programs on television?

If you are against these sins, then you are exactly the person I want on my team. I have put together a Clean Up America campaign that is going to shake this nation like it has never been shaken before. I cannot do it alone. Together we must awaken the moral conscience of our nation. The battle has just begun.

> Jerry Falwell, quoted in Gerald Strober and
> Ruth Tomczak, *Aflame for God* (1979)

If the religious right is ever to accomplish its stated goal of returning our nation to moral sanity and spiritual stability, it must humbly but determinedly *set its own course* according to the wind of the Spirit of God. It must no longer be the pawn of powers and principalities, of godless men and institutions be they left or right. In short, the religious right must not compromise.

> George Grant, *The Changing of the Guard:*
> *Biblical Blueprints for Political Action* (1987)

I had never actively solicited candidates for political office. Then, in the providence of God, I was subjected to a painful educational experience, when the church attempted to get a zoning variance passed by the city council. After three years of effort, we lost, 6 to 2. For the first time, I realized that men and women largely hostile to the church controlled our city.

> Tim LaHaye, quoted in Kathleen C. Boone,
> *The Bible Tells Them So: The Discourse of*
> *Protestant Fundamentalism* (1980)

Everyone wants to be in the "big time" politically. Everyone wants to run for governor. *Let them.* Meanwhile, we take over where today's politicians think that nothing important is happening. We should get our initial experience in ruling on a local level. We must prepare ourselves for a long-term political battle. We start out as privates and corporals, not colonels and generals. We do it God's way.

> Gary North, *Inherit the Earth: Biblical Blue-*
> *prints for Economics* (1987)

Prayer in the Schools

Supporters of prayer in school seek to restore traditional values. They call for a constitutional amendment to reaffirm and reestablish the original intent of the religious freedom clause of the First Amendment, that which has been stolen, twisted, and used against them. The issue, they insist, is the guaranteed preservation of religious liberty.

Rus Walton, *Biblical Solutions to Contemporary Problems: A Handbook* (1988)

Reconstructionism

God has a plan for the conquest of all things by His covenant people. That plan is His law. It leaves no area of life and activity untouched, and it predestines victory. To deny the law is to deny God and His plan for victory.

Rousas John Rushdoony, *God's Plan for Victory* (1977)

Christianity has given birth to the greatest prosperity, stability, and liberty known in history. To the extent that the Christian view is also the biblical view (contrary to liberalism, which attempts to separate the two), we may expect God's objective blessings upon that people whose God is the Lord, as evidenced in their law code.

Kenneth L. Gentry, Jr., *God's Law in the Modern World: The Continuing Relevance of Old Testament Law* (1993)

Religious Equality Amendment (proposed)

Section 1. Neither the United States nor any State shall abridge the freedom of any person or group, including students in public schools, to engage in prayer or other religious expression in circumstances in which expression of a nonreligious character would be permitted; nor deny benefits to or otherwise discriminate against any person or group on account of the religious character of their speech, ideas, motivations or identity.

Section 2. Nothing in the Constitution shall be construed to forbid the United States or any State to give public or ceremonial acknowledgement to the religious heritage, beliefs, or traditions of its people.

Section 3. The exercise, by the people, of any freedoms under the First Amendment or under this Amendment shall not constitute an establishment of religion.

Traditional Values Report (May–June 1995)

Right To Bear Arms

The right to defend one's life, family, liberty and property is a God-given right, supported by Scripture and illustrated in God's Law as seen in Nature. Any person, group or government which would attempt to deprive one of this right, or attempt to persecute, prosecute or punish one for exercising this right, violates God's Law and is an enemy of God's people. Weapons are essential for self-defense and Jesus admonished His followers to purchase a sword. A firearm is the modern equivalent of a sword, thus gun control in any form or manner is in opposition to God's Law.

Remnant Resolves (1988)

Secular Humanism

If the atheistic, amoral, one-world humanists succeed in enslaving our country, that missionary outlet [America] will eventually be terminated. As a Christian and as a pastor, I am deeply concerned that this ministry be extended. The eternal souls of millions of people depend on us to supply them with the good news. In addition, I am concerned that the 50 million children who will grow up in America during the next generation will have access to the truth, rather than the heresies of humanism.

Tim LaHaye, *The Battle for the Mind* (1980)

Inasmuch as humanistic curriculum programs and "values-clarification" and "moral-education" teaching strategies are based upon materialistic values found only in man's nature itself, they reject the spiritual and moral tradition of theistic faith and religion. Thus, many parents who subscribe to Judaeo-Christian belief oppose humanistic education in the tax-supported schools on grounds that such programs promote and advocate the religion of secular humanism in violation of the First Amendment to the U.S. Constitution.

Onalee McGraw, *Secular Humanism and the Schools: The Issue Whose Time Has Come* (1976)

A humanist is a humanist is a humanist! That is, he believes as a humanist, thinks as a humanist, acts as a humanist, and makes decisions as a humanist. Whether he is a politician, government official, or educator, he does not think like a pro-moral American, but like a humanist. Consequently, he is not fit to govern us or to train our young.

Tim LaHaye, *The Battle for the Mind* (1980)

Taxation

Communism is a system of private property confiscation and control. Any means of property control and confiscation used in the U.S.A. today *against* the consent of the individual is a communist practice. . . .

The graduated income tax is one of the strongest planks of the Communist Manifesto. Every Christian should be opposing it with all his strength. . . .

But, lo, most Christians and pastors criticize those brave persons who are participating in Godly resistance. In fact, many pastors and Christians preach against sodomy and abortion; but at the same time they are supporting the practice of those very sins through the graduated income tax.

Everett Sileven, *The Christian and the Income Tax* (1986)

Should we pay taxes to the government of the United States of America? Christ did not say to pay what Caesar demanded, nor did He say that God demanded anything. The individual must decide who he wishes to serve. If Caesar has a return due him for services rendered, then that which is Caesar's should be paid. But what about your God and His just dues? Did Caesar bring the sun and rain and the growth of crops and livestock? What does your government do with the tax money which you pay? Are they not paying for the murder of the unborn in abortion clinics? Are they not teaching the diabolical, satanic lie called humanism in the

schools with your taxes paying the bills? Have you been taking
that which is God's and paying for evil and wicked government?
Did not our government lie to us about Pearl Harbor, Korea, Viet
Nam, Watergate, energy shortage and social security? Your government is a liar and Satan is the father of lies and our churches
are teaching that you must render unto our wicked government
whatever they demand.

M. J. "Red" Beckman, *Born Again Republic*
(1981)

By the use of various methods of taxation, we have been deprived
of the right to property contrary to God's Law against theft. Therefore, we, God's Covenant People, call for a repentance by our
Government of all unscriptural methods of taxation as outlined in
His Law.

Remnant Resolves (1988)

Responses to the Religious Right, Scholarly and Polemical

At times it has seemed that if evangelicals were to wake up as
citizens of an African or Asian nation, their identity as followers
of Christ would be profoundly shaken. Why? Not simply because
of the differences in language, food, and culture, but because
many American evangelicals have been truly more American than
Christian, more dependent on historical myths than spiritual realities, more shaped by the flag than the cross. . . .

These tendencies came to a climax in the eighties with the rise
of religious Right. What began as an appreciation of the contribution faith made in our nation turned into a false reliance on evangelicals' social standing in America. The evangelical identity
shifted from being grounded in the source of blessing to being
grounded in the blessing itself. Their status as pilgrims in search
of the heavenly kingdom was less important than being citizens of
a "Christian America." Following the pattern of most idolatry,
something to be appreciated became a point of overattachment, a
source of reliance, and finally an idol that led to public pride and
self-deception.

John Seel, "Nostalgia for the Lost Empire,"
in Os Guinness and John Steel, eds., *No God
but God* (1992)

At least within the twentieth century, and especially since the Second World War, American fundamentalism has commonly been strongly aligned with extreme political conservatism. Christianity is, in these circles of the far right, understood to give complete sanction to the capitalist system and to a *laissez-faire* approach to society, and government intervention in social arrangements, the welfare state, mildly reformist attitudes, liberalism and socialism are all alike seen as forms of communism masquerading under another name. In such a milieu, though accusations of communism may be common coin (and even Billy Graham is said to have been called a communist by such extremists, or at least to have been accused of being "soft on communism"; an actual socialist Christian, even a mild one, is as inconceivable among conservative evangelicals as a man with two heads.
    James Barr, *Fundamentalism* (1978)

It should be recalled that conservative Christianity began to flourish at the very moment when the more sedate and rational branches of Protestantism were floundering. In the 1970s the United Presbyterian Church lost 21 percent of its members. The Episcopal Church lost 15 percent. The United Church of Christ and the United Methodists both lost 10 percent. As these moderate and liberal denominations, which recognized the complexities of modern life and resisted biblical simplification, declined, many of their former members defected . . . to conservative, born-again Christianity. They filled the thousands of new conservative churches and schools that were founded as the revival spread to every corner of the country and eventually claimed 60 million adherents. The revival became so successful that by 1980, despite the complaints of mainline Protestants and Catholics, the very word "Christian" had come to mean a born-again conservative.
    Michael D'Antonio, *Fall from Grace: The
    Failed Crusade of the Christian Right* (1989)

In the eighties, America has given birth to a new form of terror, a campaign of fear and intimidation aimed at the hearts of millions. It is in two great American arenas—religion and politics—that this new terror has raised its head. In the past few years, a small group of preachers and political strategists has begun to use religion and all that Americans hold sacred to seize power across a broad spectrum of our lives. They are exploiting this cherished and protected institution—our most intimate values and individual beliefs—along with our civil religion—our love of country—in a concerted effort to transform our culture into one altogether different from the one we have known. It is an adventurous thrust: with cross and flag to pierce the heart of America without bloodshed. And it is already well under way.

> Flo Conway and Jim Siegelman, *Holy Terror: The Fundamentalist War on America's Freedoms in Religion, Politics and Our Private Lives* (1984)

For the Religious Right, the close of the century will be a time of unprecedented evangelistic activity and preoccupation with the second coming of Christ. Adherents of the "pre-tribulation rapture" theory are anxiously packing their spiritual bags as they await departure from the planet. "Post-millenialists" [*sic*] who believe that they themselves are destined to usher in the Kingdom of God on earth will escalate their drive to transform secular institutions. Evangelicals of all stripes hope that the spiralling technological advances, political turmoil and economic instability expected in the 1990s will help them attract millions of "lost sheep" seeking answers to life's most profound questions.

> Sara Diamond, *Spiritual Warfare: The Politics of the Religious Right* (1989)

In attempting to discover if the majority of Americans actually subscribe to the New Christian Right definition of public morality, scholars have conducted a multitude of opinion surveys based on local, state, and national samples. With an unusual degree of accord, these surveys have challenged the most enthusiastic claims about the extent of broad public support for the profamily agenda. In fact, support for the core items making up the "profamily" agenda has been limited to a minority of the population and apparently has declined over the course of the 1970s and 1980s. . . . In the face of New Right efforts to the contrary, the public apparently has become more liberal on issues like abortion, tolerance for homosexuality, and women's rights.

> Kenneth D. Wald, *Religion and Politics in the United States* (1987)

Rooted in the past, connected to the political context of its times, the Christian right has demonstrated a distinctive approach to politics characterized by alternating strains of accommodation, activism, and alienation, continuing tensions between movement members, and a paradoxical synthesis of piety and protest. Far from short-lived, its redemptive approach to politics is cyclical and recurrent.

Michael Lienesch, *Redeeming America: Piety and Politics in the New Christian Right* (1993)

Notes

1. George Gallup, Jr., *Religion in America: 1990 Report* (Princeton, NJ: Princeton Religion Research Center, 1990); Robert Bezilla, ed., *Religion in America 1992–1993* (Princeton, NJ: Princeton Religion Research Center, 1990), and the 1994 Supplement.

2. Bezilla, *Religion in America 1992–1993*, p. 20.

3. Princeton Religion Research Center, *Religion in America 1992–1993*, 1994 Supplement, p. 5.

4. See Kenneth Wald, *Religion and Politics in the United States* (New York: St. Martin's, 1987), p. 64, for a detailed discussion of his classification scheme.

5. The information in Tables 3 and 5 was derived from Martin B. Bradley, Norman M. Green, Jr., Dale E. Jones, Mac Lynn, and Lou McNeil, *Churches and Church Membership in the United States, 1990: An Enumeration by Region, State and County Based on Data Reported for 133 Church Groupings* (Atlanta, GA: Glenmary Research Center, 1992).

6. Gallup, *Religion in America 1990*, pp. 48–49.

7. Gallup Poll News Service, *Recent Trends* (Princeton, NJ, 1994), p. 1.

8. The much higher proportion of single and lower proportion of married respondents among non–church members suggest that some other variable, such as age, may be intervening.

Directory of Organizations

5

The organizations listed here vary considerably in basic ideology and political influence. They differ politically from extreme right stances to more traditional conservative positions. Members of some organizations would undoubtedly object strongly to being categorized with other groups that appear here. Many of these groups presently engage actively and successfully in politics; others, influential at one time, have lost their prominence, and several never did gain wide public attention. Several organizations that were significant to the evolution of the contemporary religious right but that no longer exist are also included. Despite the wide variation, the authors believe these groups all share a family resemblance. They all profess a traditional Christian faith and advocate minimal governmental interference in people's lives, except of course with regard to specific objectives of their own, such as abortion and pornography. In order to provide a more complete landscape, the authors have also included a few organizations whose principles and objectives collide with those of the religious right.

Organizations on the Religious Right

American Association of Christian Schools (AACS)
4500 Selsa Road
Blue Springs, MO 64015
(816) 795-7709
FAX (816) 795-7709
President: Dr. Carl Herbster

Founded in 1972, this organization focuses on two major goals. First, AACS assists in the maintenance and improvement of the quality, both academic and spiritual, of Protestant Christian schools. It offers a number of services, including teacher placement and teacher certification programs, and acts as a source for instructional materials. Second, AACS provides interest-group representation in protecting the integrity of Christian schools against government interference at both the state and the national levels.

Publications: Monthly newsletter, the annual *AACS Directory,* and an occasional publication, *The Builder.*

American Center for Law and Justice (ACLJ)
1000 Centerville Turnpike
P.O. Box 64429
Virginia Beach, VA 23467
(804) 523-7570
Executive Director: Keith A. Fournier

Pat Robertson established the ACLJ in 1990 to serve as a public interest law firm and an organization concerned with defending traditional family values and the religious and civil liberties of Americans. Contending that secularism in America has led to attempts to restrict the preaching of the Gospel in public places, the organization offers legal advice and supports attorneys in cases where the rights of Christians are being challenged. The ACLJ objects to legalized abortion and what it sees as the harmful effects of social welfare agencies on the traditional family unit.

Publications: Law & Justice Journal, quarterly.

American Christian Action Council
See Council of Bible Believing Churches

American Coalition for Traditional Values (ACTV)
139 C Street SE
Washington, DC 20003
(202) 547-8570
President: Tim LaHaye

An organization of evangelical Christian leaders founded in 1983, the ACTV's original executive board, chaired by Tim LaHaye, included some of the major religious right figures of the 1980s, such as Colonel Doner, Jimmy Swaggart, Jerry Falwell, James Dobson, James Robison, Bill Bright, and Ben Armstrong. The ACTV gained unfavorable publicity in 1986 when claims were made that the organization had received financial support from Sun Myung Moon's Unification ("Moonie") Church. Reportedly disbanded by LaHaye in 1986, the organization continues to maintain a Washington office. It is dedicated to re-establishing traditional moral values in American government, the public schools, and the mass media. As a means to that end, the organization emphasizes voter registration and voting by fundamentalist Christians. In its concern for traditional values, the ACTV focuses on such issues as abortion, religious freedom, a voluntary prayer amendment to the national constitution, laws against pornography, and a strong national defense.

Publications: The Active Network, an annual report; *The Washington Report,* a monthly publication that deals with issues of concern to the organization and its members.

American Coalition of Unregistered Churches (ACUC)
P.O. Box 11
2711 South East Street
Indianapolis, IN 46206
(317) 787-0830
FAX (317) 781-2775
National Chairman: Greg Dixon

Founded in 1983 in Chicago by a group of fundamentalist ministers, the ACUC represents a group of fundamentalist pastors and churches that opposes government interference in the activities of pastors, churches, and Christians generally. The organization follows a strict policy of separation of church and state, including resistance to government regulation in such areas as building codes and permits, legally required registration or incorporation of churches, licensing of pastors, and Social Security tax payments for church employees.

Publications: Monthly newsletter and an occasional publication, *The Trumpet.*

American Council of Christian Churches (ACCC)
P.O. Box 816
Valley Forge, PA 19482
(215) 566-8154
FAX (215) 566-8942
President: Caren Howery

This organization was established in 1941 by Carl McIntire in reaction to the National (then Federal) Council of Churches (NCC), which McIntire considered too liberal. The ACCC demanded that its members maintain complete separation from the NCC. The ACCC has opposed communism and other beliefs that it considers a threat to American religious, economic, and political freedom. Dissension in the organization arose between McIntire and other leaders of the ACCC, and in 1969 the organization dropped McIntire from the executive council. In 1970 the ACCC voted to leave the International Council of Churches, another organization created by McIntire. The ACCC holds to a fundamentalist doctrine, advocates the inerrancy of the Bible, supports dissemination of the "historic Christian faith" in America and around the world, and opposes liberal, socialist, and communist doctrines. The organization is affiliated with the Council of Bible Believing Churches.

Publications: Fundamental News Service, a bimonthly newsletter that discusses social and political issues of concern to Christians.

American Family Association (AFA)
P.O. Box 2440
Tupelo, MS 38803
(601) 844-5036
Executive Director: Donald E. Wildmon

Founded by Donald Wildmon in 1977, this organization promotes what it terms the "biblical ethic of decency in American society" and focuses its attention on the perceived immorality, profanity, and violence on television and in the other mass media. The organization encourages the television networks to broadcast family-oriented entertainment. The AFA compiles data on television programming it deems objectionable and encourages boycotts of the offending networks and their sponsors. The AFA also employs petition campaigns.

Publications: Monthly publication, *AFA Journal;* pamphlets dealing with the organization's opposition to pornography and sex education in the public schools.

American Freedom Association
See Christian Patriot Association

American Freedom Coalition (AFC)
7777 Leesburg Pike, No. 314N
Falls Church, VA 22043-2403
(703) 790-8700
FAX (703) 790-8711
President: Dr. Robert G. Grant

This lobbying group, active politically at both the state and national levels, represents a recent trend of some religious right organizations to emphasize the more traditional liberal issues related to freedom. It has a more secular than religious orientation, and it places greater emphasis on activity at the state and local levels. It was created in 1987 by the leadership of Christian Voice and reportedly had the financial assistance of Sun Myung Moon's Unification Church. Organization members work in support of what they consider traditional American values, including especially First Amendment freedoms. In addition to advocating freedom of religion, the AFC supports charity and educational and children's programs. The AFC has tended to support Republican economic positions, opposed environmental groups, and advocated public school reform.

Publications: American Freedom Journal, a monthly tabloid that covers issues of concern to the organization both at the national and the local levels.

American Society for the Defense of Tradition, Family and Property (TFP)
P.O. Box 1868
York, PA 17405
(717) 225-7147
President: Raymond E. Drake

A civic organization founded in 1974 and based largely on Roman Catholic doctrine, the TFP defends traditional values, the family, and the right to property. It opposes what are considered socialist and Marxist positions on these subjects. The society is based on a concern for the perceived crisis in morality, politics, and religion and works toward educating Americans in ways to defend traditional values.

Publications: Tradition, Family, Property, a bimonthly magazine.

Americans United for God and Country (AUGC)
P.O. Box 183
Merion Station, PA 19066
(215) 224-9235
Executive Director: Leslie Harris

Begun in 1977, this organization supports tuition tax credits for private schools as a means of furthering the Judeo-Christian tradition. According to the organization, since religious citizens provide tax funds to operate public school systems, their principles deserve attention in the curriculum. These principles include patriotism and the basic governing concepts listed in the Constitution and the Bill of Rights.

Publications: None.

Anglo-Saxon Christian Patriot (ASCP)
1948 Fabersham
Snellville, GA 30278
(404) 972-4445
Contact: Pastor E. S. Hall

Originally called Christians for Truth and Religious Freedoms when formed in 1948, the ASCP, a white supremacist group, contends that the Bible supports racial segregation. The group considers "race mixing" to be a sin and a threat to racial identity.

Publications: The Bible Answers Racial Questions and *What? Where? Why?*

Associates for Biblical Research (ABR)
P.O. Box 125
Ephrata, PA 17522-0125
(717) 733-3585

Founded in 1969, this association conducts research on biblical archaeology and promotes creationism as a scientifically legitimate approach to the origins of human life. The organization conducts an educational program and sponsors an annual archaeological excavation in Israel.

Publications: Archaeology and Biblical Research (quarterly); a monthly newsletter.

Bible-Science Association (BSA)
P.O. Box 32457
Minneapolis, MN 55432
(612) 755-8606
(800) 422-4253
FAX (612) 755-8535
Contact: Gregory A. Hull

The Bible-Science Association was founded in 1963 by a group that wanted the biblical story of creation taught in public schools. The organization conducts educational programs and seminars to further its objectives and promotes books on creationism and the relationship between science and religion. The BSA maintains a library of materials on creation science.

Publications: Bible-Science Newsletter, printed nine times each year, provides information on subjects dealing with the relationship between Christian belief and science; *Technical Issues,* an occasional publication.

Campus Crusade for Christ International (CCC)
100 Sumport Lane
Orlando, FL
(407) 826-2131
President: William R. (Bill) Bright

This organization began in 1951 on the University of California–Los Angeles campus. In addition to college and university ministries, including Bible study groups, faculty groups, and student, family, and pastoral conferences, Campus Crusade has programs to reach high school students, military personnel, and prisoners. The organization is active in most countries around the world.

Publications: Worldwide Challenge, a bimonthly magazine.

Chalcedon Foundation (CF)
P.O. Box 158
Vallecito, CA 95251
(209) 728-3510
President: Rousas John Rushdoony

This organization seeks to reconstruct government and society according to biblical principles. The CF issues grants for research dealing with the relevance of biblical law and faith to contemporary life.

Publications: Monthly newsletter, *Chalcedon Report,* and the semi-annual *Journal of Reconstruction.*

Christian Action Council (CAC)
101 W. Broad Street, Suite 500
Falls Church, VA 22046
(703) 237-2100
FAX (703) 237-8276
President: Thomas Glessner

Founded in 1975, the CAC is dedicated to conforming government policy and laws to the biblical principles of the Judeo-Christian tradition. Through its more than 500 local organizations, the CAC attempts to activate Christians politically. In addition to lobbying national and state legislators in order to gain greater attention for biblical values, the organization has the more specific objective of reversing the *Roe v. Wade* (1971) Supreme Court decision on abortion. Through its Care Net ministry, the CAC provides training for staff and volunteers in over 450 pregnancy-care centers, encourages and helps local churches in offering assistance to pregnant women, makes available materials such as sermon outlines and Bible studies to pastors, and trains Christians to care for women who have experienced the ill effects of abortion.

Publications: Action Line, a monthly publication, and the quarterly *Pro-Life Advocate Magazine;* many publications on pregnancy and abortion, including the *Sanctity of Human Life Update.*

Christian Action Network (CAN)
P.O. Box 606
Forest, VA 24551
(804) 385-5156
FAX (804) 385-0115
President: Martin Mawyer

Martin Mawyer, a former official in Jerry Falwell's Moral Majority, founded Christian Action Network in 1990. The organization has focused on such issues as abortion, prayer in the public schools, child pornography, and gays in the military. The CAN became a major critic of the National Endowment for the Arts, calling for an end to funding the endowment, when controversy arose over some of the grant recipients. Its pressure eased when endowment policies became more conservative. The organization was active during the 1992 Republican National Convention and opposed Bill Clinton's presidential candidacy, running radio and television commercials attacking Clinton's policy stands on social issues such as gay rights.

Publications: Family Alert Newsletter, monthly.

Christian Advocates Serving Evangelism (CASE)
P.O. Box 64429
Virginia Beach, VA 23457
(804) 523-7239
FAX (804) 523-7546
Executive Director: Jay Sekulow

The CASE was formed in 1990 by Jay Sekulow, an attorney concerned with maintaining the right of Christians to promulgate freely their religious beliefs without government limitations. The organization offers legal support to people who believe government has violated their religious freedom. The staff of the organization includes four attorneys, including Sekulow. Sekulow has been successful in some cases, such as *Board of Airport Commissioners of Los Angeles v. Jews for Jesus*, concerning the distribution of literature in public places, and *Board of Education of the Westside Community Schools v. Mergens*, which allowed voluntary student Bible clubs.

Publications: A brochure on religious rights.

Christian Anti-Communism Crusade (CACC)
P.O. Box 890
227 East 6th Street
Long Beach, CA 90801
(231) 437-0941
President: Fred C. Schwarz, M.D.

Founded in 1953 by Fred Schwarz, originally an Australian physician, this anticommunist religious and educational group has a long history of providing information on the alleged evils of communism. Lectures and forums coordinated by the organization for citizen groups, college students, and churches stress communist strategy and philosophy in order to prepare individuals to resist more effectively the communist threat. In explaining its objective, the organization employs a medical analogy, with communism as the disease, the Crusade as pathologist, and politicians, educators, and voters as physicians. The CACC has been active not only in the United States, but also in several foreign nations, including India, the Philippines, Korea, Taiwan, Malaysia, El Salvador, and Chile.

Publications: Newsletter, issued twice monthly and sent to the president, members of Congress, Supreme Court justices, and various state officials; Schwarz's books and booklets, including *You Can Trust the Communists (To Be Communists)* and *Why Communism Kills.*

Christian Coalition (CC)
1801 Sarah Drive, Suite L
Chesapeake, VA 23320
(804) 424-2630
FAX (804) 424-9068
Executive Director: Ralph Reed

The Christian Coalition was founded in 1989 by Pat Robertson as a grass-roots political organization concerned with an alleged lack of morality in government. The organization seeks the election of legislators who have high moral values and supports legislation of concern to the Christian right, especially pro-family measures. The CC has opposed homosexuals in the military, taxpayer-funded "abortion-on-demand," condom distribution in the public schools, "socialized medicine," legal recognition of homosexual marriages, and increased government spending and taxation. Although it does not support specific candidates, the organization distributes "Congressional Scorecards," statements of candidates' issue-positions and voting records on measures considered important to Christian voters. In 1993 and 1994 the CC claimed to have distributed 29 million Congressional Scorecards and 40 million voter guides (candidates' stands on key issues) in an effort to affect election outcomes and government policy.

Publications: Christian American, a bimonthly newspaper, and a *Newsletter,* published monthly.

Christian Crusade
P.O. Box 977
Tulsa, OK 74102
(918) 665-2345
President: Billy James Hargis

Founded in 1948, the Christian Crusade has had a long history of opposition to communist and socialist ideologies, as well as to what the organization believes were attempts by supporters of such ideologies to infiltrate American government and society. The Christian Crusade (formerly Christian Echoes National Ministry) works to preserve the conservative Christian ideals upon which it believes America was founded. In addition to opposing communism, the organization has objected to American participation in the United Nations, government interference in the economy, and federal involvement in areas, such as education, it believes to be constitutionally reserved to the states. After the 1994 congressional elections, the Christian Crusade strongly supported the Republican policy agenda in Congress.

Publications: Christian Crusade Newspaper, a monthly publication that treats current events from a conservative Christian standpoint. Billy James Hargis authors many of the front-page items.

Christian Defense League (CDL)
P.O. Box 449
Arabi, LA 70032
(504) 277-5940
Executive Officer: James K. Warner

Launched in 1964, the CDL supports the perpetuation of traditional Christian values and fosters the advancement of Christian leaders in the public realm. The organization offers educational programs.

Publications: Two monthly magazines, *CDL Report* and *Christian Vanguard.*

Christian Echoes National Ministry
See Christian Crusade

Christian Family Renewal (CFR)
P.O. Box 73
Clovis, CA 93613
(209) 297-7818
(800) 345-7646
President: Dr. Murray Norris

Established in 1970, this organization focuses on problems related to the family. The CFR attempts to offer Christians ways to resolve social problems in politics, business, and education. Among the issues of concern to the organization are abortion, homosexuality, and pornography.

Publications: Jesus and Mary Are Calling You, a quarterly publication, and a newsletter.

Christian Heritage Center (CHC)
205 Watterson City West
1941 Bishop Lane, Suite 205
Louisville, KY 40218
(502) 452-1592
Executive Director: Dr. N. Burnett Magruder

A Christian patriotic organization founded in 1964, the CHC advocates a return to the basic faith and liberties of the American founding. The organization supports the introduction of prayer, Bible reading, and the teaching of the Ten Commandments in the public schools. A part of the CHC's agenda is to identify atheistic, humanistic, and communistic influences in American government and society. The organization produces the daily radio broadcast, *Liberty Radio Program.*

Publications: Two monthly periodicals, *Awake and Alert* and *Revival and Survival.*

Christian Law Association (CLA)
c/o Gibbs and Craze Law Firm
P.O. Box 30
Conneaut, OH 44030
(216) 593-3933
Executive Director: David Gibbs

The CLA began in 1977 with David Gibbs's successful defense of a couple that had been arrested and jailed for refusing to send their children to public school, preferring instead home schooling in a religious atmosphere. Attached to the Gibbs and Craze law firm, the CLA uses litigation to defend members' religious rights. The organization receives monthly dues from churches and individuals who, if they require legal assistance regarding their religious rights, will receive representation at no additional cost.

Publications: Monthly newsletter, *The Briefcase,* which offers current legal information.

Christian Patriot Association (CPA)
33838 SE Kelso Road, #6
P.O. Box 596
Boring, OR 97009
(503) 668-4941
Founder: Richard G. Flowers

Founded in 1982 as the American Freeman Association, this patriotic Christian organization concerns itself with what members believe to be abuses of constitutional limitations on government power. The organization attempts to restore to American citizens the sovereignty that government abuses have threatened. Information relevant to such abuses is gathered from mass media reports.

Publications: The Patriot Review, monthly.

Christian Research (CR)
P.O. Box 385
Eureka Springs, AR 72632
(501) 253-7185

This organization, founded in 1958, offers itself as an alternative to the secular media and the American educational system. Although the CR calls for upholding the American Constitution, as the organization interprets its original meaning, and encourages patriotism and nationalism, major emphasis is placed on obeying God's commands over any human law. The CR informs Christian Americans of their biblical heritage and responsibilities and warns them of threats to "our theocratic republic." The organization opposes Zionism, communism, the income tax, and the United Nations and supports a revisionist history of the Holocaust. Christian Research was formerly Pro-American Books.

Publications: Quarterly newsletter, *Facts for Action;* and an annual book and tape catalog that includes sources on a wide variety of subjects, including history, government and law, economics, taxation, and creationism.

Christian Research Institute (CRI)
Box 500
San Juan Capistrano, CA 92693-0500
(714) 855-4428
FAX (714) 855-4428 ext. 576
President: Hendrik Hanegraaff

The institute, established in 1960, opposes perceived threats to the Christian faith. It provides information about the direction of events in the secular world relevant to Christianity. The institute advocates "orthodox" Christianity and critically evaluates groups it considers to be heretical cults, such as the Jehovah's Witnesses and Mormons. Most recently the CRI has focused its critical attention on such popular televangelists in the "faith movement" as Benny Hinn, Kenneth and Gloria Copeland, Oral Roberts, and Trinity Broadcasting Network founder Paul Crouch and his wife, Jan. Former president Walter Martin was noted for engaging in debates with religious leaders having opposing views. The CRI sponsors the *Bible Answer Man,* a syndicated radio program. The organization is associated with Evangelical Ministries.

Publications: Christian Research Journal: Examining Today's Religious Movements/Giving Reasons for Christian Faith, a quarterly journal that examines various religious cults and the occult; bimonthly *Christian Research Newsletter,* which also deals with cults and the occult.

Christian School Action
See National Christian Action Coalition

Christian Voice (CV)

This Christian right organization, founded in 1979, became virtually nonexistent after the formation of the American Freedom Coalition in 1987. The CV grew out of the anti–gay rights movement in California and expanded through direct-mail appeals. In 1980 the organization created an associated group, Christians for Reagan, which concentrated on voter registration. The CV focused on such issues as abortion, gay rights, pornography, a school prayer amendment, and the Equal Rights Amendment. It gained publicity through the controversial use of "moral report cards" for members of Congress. In the 1980s, when the religious right concentrated its efforts on influencing the national legislative process, Gary Jarmin served as the major congressional lobbyist for the organization.

Christians for Reagan
See Christian Voice

Church League of America

George Washington Robnett, an advertising executive, formed the Church League in 1937 to combat the perceived threat of communism in America. The organization sought to advance "Christian Americanism" and to oppose centralization of political authority. It opposed President Franklin Roosevelt's "court packing" plan in 1937 and campaigned against his bid for reelection in 1940. In 1956 Edgar C. Bundy succeeded Robnett as the organization's leader. The Church League collected data on individuals and organizations suspected of communist affiliations and maintained a library of publications the organization considered subversive. One section of the library focused on John Dewey, whose works were believed to be sympathetic to communism. The organization distributed literature to ministers, informing them of the dangers of communism and socialism, and published a monthly newsletter, *News and Views*, that alerted readers to the activities of left-wing organizations. The Church League never attracted a large following and by the mid-1960s had declined into obscurity.

Coalition for Religious Freedom (CRF)
5400 Eisenhower Avenue
Alexandria, VA 22304
(703) 823-7582
Executive Director: Dan Holdgreiwe

Founded in 1984, reportedly with assistance from Sun Myung Moon's Unification Church, this nondenominational organization, formerly the Committee for Religious Freedom, assists religious groups in dealing with the various levels of government on questions involving freedom of religion. Many of the top religious figures of the 1980s, including Tim LaHaye, Jerry Falwell, Ben

Armstrong, Pat Robertson, Rex Humbard, D. James Kennedy, and Jimmy Swaggart served on the original executive board. CRF offers advice and information to churches regarding the activities of all branches and levels of government that have an impact on religious institutions. The organization has dealt with such issues as the licensing of ministries, tax laws as applied to religious groups, government health and safety codes for private religious schools, and accreditation controversies.

Publications: Religious Freedom Alert (approximately ten issues per year), a tabloid that provides information and commentary on church-state relations.

Committee for Religious Freedom
See Coalition for Religious Freedom

Concerned Women for America (CWA)
370 L'Enfant Promenade SW, Suite 800
Washington, DC 20024
(202) 488-7000
FAX (202) 488-0806
President: Beverly LaHaye

Beginning in the late 1970s with just nine members, CWA currently claims a membership of over a half-million women. It reports an annual budget of $8 million. The organization conducts educational programs that emphasize the theme of traditional American values and lobbies the national and state legislatures on issues of concern to its members. The organization has supported a number of religious right positions, including support for religious freedom, antiabortion legislation, required AIDS testing for marriage license applicants, and a strong national defense. It has opposed the Equal Rights Amendment, pornography, sex and violence in the mass media, condom advertising on television, unisex insurance rates, violence in families, and communism in the Western Hemisphere. The CWA supported President Reagan's efforts to aid the Nicaraguan contras. The CWA, along with Phyllis Schlafly's Eagle Forum, received credit in 1986 for defeating a Vermont equal rights amendment. The CWA has had success as a legal defense foundation, providing legal representation to Christian parents who have challenged local public school policy. The organization has attempted to increase religious right influence at the local level by organizing its members in congressional districts to campaign for favored candidates and to maintain contact with public officials. Members can receive training on how to run for political office, organize a campaign for board of education, and influence public school policy.

Publications: Newsletter, 11 issues per year.

Council of Bible Believing Churches
125 South Sherman
Denver, CO 80209
(303) 794-4587

Founded in 1968 as the American Christian Action Council and later known as the National Council of Bible Believing Churches, this organization was established to assist the International Council of Christian Churches in promoting fundamentalist Christian beliefs and the traditional Christian faith.

Publications: Servant, a monthly newsletter.

Creation Social Science and Humanities Society
1429 N. Holyoke
Wichita, KS 67208
(316) 683-3610
President: Paul D. Ackerman

This organization, founded in 1977, is composed primarily of individuals who hold college degrees in the social sciences and the humanities and who teach creationism. The society adheres to the following beliefs: the Bible is the inspired and unerring word of God; God created all living things, including human beings, in six days; the flood of Genesis is a historically accurate account. Members support the development of the social sciences according to creationist theory.

Publications: Creation Social Science and Humanities Quarterly, which includes articles and other material relevant to the social sciences as well as the humanities.

Eagle Forum (EF)
P.O. Box 618
Alton, IL 62002
(618) 462-5415
President: Phyllis Schlafly

Founded in 1975 by Phyllis Schlafly in part as a reaction to the Supreme Court abortion decision *Roe v. Wade,* Eagle Forum is a pro-family, conservative organization active at the local, state, and national governmental levels on issues concerning the family, education, and national defense. The EF supports "traditional morality," private enterprise, and a strong national defense, and opposes an equal rights amendment and sex education in public schools. The Forum focuses on tax policy, advocating an increase in tax exemptions for children and the elimination of what it considers discriminatory tax policy against the traditional family.

Publications: Phyllis Schlafly Report, a monthly newsletter containing information on such issues as education, economics, social policy, national defense, and foreign policy.

Family Research Council (FRC)
700 13th Street, Suite 500
Washington, DC 20005
(202) 393-2100
FAX (202) 393-2134
President: Gary Bauer

Established in 1980 as the Family Research Group, this organization acquired its present name in 1988. The FRC is an affiliate of James Dobson's radio ministry, *Focus on the Family.* As a research-oriented group, it provides information to government agencies and members of Congress on issues such as parental autonomy, the problems of single parents, tax breaks for parents with preschool children, teen pregnancy, abortion, alternatives to public school, welfare programs, and housing. The president of the organization, Gary Bauer, served as an aide to Education Secretary William Bennett and as a policy adviser to President Reagan. Although both Dobson and Bauer have rejected association with the religious right, issues of concern to the FRC indicate a close affinity to the Christian right.

Family Research Group
See Family Research Council

Focus on the Family (FF)
420 N. Cascade Avenue
Colorado Springs, CO 80903
(719) 473-4020
FAX (719) 473-9751
Executive Vice President: Paul D. Nelson

Focus on the Family was founded in 1977 as the support organization for James Dobson's radio program of the same name that provides Christian guidance to troubled families. The organization encourages the development and maintenance of the family unit in unison with Christian values. Among its many activities, the FF provides information on such family-related topics as marriage and parenting, conducts educational and charitable programs, and offers child-related programs.

Publications: Several monthly magazines, including *Focus on the Family Citizen,* which evaluates legislative activites at all levels; *Teachers in Focus,* for educators in public and private schools; and *Parental Guidance,* a newsletter examining the media and popular culture; various magazines for youth, including *Breakaway* (for teen boys), *Brio* (for teen girls), *Clubhouse* (for children), and *Clubhouse Jr.* (for preschoolers).

Foundation for a Christian Civilization (FCC)
P.O. Box 1868
York, PA 17405
(717) 225-7147
President: Raymond E. Drake

This organization attempts to instill the religious and cultural heritage of Christianity in the general public. Youth are of special concern to the organization, which supports programs dealing with family issues. Scholarships and grants are provided to support individual and institutional research and development projects. As one of its activities, the FCC campaigns against abortion.

Publications: TFP Magazine, a bimonthly newsletter, and *TFP Campus Update,* a monthly publication.

Freedom Council (FC)

Pat Robertson began the Freedom Council in 1981 and terminated it in 1986. It was headquartered in Virginia Beach, Virginia. Focusing on freedom of religion, the FC attempted to educate Christians on religious and civil liberties. The organization supported litigation on such issues as school prayer and freedom of religion in the workplace. As a grass-roots organization, the FC encouraged citizens to write to their representatives on issues related to freedom of religion. Before its termination, charges of financial irregularities arose involving the use of donations to the Freedom Council for Robertson's political activities. The organization was succeeded by the Christian Coalition.

International Council of Christian Churches (ICCC)
756 Haddon Avenue
Collingswood, NJ 08108
(609) 858-0700
President: Carl McIntire

The ICCC, formed in 1948 under the leadership of Carl McIntire, was the international version of his American Council of Christian Churches (ACCC). The organization was established in direct response to the creation of the World Council of Churches (WCC). McIntire objected to that organization's emphasis upon ecumenism among Protestant churches and its willingness to converse with Roman Catholics and Jews. In the 1950s leaders of the ICCC, along with the ACCC, cooperated with Senator Joseph McCarthy and the House Un-American Activities Committee in identifying possible communist influences in the clergy. The ICCC serves as a gathering point for fundamentalist churches worldwide and encourages a fundamentalist Christianity opposed to all forms of modernism.

Publications: Getrouw, a monthly journal written in Dutch.

John Birch Society (JBS)
P.O. Box 8040
Appleton, WI 54913-8040
(414) 749-3780
FAX (414) 749-3785
President: John F. McManus

Founded by Robert Welch in 1958, the John Birch Society, although best known for what it opposes—communism, socialism, totalitarian government, the United Nations, and federal regulatory agencies—maintains a positive, though vague, image of a future world made better through the help of God. The organization professes a belief in the traditional moral values as found in the Judeo-Christian heritage and considers the family to be the most important element in society. Local chapters conduct letter-writing campaigns to public officials and distribute the society's literature. The organization supports a speakers' bureau and a seminar program.

Publications: JBS Bulletin, a monthly publication, and the *New American*, a biweekly newsmagazine.

Liberty Federation (LF)
P.O. Box 2000
Lynchburg, VA 24506
(804) 582-7310
President: P. Gilsman

Founded in 1979 as the Moral Majority Foundation by Jerry Falwell and given its present name in 1986, the organization never reached the prominence of its forerunner. The Liberty Federation has not been active since the Moral Majority was terminated in 1989. It still maintains an address and phone number in Lynchburg, Virginia, claims a membership of 72,000 ministers and 4 million laypersons, and reports active engagement in persuading conservatives to register and vote for candidates that support traditional values as a way of responding to moral decline in America. The organization points to legalized abortion and pornography and the advocacy of homosexual rights as evidence of that decline.

Publications: None.

Moral Majority (MM)

Formed in 1979 and terminated in 1989, three years after its activities had been shifted to a new organization, the Liberty Federation, Moral Majority was the best known of the religious right organizations of the 1980s. It was established in order to activate the religious right politically. Moral Majority concentrated on the major religious right issues, including opposition to gay rights, abortion rights, pornography, and the Equal Rights Amendment and support for school prayer. The organization consisted of the Moral Majority Foundation, which claimed tax exemption, Moral Majority, Inc., which served as the political lobbying branch, and the Moral Majority Political Action Committee, the part of the organization responsible for raising campaign funds to support candidates for public office. The organization published the periodical *Moral Majority Report.* Although Moral Majority gained influence over the national political agenda during the early 1980s, it acquired a negative public image due in part to the aggressive lobbying activities of the organization and its leader, Jerry Falwell. Falwell resigned as president in November 1987.

National Association of Evangelicals (NAE)
P.O. Box 28
Wheaton, IL 60189
(708) 665-0500
FAX (708) 665-8575
Executive Director: Dr. Billy A. Melvin

This interdenominational organization was founded in 1942 to provide an alternative to the National (then Federal) Council of Churches and to serve as a medium of cooperation among evangelical churches and organizations. Reporting a membership of 15 million, the NAE includes 50,000 churches representing more than 77 denominations. Such groups as Assemblies of God, Baptists, and evangelical wings of the Lutheran, Methodist, and Presbyterian denominations are represented in the membership. The organization sponsors various events, such as the Washington Insight Briefing and the Washington Student Seminar. The NAE has demonstrated explicitly conservative political preferences. For instance, in 1983 President Ronald Reagan chose an NAE meeting to make a well-publicized speech in which he referred to the former Soviet Union as the "evil empire." President Reagan spoke before the organization again in 1984, calling for a school prayer amendment to the Constitution. The NAE is associated with the Evangelical Fellowship of Mission Agencies and National Religious Broadcasters.

Publications: NAE Washington Insight, a monthly newsletter reporting on national government activites of concern to evangelical leaders; *National Association of Evangelicals—Dateline,* a quarterly newsletter providing a preview of events and meetings and information on state organizations; *National Evangelical Directory,* a bienniel publication listing various evangelical organizations; *United Evangelical Action: A Call to Action from the NAE,* a bimonthly reporting on organization activities and providing a calendar of future events.

National Christian Action Coalition (NCAC)

No longer in existence, this organization was established by Robert Billings in 1978. Billings left the organization after one year to become the first executive director of Moral Majority. He was succeeded at the NCAC by his son, William Billings. The NCAC was preceded by Christian School Action, an organization that Robert Billings formed in 1977. Billings initiated the NCAC in reaction to the Internal Revenue Service's attempts to withdraw the tax-exempt status of those private schools that were judged racially discriminatory. The organization included the Christian Voter's Victory Fund (a political action committee), the Christian Education and Research Foundation, and the New Century Foundation (a publishing enterprise). Support declined during the early 1980s, and William Billings finally terminated the organization in 1985.

National Coalition Against Pornography (N-CAP)
800 Compton Road
Cincinnati, OH 45231
(513) 521-6227
President: Jerry R. Kirk

In 1983 Rev. Jerry Kirk, concerned about the spread of pornography in the United States, established N-CAP, an ecumenical organization devoted to assisting religious, civic, and legal groups opposed to obscenity and child pornography. The organization calls for strict enforcement of obscenity and child protection laws and participates in efforts to strengthen those laws. The organization plays an educational role by distributing written materials and video and audio tapes that give advice on how to combat pornography.

Publications: Bimonthly newsletter, *Standing Together.*

National Legal Foundation (NLF)
6477 College Park Square, Suite 306
Virginia Beach, VA 23464
(804) 424-4242
FAX (804) 420-0855
Executive Director: Robert Skolrood

This public interest law firm, founded in 1985 by Pat Robertson and originally financed by the Christian Broadcasting Network, offers legal services to defend constitutional liberties, especially religious freedom. The organization prepares legal briefs and educational materials dealing with church-state issues. Attorneys associated with the foundation choose to become involved in cases that are potentially precedent-setting and that have national application. In the Supreme Court case *Westside Community Schools v. Mergens,* the foundation's attorneys successfully argued for the right of students to form a campus Bible club under the 1984 Equal Access Act.

Publications: The NLF Minuteman, a quarterly newsletter.

National Religious Broadcasters (NRB)
7839 Ashton Avenue
Manassas, VA 22110
(703) 330-7000
FAX (703) 330-7100

The membership of this organization includes religious radio and television producers, owners, and operators in the United States and worldwide. Founded in 1940, the NRB is a major data source about Christian broadcasting. The organization protects religious broadcasters' access to the airwaves and conducts meetings at which fundraising techniques and new technology can be shared among members. The NRB provides religious programming to its members and operates religious radio and television stations. In 1988 the organization adopted a new financial code of ethics as a result of scandals involving television evangelists. The new code requires member organizations to provide annual income and expenditure statements to the NRB's executive committee. The organization's leaders have shown a preference for conservative political candidates. For instance, in 1988 all major Republican presidential hopefuls spoke at the NRB convention, whereas no Democratic candidates were invited. The NRB is associated with the National Association of Evangelicals.

Publications: Directory of Religious Broadcasters, an annual listing of those engaged in religious broadcasting, including radio and television stations and programmers; *Religious Broadcasting,* a monthly magazine.

National Right to Life Committee (NRLC)
419 Seventh Street NW, Suite 500
Washington, DC 20004
(202) 626-8800
FAX (202) 737-9189
Executive Director: David N. O'Steen

Formed in 1973 in reaction to the Supreme Court's *Roe v. Wade* abortion decision, this organization employs a wide variety of strategies, including testifying at congressional hearings, writing legislation, and litigating to protect "all innocent human life" threatened by abortion, euthanasia, and infanticide. The organization supports an amendment to the Constitution that would prohibit abortions. Due to the NRLC's willingness to compromise and its opposition to civil disobedience, this antiabortion organization is considered more moderate than other groups.

Publications: Two biweekly publications, *National Right to Life Chapter Newsletter* and *National Right to Life News.*

Operation Rescue (OR)
P.O. Box 127
Summerville, SC 29484
(803) 821-8441
Executive Director: Keith Tucci

Operation Rescue, which calls Americans to "repentance" for more than 25 million abortions since 1973, was originally founded as Project Life in 1984 by Randall Terry and his wife, who attempted to dissuade women from entering an abortion clinic. The organization took on its present name in 1986 when it began the more confrontational tactic of blocking entrances to abortion clinics and conducting large demonstrations and sit-ins in order to "rescue" innocent children. Demonstrators would refuse to leave, thus forcing police to arrest and carry them away. Over 43,000 arrests have resulted from such demonstrations. The organization has attempted to discourage doctors who perform abortions by publicizing their names and confronting them in public places.

Publications: Pro-Life Newsbrief, a monthly publication; *To Rescue the Children: A Manual for Christ-Centered Pro-Life Activism;* and *The Right and Responsibility to Rescue.*

Order of the Cross Society (OCS)
P.O. Box 7638
Fort Lauderdale, FL 33338
(305) 564-5588
Steward: Rev. K. Chandler

Initiated in 1975, the OCS advocates the introduction of biblical principles into governmental organization and operation. Strong family ties and honest business practices are the organization's basic goals. The OCS encourages citizens not to accept government actions inconsistent with Christian principles. Unacceptable government policies include legalized abortion, government subsidies, and Social Security.

Publications: Envoy.

Plymouth Rock Foundation (PRF)
Fisk Mill
P.O. Box 577
Marlborough, NH 03455
(603) 876-4685
Executive Director: Rus Walton

This organization, founded in 1970, wants to base American society and government on biblical principles. The foundation wishes to "restore" America as a Christian republic through the activities of Christians on an individual basis. Christian committees of correspondence have been established to promote action at the local level. The foundation holds workshops and seminars for Christian leaders that focus on biblical understandings of government and education and the nation's Christian history.

Publications: American Christian Heritage Series and the *American Christian Statesmen Series; The Correspondent,* a monthly newsletter that provides information about local committee activities.

Pro-American Books
See Christian Research

Reasons to Believe (RTB)
P.O. Box 5978
Pasadena, CA 91117
(818) 335-1480
FAX (818) 852-0178
President: Hugh Ross

This organization, founded in 1986, strives to develop an explanation for creation that is compatible with the Bible and at the same time scientifically sound. It is affiliated with Campus Crusade for Christ International and the National Association of Evangelicals. The RTB seeks to answer skeptics and to offer Christians a stronger foundation for their faith.

Publications: Facts and Faith, a quarterly that deals with scientific issues relevant to the Bible.

Religious Heritage of America (RHA)
1750 South Brentwood Boulevard, Suite 302
St. Louis, MO 63144
(314) 962-0001
(800) 325-3016

The Religious Heritage of America, founded in 1951 as Washington Pilgrimage, seeks to preserve traditional American values and attempts to provide individuals with a clearer definition of those values. In 1954 the organization lobbied successfully for the inclusion of "under God" in the Pledge of Allegiance. Each year the RHA sponsors trips to religious, cultural, and historical sights.

Religious Roundtable (RR)
P.O. Box 11467
Memphis, TN 38111
(901) 458-3795
President: Edward E. McAteer

Founded in 1979 by Ed McAteer to recruit fundamentalist ministers and their congregations into politics, the Religious Roundtable is concerned with the moral conditions of America, which the organization associates with the very survival of the Judeo-Christian tradition and Western civilization. James Robison was initially the organization's vice president. The Roundtable became active in the 1980 presidential campaign, sponsoring a National Affairs Briefing in Dallas, Texas, and organizing ministers in support of Ronald Reagan. After McAteer failed to win a U.S. Senate seat in 1984, the group became less prominent. The Religious Roundtable has emphasized such issues as child abuse, homosexuality, and pornography and has lobbied to preserve a strong national defense.

Publications: None.

Rutherford Institute (RI)
P.O. Box 7482
1445 East Rio Road
Charlottesville, VA 22906-7482
(804) 978-3888
FAX (804) 978-1789
President: John Whitehead

John Whitehead began the institute in 1982, naming it after Samuel Rutherford, a seventeenth-century Scottish minister who argued that all persons, including royalty, must abide by the civil law. The institute has experienced success using litigation and the threat of litigation to support individuals believed to have been denied their right to religious liberty. The institute concentrates its efforts on such issues as freedom of speech, parental rights, family values, school prayer, home schooling, and abortion.

Publications: Rutherford Journal, a monthly magazine, and other publications including *Home Education Reporter, The Religious Liberty Bulletin,* and *Home School Briefs.*

Traditional Values Coalition (TVC)
P.O. Box 940
Anaheim, CA 92815-0940
(714) 520-0300
Chairman: Rev. Louis P. Sheldon

Originally formed as the California chapter of Tim LaHaye's American Coalition for Traditional Values, the Traditional Values Coalition is concerned with educating Christians about contemporary issues, with the intention that they will become politically active in support of traditional Christian and pro-family values. The coalition focuses on such issues as public school prayer, abortion, sex education in the public schools, and gay-rights legislation. The organization is currently promoting a Religious Equality Amendment to the U.S. Constitution. It opposes any proposal to allow professed homosexuals in the military. The TVC has reportedly succeeded in soliciting the support of African American conservative Christians, especially in California, on issues such as gay rights and condom distribution in public schools.

Publications: Traditional Values Report, an occasional newsletter.

Voice of Liberty Association (VLA)
692 Sunnybrook Drive
Decatur, GA 30033
(404) 633-3634
Executive Secretary: Martha O. Andrews

This organization focuses its efforts on opposing secular humanism. The VLA considers humanism to be a state religion that intends to replace the deity of God with the deity of man. The organization offers educational programs.

Publications: Semiannual newsletter, *Voice of Liberty.*

World's Christian Fundamentals Association (WCFA)

The WCFA, founded in 1919 under the leadership of William Bell Riley and other noted conservative leaders such as J. Frank Norris and John Roach Straton, played a major role in forming the tenets of fundamentalist Christian belief. At its inaugural meeting in Philadelphia, the association adopted a nine-point Confession of Faith that included belief in the verbal inerrancy of the Bible, the premillennial return of Christ, the trinity, the deity of Jesus, the sinfulness of man, "substitutionary atonement," the bodily resurrection of Jesus, justification by faith, and the bodily resurrection of the just and the unjust. During the 1920s the association became embroiled in the question of evolution, supporting antievolution legislation in 20 states. The WCFA selected William Jennings Bryan to serve as its attorney at the famous Scopes Trial in 1925. Riley resigned the presidency in 1929 and the organizational effectiveness of the association declined thereafter. A number of factors led to the WCFA's decline, including the extreme individualism of its leaders, the coming of the depression that diverted attention away from the concerns of the organization, and the ill-fated struggle over evolution. The association lingered into the early 1950s.

Organizations Critical of the Religious Right

American Humanist Association (AHA)
7 Hardwood Drive
P.O. Box 1188
Amherst, NY 14226-7188
(716) 839-5080

The religious right finds many of the principles of this organization to be antithetical to its beliefs. The AHA holds that human beings are dependent on natural and social foundations alone and denies the relevance of any supernatural being. The organization encourages education in ethics as a substitute for religious training. Humanist counselors are certified with the same legal status as pastors or priests. Among the awards the AHA confers is the annual John Dewey Humanist Award.

Publications: The Humanist, a bimonthly magazine; *Free Mind,* a bimonthly newsletter. The organization also has a list of publications and audio- and videotapes critical of the religious right.

Anti-Defamation League (ADL)
823 United Nations Plaza
New York, NY 10017
(212) 490-2525
Director: Abraham H. Foxman

Founded in 1913, the ADL, also known as the Anti-Defamation League of B'nai B'rith, states as its goals the elimination of anti-Semitism and the achievement of justice for all individuals. The organization encourages better relations among differing religious faiths. The ADL supports democratic values and opposes extremist groups it considers threats to democracy. In recent years the organization has published materials, such as its 1994 report, *The Religious Right: The Assault on Tolerance and Pluralism in America,* that are critical of religious right groups and leaders.

Publications: ADL on the Frontline, ten issues per year.

Freedom from Religion Foundation (FFRF)
P.O. Box 750
Madison, WI 53701
(608) 256-8900
President: Anne Nicol Gaylor

Founded in 1978, this organization of atheists, agnostics, secularists, and humanists campaigns against fundamentalist religious beliefs, supports the separation of church and state, and opposes fundamentalist religious attacks on the rights of women and homosexuals. The organization has worked to end prayer in schools and at public events and investigates charges of sexual abuse made against the clergy. Films and public service announcements for television have been produced.

Publications: Freethought Today, a newspaper published ten times per year.

Fundamentalists Anonymous (FA)
P.O. Box 20324, Greeley Square Station
New York, NY 10001-9992
(212) 696-0420
Assistant Executive Director: James J. D. Luce

The membership of this organization consists of former members of pentecostal and charismatic fundamentalist groups and the families and friends of fundamentalists. Formed in 1985, the group claims a membership of 65,000. The FA perceives the fundamentalist perspective to be authoritarian, overly concerned with control, and intolerant of ambiguity and uncertainty. According to the FA, fundamentalists tend to view the world in absolute terms of good and evil. The organization assists people who claim to have been harmed mentally or socially by an experience with fundamentalism and attempts to inform the general public regarding the potential psychological ill effects of fundamentalist experiences. The organization offers support groups.

Publications: Booklet entitled *There Is a Way Out.*

People for the American Way (PFAW)
2000 M Street NW, Suite 400
Washington, DC 20036
(202) 467-4999
President: Arthur J. Kropp

Television producer Norman Lear established the PFAW in 1980 to counter the alleged antidemocratic and discordant effects on the American political process of religious right leaders and organizations such as Jerry Falwell and the Moral Majority. The religious right is seen as using religion to further its own political ambitions. According to the PFAW, traditional American values include cultural diversity, pluralism, the continuing importance of the individual, and freedom of expression. The organization works for tolerance and respect for diversity by monitoring religious right activities, opposing censorship, and supporting such rights as reproductive choice.

Publications: Attacks on the Freedom To Learn, an annual publication; occasional papers and reports.

Selected Print Resources 6

Works about the Religious Right

The works listed in this section are divided into three categories. The biographical section presents a sampling of studies on important figures in the development of the religious right. The section on general religious studies includes works that investigate more broadly the relationship between religion and the social and political environment. The last section contains sources on the religious right and its activities in American society and politics.

Biography

Coletta, Paolo E. *William Jennings Bryan, Volume III: Political Puritan, 1915–1925.* Lincoln: University of Nebraska Press, 1969.

This volume focuses on the last years of Bryan's life, during which he shifted his main concern from progressive political causes to a defense of fundamentalist Christianity. The account of Bryan's crusade against evolution ends with the famous Scopes trial in Dayton, Tennessee, in 1925.

Felsenthal, Carol. *The Sweetheart of the Silent Majority: The Biography of Phyllis Schlafly.* New York: Doubleday, 1981.

This biography depicts the conservative activist and opponent of the Equal Rights Amendment during the early days of the "New Christian Right." The author interviews Schlafly supporters as well as opponents to develop this generally positive treatment of an important figure on the secular and religious right.

Frady, Marshall. *Billy Graham: A Parable of American Righteousness.* Boston: Little, Brown, 1979.

Well researched and based on extensive interviews, this biography provides a largely sympathetic portrait of the famous evangelist. The author emphasizes Graham's basic innocence, which led to his failure to deal adequately with political events, especially during the turbulent 1960s.

Harrell, David Edwin, Jr. *Pat Robertson: A Personal, Religious, and Political Portrait.* San Francisco: Harper and Row, 1987.

A political biography written shortly before Robertson's 1988 presidential bid, this book is a balanced and useful study of the Virginia televangelist. Divided into three parts, the work presents a biographical overview, a survey of Robertson's religious views, and a brief review of his political thinking on a variety of issues. Harrell also discusses Robertson's success in establishing the Christian Broadcasting Network. Although the book is far from definitive, it is the best biography currently available.

Lippy, Charles H., ed. *Twentieth-Century Shapers of Popular Religion.* Westport, CT: Greenwood Press, 1989.

This biographical volume includes entries on over 60 people who have played important roles in the development of popular religious movements in the United States. Many of the biographical sketches are of religious right leaders.

Quebedeaux, Richard. *I Found It! The Story of Bill Bright and Campus Crusade.* San Francisco: Harper and Row, 1979.

This is a relatively uncritical treatment of Bright's Campus Crusade for Christ ministry and its off-shoot organizations, such as "Christian Embassy" and "Christian Graduate School." The title is derived from Bright's evangelical campaign in the late 1970s that drew criticism because of Bright's association with conservative political causes.

Russell, Charles Allyn. *Voices of American Fundamentalism: Seven Biographical Studies.* Philadelphia: Westminster Press, 1976.

This exceptionally good study illustrates the diversity and complexity of fundamentalism through the careers of seven prominent fundamentalists—J. Frank Norris, John Roach Straton, William Bell Riley, Jasper C. Massee, J. Gresham Machen, William J. Bryan, and Clarence E. Macartney. Although a varied and colorful group, they were unified in their opposition to "modernism."

Straub, Gerard Thomas. *Salvation for Sale: An Insider's View of Pat Robertson's Ministry.* New York: Prometheus, 1986.

Straub, former producer for Pat Robertson's *700 Club* television program, writes of his increasing doubts about Robertson and televangelism in general. Writing prior to Robertson's presidential bid, the author questions Robertson's media strategies.

Religious Studies

Ahlstrom, Sydney E. *A Religious History of the American People.* New Haven, CT: Yale University Press, 1972.

An extensive analysis of America's religious history, this book examines the moral development of Americans through the evaluation of varied religious movements, especially in the nineteenth and twentieth centuries. Ahlstrom examines such topics as regional beliefs, separation of church and state, and the relationship between religion and scientific progress. The book provides an excellent context for studying the Christian right.

Allen, Leslie H., ed. *Bryan and Darrow at Dayton.* New York: Russell and Russell, 1925.

Allen offers an account of the famous trial of John T. Scopes, who was prosecuted for violating a state law that forbade teaching evolution in the public schools of Tennessee. Published soon after the trial, the book provides portions of the official court record. In an attempt to be impartial, the editor includes an appendix in which appear excerpts from Genesis and a biology textbook of the times.

Ammerman, Nancy Tatom. *Bible Believers: Fundamentalists in the Modern World.* New Brunswick, NJ: Rutgers University Press, 1987.

A noted sociologist examines the conflict between "moderates" and "fundamentalists" within the Southern Baptist Convention, a conflict which by 1989 had been resolved in favor of the fundamentalists. According to Ammerman, a "gentlemanly consensus" among Southern Baptists of varying degrees of theological conservatism eroded as the South became more urban. Frightened by the changes inherent in urbanization, fundamentalists not only sought security in the "inerrant Word," but also outmaneuvered moderates for control of the convention.

Balmer, Randall. *Mine Eyes Have Seen the Glory: A Journey into the Evangelical Subculture in America.* New York: Oxford University Press, 1993.

This highly readable religious travelogue through America's heartland focuses on fundamentalists, charismatics, and Pentecostals. Balmer illuminates the diversity of America's evangelical subculture. His journey took him from a holiness meeting in Florida to an Indian reservation in the Dakotas to a fundamentalist Bible camp in New York. This work is a must for anyone prone to easy generalization about evangelicalism.

Barr, James. *Fundamentalism.* Philadelphia: Westminster Press, 1978.

A British scholar, Barr has spent considerable time in America. This insightful study calls attention to links between British and American fundamentalism. According to Barr, fundamentalism has been more denominational in America than in Britain, resulting in bitter intradenominational splits in the United States. By contrast, fundamentalism in Britain has been nondenominational.

Bloom, Harold. *The American Religion: The Emergence of the Post Christian Nation.* Hyattsville, MD: Daedalus, 1992.

Although he claims that America is not a Christian nation but rather is dominated by a form of Gnosticism, Bloom nonetheless observes that the nation is "religion-soaked." Americans tend to believe in a personal and loving God. The author examines a number of Christian organizations, including Pentecostalism, Jehovah's Witnesses, Seventh-Day Adventism, and the New Age movement, and gives special attention to Mormons and Southern Baptists.

Boone, Kathleen C. *The Bible Tells Them So: The Discourse of Protestant Fundamentalism.* Albany: State University of New York Press, 1989.

Boone focuses on biblical inerrancy, a principle of utmost importance to fundamentalism, and the doctrine of dispensational premillennialism. The author argues against the plausibility of inerrancy, referring to the lack of original texts and to the fact that interpreters tend to disagree over the meaning of biblical texts. Even inerrantists, Boone argues, have difficulty with words like "day" and "hour," resulting in questionable interpretations.

Boyer, Paul. *When Time Shall Be No More: Prophecy Belief in Modern American Culture.* Cambridge, MA: Belknap Press, 1992.

This study is the best available about the influence on contemporary American society of apocalyptic literature, a genre that reached fruition among the ancient Hebrews between the eighth and sixth centuries B.C. The post–World War II threat of nuclear destruction bred an intense concern about the end of time, exemplified by the popularity of Hal Lindsey's *The Late Great Planet Earth.* According to Boyer, American foreign policy since the 1940s cannot be fully understood without some understanding of dispensational premillennialism. Such religious thinking helps explain President Ronald Reagan's reference to the Soviet Union as an "evil empire."

Burgess, Stanley, and Gary McGee, eds. *Dictionary of Pentecostal and Charismatic Movements.* Grand Rapids, MI: Zondervan, 1989.

This reference work includes more than 800 entries on Pentecostal and charismatic movements primarily in the United States, but also in Europe. Individual entries focus on denominations, specific individuals within the movement, and varied topics such as the Healing Movement and Christian Perfection. The book includes entries on Jim Bakker and Jimmy Swaggart, detailing their fall from grace.

Caplan, Lionel, ed. *Studies in Religious Fundamentalism.* Albany: State University of New York Press, 1987.

The contributors to this volume examine Islamic, Jewish, Sikh, Hindu, West African Islamic, and American Protestant fundamentalism in an effort to discover crosscultural similarities. Although aware that fundamentalism in different parts of the world cannot be understood apart from its specific cultural context, the authors cautiously suggest several parallels. Interestingly, fundamentalists in many parts of the world tend to identify the erosion of male authority and the growing assertiveness of women with spiritual and national decline.

Carter, Stephen L. *The Culture of Disbelief: How American Law and Politics Trivialize Religious Devotion.* New York: Basic Books, 1993.

Carter deals with the dilemmas of religious involvement in the public arena that arise from an American society that is basically secular, despite the widespread expressions of religious belief. Though critical of the religious right, the author is concerned with establishing an appropriate balance in the principle of separation of church and state, recognizing that religion can strengthen those values Americans esteem.

Cox, Harvey. *Religion in the Secular City: Toward a Postmodern Theology.* New York: Simon and Schuster, 1984.

The author examines recent trends in Christianity from Catholic and Protestant (both liberal and fundamentalist) perspectives. Cox offers a theological perspective of Christian involvement in social, political, and economic areas.

Davidson, James West. *The Logic of Millennial Thought.* New Haven, CT: Yale University Press, 1977.

This treatment of millennialist thought in New England during the eighteenth century provides a background for understanding an idea important to much contemporary religious right thinking.

Davidson focuses on the combination of millennialism with events of the times, particularly the French and Indian War and the American Revolution.

Davis, Edward B., ed. *The Antievolution Pamphlets of Harry Rimmer.* Hamden, CT: Garland, 1995.

Volume six in the Creationism in Twentieth-Century America series (Ronald L. Numbers, general editor) contains 16 of Henry Rimmer's works criticizing the theory of evolution. Rimmer, the most noted antievolutionist until his death in 1952, was a Presbyterian minister. Among the works included are "Modern Science, Noah's Ark, and the Deluge" (1925), "Modern Science and the First Fundamental" (1928), and "It's the Crisis Hour in Schools and Colleges" (no date).

Dayton, Donald. *Theological Roots of Pentecostalism.* Metuchen, NJ: Scarecrow, 1987.

This volume examines the history of Pentecostalism, tracing its Wesleyan roots to Great Britain. Dayton identifies four basic elements of this Christian belief: Christ as savior, Christ as baptizer in the Holy Spirit, Christ as healer, and Christ as the future king.

Dunn, Charles W., ed. *Religion in American Politics.* Washington, DC: CQ Press, 1989.

The contributors to this volume examine the conflicts that have arisen in the relationship between religion and politics in America. Individual articles deal with such topics as the First Amendment, the role of religion in maintaining community, religious right involvement in party politics, and religious lobbying efforts.

————. *American Political Theology: Historical Perspective and Theoretical Analysis.* New York: Praeger, 1984.

This book provides an excellent selection of religious documents from the Mayflower Compact in 1620 to the Resolutions of the World Congress of Fundamentalists in 1980 and 1983. Dunn concludes with chapters on the theology of American presidents and theoretical propositions regarding American political theology.

Edel, Wilbur. *Defenders of the Faith: Religion and Politics from the Pilgrim Fathers to Ronald Reagan.* Westport, CT: Praeger, 1987.

Edel's purpose is to expose the myths and misunderstandings about America's religious heritage, myths that some groups and individuals allegedly exploit in order to gain political office. He explores the role of religion in public life throughout American history and observes that religious organizations have recently become significantly more involved in varied public policy issues. Edel notes with concern the desire of some political leaders to return to a relationship between church and state that existed in colonial times.

Elwell, Walter A., ed. *Evangelical Dictionary of Theology.* Grand Rapids, MI: Baker Book House, 1984.

Containing approximately 1,200 entries, this book is an excellent reference. Whether dealing with church history, biography, or the Bible, its emphasis is on the entry's theological significance. While the contributors are sympathetic to their subjects, they are not uncritical. This is a useful took for anyone interested in Christianity.

Fitzgerald, Frances. *Cities on a Hill: A Journey through Contemporary American Cultures.* New York: Simon and Schuster, 1986.

The author critically examines four separate American subcultures, including Jerry Falwell's Thomas Road Baptist Church in Lynchburg, Virginia. The other three communities—the gay district in San Francisco, the Sun City, Florida, retirement community, and Bhagwan Shree Rajneesh's Oregon commune—may appear to have little in commmon, but Fitzgerald sees each as an example of the belief that lives can be rebuilt.

Gamwell, Franklin I. *The Meaning of Religious Freedom: Modern Politics and the Democratic Revolution.* Albany: State University of New York Press, 1994.

This religious-philosophical-political work examines religious freedom in the context of First Amendment protections, over which there has been much disagreement. Gamwell argues that religious pluralism can lead to political agreement only through free discussion among the varying religious commitments.

Gasper, Louis. *The Fundamentalist Movement.* The Hague: Mouton, 1963.

This book is a historical treatment of fundamentalism, primarily from 1930 to the early 1960s, and it contrasts two groups that developed during this period: the militant American Council of Christian Churches and the more moderate National Association of Evangelicals. The author records the development of youth organizations and Bible institutes, the move toward nationalism, and the rise of evangelist Billy Graham.

Gatewood, Willard B., ed. *Controversy in the Twenties: Fundamentalism, Modernism, and Evolution.* Nashville, TN: Vanderbilt University Press, 1969.

Through this useful collection of documents, Gatewood shows that the modernist-fundamentalist conflict originated long before the 1920s and that its impact was more pervasive and enduring than other scholars suggest. The struggle within the churches was a reaction to processes, such as industrialization, urbanization, and scientific advancement, that had gradually undermined orthodox Protestantism and had raised moral issues for which orthodox Protestants had few relevant answers.

Gritsch, Eric W. *Born Againism: Perspectives on a Movement.* Philadelphia: Fortress Press, 1982.

This brief work on the "born-again" movement distinguishes among various member groups, including fundamentalists, millennialists, and charismatics. The author also deals with biblical inerrancy.

Handy, Robert T. *A Christian America: Protestant Hopes and Historical Realities.* New York: Oxford University Press, 1971.

This study of the history of religion in America proceeds from the nineteenth century to the date of publication. Given subsequent events on the religious right, the author's conclusion is interesting. He argues that Christians have accepted pluralism, having failed to achieve a distinctly Christian America.

Harrell, David Edwin, Jr., ed. *Varieties of Southern Evangelicalism.* Atlanta, GA: Mercer University Press, 1981.

Written by six scholars of American religion, these essays illustrate the rich and complex texture of southern religion. To identify the South with only evangelicals and fundamentalists is to overlook the region's Catholic, Episcopal, Enlightenment, and African American heritages. The volume is a good starting point for the reader interested in southern religion.

Hatch, Nathan O. *The Democratization of American Christianity.* New Haven, CT: Yale University Press, 1989.

This book is a good background for the study of contemporary conservative Christianity. The author examines the development of eighteenth- and nineteenth-century Protestant denominations, focusing on the emergence of the Baptist and Methodist denominations, as well as the Mormon and Christian movements.

Hollenweger, Walter J. *The Pentecostals: The Charismatic Movement in the Churches.* Minneapolis, MN: Augsburg, 1972.

This analysis of worldwide Pentecostalism examines the history, theology, and activities of the movement. It highlights Pentecostalism in the United States, Germany, and South America.

Horsfield, Peter G. *Religious Television: The American Experience.* New York: Longman, 1984.

Written before the fall of Jim Bakker and Jimmy Swaggart, this book discusses the rise of evangelical television and the decline of more traditional religious programming. The author notes the tendency of televangelists to offer a bland version of Christianity.

Hunter, James Davison. *Evangelicalism: The Coming Generation.* Chicago: University of Chicago Press, 1987.

Hunter bases this study of evangelicalism on a survey of faculty and students at 16 evangelical colleges and seminaries. The major focus is the encounter between religious beliefs and the modern secular world. The book is a good presentation of contemporary evangelical thought and culture.

————. *American Evangelicalism: Conservative Religion and the Quandary of Modernity.* New Brunswick, NJ: Rutgers University Press, 1983.

Hunter investigates tensions in the twentieth century between conservative American Protestantism and modern secularism. The book analyzes evangelicalism from a sociological and demographic perspective. Aspects of the evangelical view of the world, Hunter claims, have in fact been adjusted to modernity. Hunter employs survey data and the analysis of evangelical documents.

Hutchison, William R. *The Modernist Impulse in American Protestantism.* Oxford: Oxford University Press, 1976.

Hutchison provides one of the better accounts of the development of liberalism, the intellectual foundation of the modernist impulse, within American Protestantism from the early 1800s through the 1920s. Like fundamentalism, modernism can be defined in varying ways. But as used by Hutchison, the term involves three ideas: the conscious adaptation of religious ideas to modern culture, the immanence of God in human cultural development, and the movement of human society toward the Kingdom of God.

Katloff, Mark A., ed. *Creation and Evolution in the Early American Scientific Affiliation.* Hamden, CT: Garland, 1995.

The tenth volume in the Creationism in Twentieth-Century America series contains 46 articles written by various authors associated with the American Scientific Affiliation Society, a group founded in 1941 by evangelical scientists. Among the articles are "Biology and Christian Fundamentals" (R. L. Mixter, 1950), "Why God Called His Creation Good" (William J. Tinkle, 1950), and "The Origin of Man and the Bible" (J. Frank Cassel, 1960).

Kurtz, Paul. *In Defense of Secular Humanism.* Buffalo, NY: Prometheus, 1983.

In this collection of papers written over a 30-year period, Kurtz attempts to defend secular humanism, while acknowledging that most attention given to the idea today originates with the religious right. Kurtz argues that much improvement can occur in morals and politics without religion.

Lawrence, Bruce B. *Defenders of God: The Fundamentalist Revolt against the Modern Age.* New York: Harper & Row, 1989.

This is an effort to place Islamic, Judaic, and Christian fundamentalism within a global context. Lawrence portrays fundamentalists as "moderns" who use science, technology, and the mass media to challenge the "heresies" of the modern age—rationalism, relativism, pluralism, and secularism. These "defenders of God" use modern means to uphold ancient, transcendent values.

Marsden, George M. *Reforming Fundamentalism: Fuller Seminary and the New Evangelicalism.* Grand Rapids, MI: Eerdmans, 1987.

This is an account of Fuller Theological Seminary in Pasadena, California. Founded in 1947, this seminary soon became a focal point of sorts for an intellectual tug-of-war within fundamentalism itself. The Fuller fundamentalists, such as Charles Fuller, Harold Ockenga, Wilbur Smith, and Carl F. H. Henry, were determined to defend the supernatural aspects of Christianity, but they could not fully embrace the rigid separatism and dispensational premillennialism of the more intractable voices of the religious right, such as Carl McIntire. By the early 1950s the Fuller fundamentalists had begun to call themselves "evangelicals."

————. *Fundamentalism and American Culture: The Shaping of Twentieth-Century Evangelicalism, 1870–1925.* New York: Oxford University Press, 1980.

An excellent overview, this study traces fundamentalism from the latter nineteenth century through the 1920s. Marsden claims that fundamentalists underwent a drastic alteration in their relationship to culture. From respected evangelicals in the 1870s, they had become a laughingstock by the 1920s. This fine study furthers an understanding of that transformation.

————, ed. *Evangelicalism and Modern America.* Grand Rapids, MI: Eerdmans, 1984.

Containing essays by 13 scholars, this collection probes the diversity and unity of fundamentalism. Arranged in two parts, the essays first treat the rise of fundamentalism since World War II more or less chronologically, then move on to topics such as women, science, the arts, modernity, and biblical authority. The book is an excellent guide for anyone interested in the emergence and recent prominence of fundamentalism.

Marty, Martin. *Religion and Republic: The American Circumstance.* Boston: Beacon, 1987.

This series of articles looks to the achievement of consensus in a pluralistic society by discovering a common framework for diverse religious communities. The author examines what he considers the major characteristics of religion in America, such as the notion of civil religion and the perceived status of the Bible in Christian belief.

————. *Modern American Religion, Volume I, 1893–1919: The Irony of It All.* Chicago: University of Chicago Press, 1986.

This broad examination of American religion, including treatment of mainline churches as well as evangelical and fundamentalist movements, emphasizes the difficulties Christians face when attempting to respond to change and modernization. Marty identifies both the theological and political consequences of the resulting tension.

————. *Righteous Empire: The Protestant Experience in America.* New York: Dial, 1970.

This treatment of Protestantism in America can be contrasted with the later narratives that religious right authors have developed. Marty emphasizes the unfortunate results, including racism and slavery, of the assumption of early settlers that they were superior, God-chosen people with a special destiny. The author analyzes more recent changes in religious movements.

Marty, Martin E., and R. Scott Appleby. *Fundamentalisms Observed.* Chicago: University of Chicago Press, 1991.

The first in a projected multivolume series, this book is an excellent study of international movements of religious reaction in the twentieth century. Following a thematic approach, it examines the political, social, cultural, and religious context within which each movement emerges; its distinguishing beliefs; and the way in which each has responded to the modern world. This work demonstrates that American fundamentalism was part of a global phenomenon.

Mead, Sidney E. *The Nation with a Soul of a Church.* New York: Harper and Row, 1975.

This group of essays examines the religious aspects of American patriotism and, conversely, the patriotic emphasis demonstrated by many religious leaders. Each can be attributed to a combination of secular elements, such as the Constitution and Supreme Court decisions, and varied religious traditions. Mead associates this unique combination of religion and patriotism to the role that both belief in God and a commitment to liberty played in the founding of America.

Moen, Matthew C., and Lowell S. Gustafson, eds. *The Religious Challenge to the State.* Philadelphia: Temple University Press, 1992.

These essays provide a comparative view of the relationships between religion and politics. Individual essays treat topics such as religion in revolutionary Cuba, religion and politics in Israel, Islamic fundamentalism in Africa, and church-state relations in Mexico and Argentina.

Moore, R. Laurence. *Selling God: American Religion in the Marketplace of Culture.* New York: Oxford University Press, 1994.

This social history of religion in America investigates the use of commercial methods by religious leaders to further religious causes. Moore also looks at business leaders who have employed religion to advance commercial interests. This book provides insightful background information for the study of the religious right and contemporary religion generally.

Nelson, John Wiley. *Your God Is Alive and Well and Appearing in Popular Culture.* Philadelphia: Westminster Press, 1976.

This study focuses on examples of popular culture, such as television, music, magazines, and detective fiction, and discovers religious values being expressed in them. Nelson's book is especially interesting, given the appeal televangelism has had for many Americans.

Nelson, Paul, ed. *The Creationist Writings of Byron C. Nelson.* Hamden, CT: Garland, 1995.

The fifth volume in the Creationism in Twentieth-Century America series (Ronald L. Numbers, general editor) includes four works by Byron C. Nelson, a Lutheran supporter of creationism and a founder of the Religion and Science Association in 1935. Among the works are "Before Abraham: Prehistoric Man in Biblical Light" (1948) and "A Catechism on Evolution" (1937).

Neuhaus, Richard John. *The Naked Public Square: Religion and Democracy in America.* Grand Rapids, MI: Eerdmans, 1984.

This is a general treatment of the role of religion in American government and politics. The author's major theme is that politics and the Judeo-Christian faith are compatible. Therefore, religion can play an important role in the American political process by helping to keep the public sphere viable.

Neuhaus, Richard John, ed. *Unsecular America.* Grand Rapids, MI: Eerdmans, 1986.

This group of essays is drawn from a 1985 conference on the relationship between religion and society conducted by the Rockford Institute Center on Religion and Society. Among the topics discussed are the interdependence of capitalism, democracy, and religion; the ability of religion and modernization to coexist; secular humanism as a religion; and the American commitment to evangelicalism. Results of religious opinion surveys are also included.

Noll, Mark A. *A History of Christianity in the United States and Canada.* Grand Rapids, MI: Eerdmans, 1992.

This book focuses on the rise and more recent decline of Protestantism in the United States. The author traces the development of a uniquely American brand of Christianity through the "great awakening" and the American Revolution. He associates the decline of evangelicalism with the emergence of modernism and the social gospel. Noll suggests that pluralism represents the future for religion in America.

Noll, Mark A., Nathan O. Hatch, and George M. Marsden. *The Search for Christian America.* Westchester, IL: Crossway, 1983.

This book contributes to the debate over the religious status of the Founding Fathers, which is an important issue for the religious right. Unlike many on the religious right who claim that the Founding Fathers based the nation on Christian principles, the authors, who are evangelical historians, argue that the notion of a Christian America is complex and difficult to demonstrate.

Numbers, Ronald L., ed. *Antievolution before World War I.* Hamden, CT: Garland, 1995.

This first volume in the Creationism in Twentieth-Century America series (Ronald L. Numbers, general editor) includes four important critiques of evolution that were written prior to the antievolution movement of the 1920s. Authors are Alexander Patterson, Eberhard Denhert, Luther Tracy Townsend, and G. Frederick Wright.

————. *Creation-Evolution Debates.* Hamden, CT: Garland, 1995.

The second volume in the Creationism in Twentieth-Century America series (Ronald L. Numbers, general editor) contains seven debates between creationists and evolutionists during the 1920s and 1930s. One such debate between William Jennings Bryan and Henry Fairchild Osborn appeared in the *New York Times* in 1922.

————. *The Antievolution Works of Arthur I. Brown.* Hamden, CT: Garland, 1995.

This third volume in the Creationism in Twentieth-Century America series (Ronald L. Numbers, general editor) is composed of seven antievolution pamphlets by Arthur I. Brown, a surgeon whom fundamentalists in the 1920s regarded as a great scientist. Among the pamphlets are "Evolution and the Bible" (1920s) and "Men, Monkeys and the Missing Link" (1923).

————. *Selected Works of George McCready Price.* Hamden, CT: Garland, 1995.

Volume seven in the Creationism in Twentieth-Century America series (Ronald L. Numbers, general editor) includes four of George Price's works on creationism. Price is given credit for establishing a geology of the flood, which ultimately came to be known as scientific creationism. Among the works are "Q.E.D. or New Light on the Doctrine of Creation" (1917) and "Theories of Satanic Origin" (no date).

———. *The Early Writings of Harold W. Clark and Frank Lewis Marsh.* Hamden, CT: Garland, 1995.

This eighth volume in the Creationism in Twentieth-Century America series (Ronald L. Numbers, general editor) includes two works by Clark ("Back to Creation" [1929] and "The New Diluvialism" [1946]) and one by Marsh ("Fundamental Biology" [1941]). The authors, all students of creationist George McCready Price, were educated as biologists.

———. *Early Creationist Journals.* Hamden, CT: Garland, 1995.

The ninth volume in the Creationism in Twentieth-Century America series (Ronald L. Numbers, general editor) presents issues from three early creationist journals: *Creationist* (1937–1938), *Bulletin of Deluge Geology* (1941–1945), and its continuation, *Forum for the Correlation of Science and the Bible* (1946–1948).

Packer, J. I. *"Fundamentalism" and the Word of God.* Grand Rapids, MI: Eerdmans, 1958.

Written from a sympathetic viewpoint, this work is a good introduction to fundamentalism. With wit and humor, the author covers the usual territory of biblical authority and inerrancy and takes exception to the view of fundamentalists as obscurantists and unthinking biblical literalists. The tendency to use fundamentalism and evangelicalism synonymously is a major flaw in Packer's treatment.

Perry, Michael J. *Love and Power: The Role of Religion and Morality in American Politics.* New York: Oxford University Press, 1991.

This excellent, scholarly work examines the appropriate relationship between religious morality and politics in a morally pluralistic society. The author suggests that a more "ecumenical politics" might allow moral positions, especially about what is good for human beings, to contribute to political arguments.

Quebedeaux, Richard. *The Worldly Evangelicals.* New York: Harper and Row, 1978.

This book, published just before the formation of the Moral Majority, includes an overview of the various movements, individuals, and issues relevant to evangelicalism at that time. Quebedeaux's analysis is interesting in light of the subsequent development of the religious right in the 1980s.

————. *The Young Evangelicals: Revolution in Orthodoxy.* New York: Harper & Row, 1974.

Examining trends in evangelicalism, the author recommends an association of differing elements within American Protestantism, including a move away from conservatism and toward a greater compassion more often associated with liberal thought.

Reichley, A. James. *Religion in American Public Life.* Washington, DC: Brookings, 1985.

This general treatment of religion and politics deals with historical interpretations of the First Amendment protection of religion and religious influence on policymaking. Reichley examines such topics as the intentions of the constitutional framers and the positions denominations took on public issues during the Vietnam War era.

Sandeen, Ernest Robert. *The Roots of Fundamentalism: British and American Millenarianism, 1800–1930.* Chicago: University of Chicago Press, 1970.

The author contends that fundamentalism may best be understood in the context of the history of millenarianism. The book traces the development of fundamentalism during the nineteenth and early twentieth centuries, discussing the importation of millenarianism from Great Britain to the United States and the development of dispensationalism. Whereas some scholars see publication of *The Fundamentals* and creation of the World's Christian Fundamentals Association as the beginning of the fundamentalist movement, one that climaxed in the 1920s, Sandeen argues instead that the unity of fundamentalism was already dissolving by about 1910. From that point on, divisive factionalism plagued the fundamentalists.

Schultze, Quentin J., ed. *American Evangelicals and the Mass Media.* Grand Rapids, MI: Zondervan, 1991.

This collection of essays deals with how various aspects of the evangelical movement have been treated in the secular media. Individual essays focus on televangelism and the response to it by the secular media. Additional essays cover other examples of the media, including books, magazines, and music.

Schultze, Quentin J. *Televangelism and American Culture: The Business of Popular Religion.* Grand Rapids, MI: Baker Book House, 1991.

Schultze argues that mass-media evangelism has strong ties to secular commercial broadcasting. Televangelists are portrayed as encouraging a religious belief related to a society of affluence and individualism, but the author concludes that there are likely very few "charlatans" engaged in the enterprise.

Trollinges, William Vance, and Edwin Grant Conklin, Jr., eds. *The Antievolution Pamphlets of William Bell Riley.* Hamden, CT: Garland, 1995.

The fourth volume in the Creationism in Twentieth-Century America series (Ronald L. Numbers, general editor) includes ten pamphlets by William Bell Riley, pastor of the First Baptist Church in Minneapolis, Minnesota. Riley was founder of the World's Christian Fundamentals Association, a major antievolution group in the 1920s. Among the pamphlets are "Are the Scriptures Scientific?" (no date), "Darwin's Philosophy and the Flood" (no date), and "The Scientific Accuracy of the Sacred Scriptures" (no date).

Tuveson, Ernest Lee. *Redeemer Nation: The Idea of America's Millennial Role.* New Haven, CT: Yale University Press, 1977.

This book provides an interesting and enlightening treatment of the background and consequences of millennialist thought. Tuveson traces the development of the belief that America has been chosen as the instrument to achieve God's purposes in the final days.

Watt, David Harrington. *A Transforming Faith: Explorations of Twentieth-Century American Evangelicalism.* New Brunswick, NJ: Rutgers University Press, 1991.

This brief treatment of evangelicalism covers the period 1925 to 1976. The author focuses on recent cultural changes in politics, the status of the public and private realms, the role of women in society, and contributions in psychology. This approach illuminates the interaction of evangelicalism with the larger culture.

Weber, Timothy P. *Living in the Shadow of the Second Coming: American Premillennialism, 1875–1925.* New York: Oxford University Press, 1979.

This book is a good treatment of the rise of the premillennialist movement in America in the late nineteenth and early twentieth centuries. The author, a Baptist church historian, focuses on the social consequences of premillennialism, a doctrine that attempted to preserve orthodox beliefs against modernism and faith in social progress.

Wells, David F., and John D. Woodbridge, eds. *The Evangelicals.* Nashville, TN: Abingdon, 1975.

The essays in this volume deal largely with evangelical doctrine rather than with empirical questions of the development and nature of organizations and social characteristics of evangelicals. The authors show the wide disagreements among the various groups broadly labeled as evangelical.

White, Ronald C., Jr., and Albright G. Zimmerman, eds. *An Unsettled Arena: Religion and the Bill of Rights.* Grand Rapids, MI: Eerdmans, 1991.

Written by a group of distinguished scholars, these essays confront the problem of maintaining a religious heritage in a pluralistic society. Such issues as prayer in public schools, public aid to parochial schools, the teaching of creationism, and the inclusion of religious ceremony in public events have led to nationwide debates about the meaning of the First Amendment and its applicability to contemporary America.

Wilcox, Clyde. *The Latest American Revolution? The 1994 Elections and Their Implications for Governance.* New York: St. Martin's, 1995.

This brief work discusses the importance of the religious right to the outcome of the 1994 elections. An appendix includes the House Republican "Contract with America," which discloses the influence of the religious right on that party's agenda. Among the promised measures are a "personal responsibility act" to discourage illegitimacy and teen pregnancy; a "family reinforcement act" that includes more stringent enforcement of child support, parents' rights in the education of their children, and stronger child pornography laws; and a stronger anticrime act.

Wills, Gary. *Under God: Religion and American Politics.* New York: Simon and Schuster, 1990.

With his usual grace, Wills explores American history from Roger Williams to Pat Robertson, focusing on those points of collision between religion and politics. Separation of church and state to the contrary notwithstanding, religion has always been a vital force in American society, and its influence has often been positive. As Wills writes, the abolitionist, women's, and civil rights movements derived considerable strength from the churches.

Wuthnow, Robert. *The Restructuring of American Religion: Society and Faith since World War II.* Princeton, NJ: Princeton University Press, 1988.

In this study of religious-political relationships, the author examines the divisions between liberal and conservative religious groups and their respective views of the role religion should play in the public sphere. A major topic is the question of separation of church and state.

The Religious Right and Politics

Benson, Peter, and Dorothy L. Williams. *Religion on Capitol Hill: Myths and Realities.* New York: Harper and Row, 1982.

This book summarizes the findings of a statistical study of the religious attitudes of members of Congress. Based on interviews with 80 members, this work discovers a high level of religious belief among congressmen. Moreover, many congressmen appear to rely upon religious principles when casting important votes.

Bromley, David G., and Anson Shupe, eds. *New Christian Politics.* Macon, GA: Mercer University Press, 1984.

These essays examine various aspects of the religious right, including its origins and its bases of support in society, the phenomenon of televangelism, and the potential political effects of the movement. The authors generally see the current appeal of the religious right as related to the resurgence of conservatism within society at large.

Bruce, Stephen. *The Rise and Fall of the Christian Right.* New York: Oxford University Press, 1988.

Employing a sociological perspective, Bruce examines the efforts of the Christian right in the 1970s and 1980s to organize politically and influence election outcomes. Although predictions of the religious right's downfall have proven premature, the problems involved in attempting to establish effective political coalitions are still relevant to the fortunes of the movement.

Bruce, Stephen, Peter Kivisto, and William H Swatos, Jr., eds. *The Rapture of Politics: The Christian Right as the United States Approaches the Year 2000.* New Brunswick, NJ: Transaction, 1994.

These essays examine the current influence of the religious right on American politics. The authors provide differing perspectives, from highly critical to sympathetic, on the efforts of this movement to combine religious and political concerns in the public arena.

Capps, Walter H. *The New Religious Right: Piety, Patriotism, and Politics.* Columbia: University of South Carolina Press, 1990.

This is an excellent account of the better-known Christian right personalities of the 1980s. The author deals in depth with Jerry Falwell, interviewing him at the Thomas Road Baptist Church; Bob Jones, Jr., and Bob Jones III and their court battle over Bob Jones University; Francis A. Schaeffer, the famous theologian of the religious right; the rise and fall of Jim and Tammy Bakker; and Pat Robertson's failed bid for the Republican presidential nomination.

Clabaugh, Gary K. *Thunder on the Right: The Protestant Fundamentalists.* Chicago: Nelson-Hall, 1974.

Written from the perspective of a seventh-grade teacher who endured the wrath of the religious right for discussing evolution in the classroom, this book is an account of the relationship between the religious right and politics in the 1950s and 1960s. Clabaugh's bias is readily apparent. To him, the "Fundamental Protestant Radical Right" is "scurrilous," "irresponsible," and "akin to Fascism."

Conway, Flo, and Jim Siegelman. *Holy Terror: The Fundamentalist War on America's Freedoms in Religion, Politics and Our Private Lives.* New York: Dell, 1984.

This highly critical and nonacademic account of the contemporary religious right concentrates on what the authors consider threats to political and personal freedoms. The authors point to the religious right's use of the mass media, computerized mass mailings, and fund-raising techniques to further conservative causes.

Crawford, Alan. *Thunder on the Right: The "New Right" and the Politics of Resentment.* New York: Pantheon, 1980.

Crawford, a traditional conservative, criticizes the "New Right" for being a radical, anti-intellectual movement that opposes the status quo institutions of business, labor, and government. The author discusses many aspects of the movement, including geographical concentrations, fund-raising techniques, and issues of concern.

Cromartie, Michael, ed. *Disciples and Democracy: Religious Conservatives and the Future of American Politics.* Washington, DC: Ethics and Public Policy Center, 1994.

These essays, originally presented at an Ethics and Public Policy Center Conference, examine the current status of the religious right mostly from a sympathetic perspective. Individual essays deal with the religious right's impact on the 1992 presidential election, media treatment of the movement, and the relationship to the Republican Party.

————. *No Longer Exiles: The Religious New Right in American Politics.* Washington, DC: Ethics and Public Policy Center, 1993.

This volume from a conference on the religious right includes four major chapters, dividing the book into discussions of the history of the religious right, future prospects for the movement, past failures, and evangelical voting patterns from 1976 to 1988.

————. *Evangelicals and Foreign Policy: Four Perspectives.* Washington, DC: Ethics and Public Policy Center, 1989.

These essays examine the applicability of evangelical Christian beliefs to American foreign policy and international relations. The

Bible is seen as establishing possible tenets for foreign policy makers, including positions on terrorism and tyranny. People on the political left are criticized for failing to separate political systems that are flawed from those that are fundamentally evil.

D'Antonio, Michael. *Fall from Grace: The Failed Crusade of the Christian Right.* New York: Farrar, Straus, and Giroux, 1989.

This book examines the Christian right through a series of interesting personal profiles of individuals committed to the movement. The book also deals with the fall of major televangelists like Jim Bakker and Jimmy Swaggart in the late 1980s and recounts Pat Robertson's failed campaign for the presidency.

Diamond, Sara. *Spiritual Warfare: The Politics of the Christian Right.* Boston: South End Press, 1989.

In her highly critical account of the religious right, Diamond examines the various aspects of the movement, including religious broadcasting networks, extremist political activity such as bombing abortion clinics, and activities in foreign nations in support of a conservative American foreign policy.

Edel, Wilbur. *Defenders of the Faith: Religion and Politics from the Pilgrim Fathers to Ronald Reagan.* Westport, CT: Praeger, 1987.

Edel examines the historical relationships between religion and politics. He focuses on important periods in American history, such as the Revolution and the writing of the Constitution. The author provides a critical examination of the religious context of Ronald Reagan's policy decisions.

Fackre, Gabriel. *The Religious Right and Christian Faith.* Grand Rapids, MI: Eerdmans, 1982.

Fackre, a theologian, raises serious questions regarding the religious right's involvement in politics. He observes that the religious right employs the Christian faith to justify particular political positions. He also faults the movement's focus on a type of human perfectibility that ironically parallels secular humanism.

Flake, Carol. *Redemptorama: Culture, Politics, and the New Evangelicalism.* Garden City, NY: Doubleday, 1984.

Although critical at points, this book is a sympathetic account of evangelicalism in the late 1970s and 1980s. The emphasis is on personalities, including such sports figures as Tom Landry, former coach of the Dallas Cowboys. Flake criticizes the contemporary conservative Christian movement for its uncompromising moral stand and its alliance with conservative political forces.

Forster, Arnold, and Benjamin R. Epstein. *Danger on the Right.* New York: Random House, 1964.

Written at the request of the Anti-Defamation League of B'nai B'rith, this work examines the attitudes, personnel, and influence of the radical right and extreme conservatism since World War II. Whereas the radical right, represented by people like Robert Welch and Billy James Hargis, sees a communist conspiracy at the root of America's ills, extreme conservatives, such as William F. Buckley, Jr., and James L. Wick, usually fault the alleged stupidity and bungling of liberals in high places.

Fowler, Robert Booth. *Religion and Politics in America.* Metuchen, NJ: Scarecrow, 1985.

This study of religious influences on American politics investigates voting behavior, interest groups, executive branch politics, and Supreme Court decisions dealing with religious issues. Although he recognizes the role played by religious belief in forming American political attitudes, Fowler concludes that religious pluralism limits the ability of any group, including the religious right, to dominate the political process.

Guth, James L., and John C. Green, eds. *The Bible and the Ballot Box: Religion and Politics in the 1988 Election.* Boulder, CO: Westview, 1991.

The authors examine the wide variety of religious influences on the 1988 presidential campaign in which two Baptist ministers—Jesse Jackson, a liberal Democrat, and Pat Robertson, a conservative Republican—vied in their respective parties for the nomination. One suggestion is that the United States may be moving toward a party system similar to European nations, with a conservative religious party competing against a liberal and secular one.

Hadden, Jeffrey K., and Anson Shupe, eds. *Secularization and Fundamentalism Reconsidered.* New York: Paragon House, 1989.

In the wake of renewed religious right activity in the 1980s, the contributors to this volume, who are sociologists of religion, examine the relationship between religion and politics in the United States and other nations. Of primary concern is the status of secularization theory in light of recent religious developments. Other topics include the role of the mass media in religious-right successes, religious attitudes toward the capitalist system, and religious right involvement in presidential elections.

Halsell, Grace. *Prophecy and Politics: Militant Evangelists on the Road to Nuclear War.* Westport, CT: Lawrence Hill, 1986.

Halsell investigates the alliance between elements of the Christian right and the government of Israel. Whereas conservative Christians look toward the battle of Armageddon after Israel regains control of the Holy Land, the Israeli government wishes to obtain land biblically given to Israel. The author discusses her fear of the possible military consequences of Christian financial and political support for Israel.

Hertzke, Allen. *Representing God in Washington: The Role of Religious Lobbies in the American Polity.* Nashville, TN: University of Tennessee Press, 1988.

The empirical research for this study includes interviews with policy makers and lobbyists. The analysis of lobbying activities of religious groups involves not only fundamentalist and evangelical organizations, but also Catholic and Jewish groups. Lobbyists' concerns vary from abortion to peace and world hunger.

Hill, Samuel S., and Dennis E. Owen. *The New/Religious Right in America.* Nashville, TN: Abingdon Press, 1982.

This study of conservative politics and religion focuses on the relationship between religious belief and social preferences. The authors provide a historical background to the contemporary religious right and analyze the goals of present-day activists. The views of religious groups not likely to be associated with the religious right are also treated.

Jelen, Ted G. *The Political Mobilization of Religious Beliefs.* New York: Praeger, 1991.

This book is based on an attitude survey Jelen conducted in 15 churches in Greencastle, Indiana. The book contains a wealth of data on the political attitudes of those who support the Christian right. Of great interest is Jelen's discussion of the relation between the political activities of the religious right and opposition to other groups in society, including feminists, homosexuals, and atheists.

Jorstad, Erling. *The New Christian Right, 1981–1988: Prospects for the Post-Reagan Era.* Lewiston, NY: Edwin Mellen, 1987.

Jorstad discusses the relationship between the Reagan administration and the new Christian right in the 1980s, focusing on such figures as Jerry Falwell, Pat Robertson, and Tim LaHaye and their assistance in Reagan's 1984 reelection campaign. The book also deals with the religious right's efforts leading up to the 1988 election and adjustments in its agenda.

————. *The Politics of Moralism: The New Christian Right in American Life.* Minneapolis, MN: Augsburg Publishing House, 1981.

This early treatment of the "New Christian Right" describes the movement's evolution from its predecessors in the 1960s. The author discusses the newly acquired techniques of the movement, such as use of direct-mail campaigns and sophisticated organizational skills. Moralizing—determining the only correct alternative on a question—is seen as a major phenomenon of the movement. Jorstad also identifies distinctions among fundamentalist and evangelical groups.

————. *The Politics of Doomsday: Fundamentalists of the Far Right.* Nashville, TN: Abingdon Press, 1970.

This work provides a good history of the political involvement of Carl McIntire, the American Council of Christian Churches, and related organizations. Jorstad discusses the fundamentalist doctrines of the religious right and how these doctrines are translated into action.

Liebman, Robert C., and Robert Wuthnow, eds. *The New Christian Right: Mobilization and Legitimation.* New York: Aldine, 1983.

Composed of 12 articles written largely by social scientists, this edited work provides a balanced treatment of the religious right of the early 1980s. The articles cover such topics as sociological aspects of the movement, including possible explanations for its formation and its significance to American culture; lobbying and political action committees; the strategies of such groups as Christian Voice, Religious Roundtable, and Moral Majority; the liberal reaction; and sources of support for the religious right.

Lienesch, Michael. *Redeeming America: Piety and Politics in the New Christian Right.* Chapel Hill: University of North Carolina Press, 1993.

This excellent work provides an in-depth view of social and political positions crucial to the religious right. Lienisch presents an intricate and fascinating analysis of conservative Christian writings. Among the topics included are the perceived social roles of men and women, defenses of capitalism, attitudes toward the political system, and the role of the United States as a redeemer nation.

Lopatto, Paul. *Religion and the Presidential Election.* New York: Praeger, 1985.

In this contribution to an understanding of religious right influence in elections, Lopatto employs survey research data gleaned from elections from 1960 to 1980. He focuses on the influence of various religious groups, including Protestant and Catholic, liberal, moderate, and conservative, and analyzes the relationship between religious beliefs and such variables as party identification and candidate preference.

McIntyre, Thomas J. *The Fear Brokers.* Boston: Pilgrim Press, 1979.

This book is a nonscholarly and highly biased treatment of the radical right by a former U.S. senator who was defeated for reelection, partly due to conservative opposition. McIntyre gives a personal account of his own encounters with the political right in New Hampshire. He also includes some general material on conservative political activity and positions on issues.

Maguire, Daniel C. *The New Subversives: Anti-Americanism of the Religious Right.* New York: Continuum, 1982.

This book presents a highly critical look at the religious right. Maguire considers the religious right a threat to American society because of the movement's alleged racist, militaristic, and anti-Semitic positions.

Moen, Matthew C. *The Transformation of the Christian Right.* Tuscaloosa: University of Alabama Press, 1992.

This examination of changes in the religious right during the 1980s is crucial to understanding the present status of the movement. Moen documents the religious right's shift away from uncompromising positions on the national level to a politically more sophisticated strategy that includes a greater regional and local emphasis.

————. *The Christian Right and Congress.* Tuscaloosa: University of Alabama Press, 1989.

This well-done empirical study examines the influence of the religious right in Congress, focusing on the years 1981 through 1984. Moen examines the major legislative efforts (antiabortion legislation, a school prayer amendment, and tuition tax credits for parents with children in private schools) and the religious right's failure to achieve its objectives. The author notes the lesser successes of the movement.

Neuhaus, Richard John, and Michael Cromartie, eds. *Piety and Politics: Evangelicals and Fundamentalists Confront the World.* Lanham, MD: University Press of America, 1987.

This work provides a variety of views about, and from, the religious right. Articles feature the origins of evangelicalism and fundamentalism and the contemporary political significance of Christian conservatives. Articles by individuals within the movement provide assessments of the United States and the problems it faces.

Ribuffo, Leo P. *The Old Christian Right: The Protestant Far Right from the Great Depression to the Cold War.* Philadelphia: Temple University Press, 1983.

The author places the new resurgence of the Christian right into the context of twentieth-century America from the 1930s to the 1950s. Ribuffo presents historical examples of religious right activity that are intended to trouble the reader.

Roy, Ralph Lord. *Apostles of Discord: A Study of Organized Bigotry and Disruption on the Fringes of Protestantism.* Boston: Beacon Press, 1953.

This early treatment of the religious right and left criticizes extremists within American Protestantism who threaten Christian principles and American democracy. Carl McIntire and his American Council of Christian Churches are faulted for their tactics in opposing Christian ecumenism. The author attacks such tendencies in Protestantism as racism and anti-Catholicism, but also calls attention to ministers who supposedly have come under the influence of the Communist Party.

Shriver, Peggy L. *The Bible Vote: Religion and the New Right.* New York: Pilgrim Press, 1981.

This early treatment of the Moral Majority and other religious right groups relies heavily on the work of others. An appendix contains speeches and writings by other authors.

Smidt, Corwin, ed. *Contemporary Evangelical Political Involvement: An Analysis and Assessment.* New York: University Press of America, 1989.

This volume contains both analytic and evaluative articles on the religious right. Contributors to the volume discuss such topics as the party identification of evangelicals, possible commonalities between evangelicals and secular humanists, the need for political sophistication among evangelicals, and possible limitations on the goals of a religious movement in a secular society.

Snowball, David. *Continuity and Change in the Rhetoric of the Moral Majority.* Westport, CT: Praeger, 1991.

This study of the Moral Majority examines the history of the organization from 1979 to 1985, focusing on the rhetorical style its leaders employed to convey messages on such issues as abortion and pornography. The author investigates the interesting use of metaphor in organization statements and concludes with an evaluation of the Moral Majority, suggesting possible reasons for its termination.

Wald, Kenneth D. *Religion and Politics in the United States.* New York: St. Martin's Press, 1987; 2d ed., 1991.

Wald's overview of religion and politics in America extends beyond evangelical religious activity to include other religious influences. Although the author notes the secular nature of American society, he recognizes the importance of traditional interactions between religion and politics.

Walker, Brooks R. *The Christian Fright Peddlers.* Garden City, NY: Doubleday, 1964.

This critical examination of the religious right during the 1960s takes a personal perspective in describing religious right personalities and organizations. Some of the major figures of the time are discussed, such as Carl McIntire, Billy James Hargis, Robert Welch, and Fred Schwarz. Walker criticizes the religious right for its extremist politics and predominantly negative goals.

Weber, Paul J., and W. Landis Jones. *U.S. Religious Interest Groups.* Westport, CT: Greenwood Press, 1994.

The authors present information on 120 national religious organizations in the United States. Although not limited to conservative groups, the volume includes a number of organizations on the religious right. The book contains a chapter on the history of religious interest groups in America.

Webber, Robert E. *The Moral Majority: Right or Wrong?* Westchester, IL: Cornerstone Books, 1981.

In attempting to maintain a moderate position, the author finds fault with both the Moral Majority and the World Council of Churches. The conservative Moral Majority is too closely aligned with nationalism and capitalism, and the liberal World Council is too closely associated with socialism. Webber recommends that religious groups not become too closely involved with any worldly ideological system.

Welch, Robert. *The Blue Book of the John Birch Society.* Appleton, WI: Western Islands, 1959, 1961, 1992.

This book is a transcript of the two-day presentation Robert Welch made at a meeting with 11 other men in 1958 that began the organization named for a fundamentalist Baptist missionary. Welch observes the loss of faith among fundamentalists of all religions and warns that this faith is being replaced by opportunism and hedonism. Communists are taking advantage of this loss. Though believing that fundamentalist faith cannot be restored, Welch suggests a broader faith that will be acceptable to "the most fundamentalist Christian or the most rationalistic idealist."

Wilcox, Clyde. *God's Warriors: The Christian Right in Twentieth-Century America.* Baltimore, MD: Johns Hopkins University Press, 1992.

This study of religion and conservative politics provides a historical survey of the religious right through the twentieth century and examines previous efforts that used statistical analysis to explain religious activism. The book explores not only the Christian right and anticommunist movement of the 1950s, but also the more current fundamentalist and pentecostal movements led by Jerry Falwell and Pat Robertson.

Willoughby, William. *Does America Need the Moral Majority?* Canoga Park, CA: Logos, 1981.

The author defends the Moral Majority against allegedly unfair and inaccurate attacks. Although he refers to some shortcomings of the organization, Willoughby argues that the movement has focused attention on moral issues that may lead to revolutionary change in America.

Young, Perry Deane. *God's Bullies: Native Reflections on Preachers and Politics.* New York: Holt, Rinehart and Winston, 1982.

This highly critical treatment of the religious right by a journalist with fundamentalist roots warns against possible threats to constitutional liberties. Young deplores the activities of such contemporary figures as Jerry Falwell and Phyllis Schlafly as well as historical personalities in the Christian right.

Works from the Religious Right

This section includes works on a wide variety of subjects relevant to the religious right: general worldview, political and economic issues, and personal and family concerns. There is of course unavoidable overlap among the various sections, as the writers range from personal accounts of the development of their personal beliefs to explorations of how those beliefs relate to the contemporary world.

The Religious Right Worldview

Ackerman, Paul D. *In God's Image after All: How Psychology Supports Biblical Creationism.* Grand Rapids, MI: Baker Books, 1990.

Ackerman relates psychological notions such as personality, self-will, perception, and self-image to biblical accounts. The author concludes that psychological data support the truth of scripture and the creation story.

Anderson, Kerby, ed. *A Christian Worldview.* Grand Rapids, MI: Zondervan, 1984.

This edited work deals with the application of the philosophical and theological aspects of a Christian perspective to contemporary life. Among the subjects treated are education, government, bioethics, political action, and the mass media.

Ball, William B., ed. *In Search of a National Morality: A Manifesto for Catholics and Evangelicals.* Grand Rapids, MI: Baker Books, 1992.

These articles by Catholic and evangelical Protestant scholars present moderate religious right positions on which it is hoped many Catholics and Protestants can agree. Among the topics analyzed are government and politics, secularization, abortion, education, family values, and morality.

Blamires, Harry. *The Christian Mind.* Ann Arbor, MI: Servant Books, 1963, 1980.

Blamires argues that there will be a clash between Christianity and secularism. Christians should not allow themselves to be influenced by secular understandings of reality. The author examines the preconditions to developing the Christian mind to combat secularism.

Bright, Bill, and Ron Jenson. *Kingdoms at War: Tactics for Victory in Nine Spiritual War Zones.* San Bernardino, CA: Here's Life Publishers, 1986.

Bright and Jenson portray Christians as engaged in a war for the minds of Americans. The enemy is humanism. It is a war that requires commitment and sacrifice and does not allow for neutrality. This war entered a new phase when the Supreme Court in 1963 restricted Bible reading in public schools. The authors blame this decision for a series of evils, including political assassinations.

Brooks, Pat. *The Return of the Puritans.* Fletcher, NC: New Puritan Library, 1979.

Brooks argues that humanists have conspired to establish a new world order and are close to achieving their goal. Among those identified with the conspiracy are the Rockefeller family, the Trilateral Commission, Henry Kissinger, and the Club of Rome. A Puritan minority remains to oppose the conspiracy.

Duncan, Homer. *Secular Humanism: The Most Dangerous Religion in America.* Lubbock, TX: Missionary Crusader, 1979.

Duncan, in opposing secular humanism, compares its objectives to those of communism. Humanism is claimed to be a fundamentally anti-Christian doctrine that intends to alter human beings through genetic and social engineering.

Falwell, Jerry. *Finding Inner Peace and Strength.* New York: Doubleday, 1982.

Falwell, leader of the Moral Majority, deals here with largely nonpolitical themes that nonetheless provide insight into his political positions. He emphasizes biblical infallibility and the need of all people for Christian regeneration.

Geisler, Norman L. *Is Man the Measure?* Grand Rapids, MI: Baker Books, 1983.

Geisler examines from a Christian perspective the varieties of secular humanism and their effects on our culture. Among the types of humanism investigated are evolution, behaviorism, existentialism, pragmatism, and Marxism.

Guiness, Os, and John Seel, eds. *No God But God: Breaking with the Idols of Our Age.* Chicago: Moody Press, 1992.

This group of essays deals with the perceived problems of contemporary evangelicalism. An over-reliance on marketing and management techniques, psychology, and politics has created idols that threaten the true Christian mission. The authors ask American evangelicals to recall their long past, confront modern idolatry, and campaign for religious freedom for all.

Ham, Ken, Andrew Snelling, and Carl Wieland. *The Answers Book.* Colorado Springs, CO: Master Books, 1991.

The authors attempt to answer questions of concern to supporters of the biblical creation thesis. The authors tackle such topics as dinosaurs and their extinction, the ice ages, the origin of different races, and the origin of animals in Australia.

Hanegraph, Hank. *Christianity in Crisis.* Eugene, OR: Harvest House, 1993.

Hanegraph, president of Christian Research Institute International, offers an evangelical warning against the "faith movement" and its leaders, among whom are Kenneth Copeland, Charles Capps, and Paul Crouch. Those in the faith movement, by emphasizing such things as physical healing and financial prosperity, stray from the orthodox Christian understanding of God. The book demonstrates the sort of disagreements that can arise within conservative Christianity.

Hitchcock, James. *What Is Secular Humanism?* Ann Arbor, MI: Servant, 1982.

This is a historical overview of secular humanism, a philosophy the author believes has been victorious in contemporary society. Hitchcock argues that secular humanism, with its supposedly neutral values, in fact introduces its own highly questionable values into politics, the mass media, and public education.

Howard, Donald R. *To Save a Nation.* Garland, TX: Accelerated Christian Education, 1976.

Howard focuses on the tendency of humanism to undermine American values. He outlines steps that Christians need to take to reform American society and return the nation to a godly course.

Huse, J. P., ed. *The Collapse of Evolution.* Grand Rapids, MI: Baker Books, 1986.

Huse contends that although evolution has been generally adopted as "fact," especially since the Scopes trial in the 1920s, organic evolution is an absurd notion. The author claims to reveal the errors in evolution theory and provides arguments for biblical creationism. Evolution and creationism are seen as incompatible.

Ingram, T. Robert. *World under God's Law: Criminal Aspects of the Welfare State.* Houston, TX: St. Thomas, 1962.

Basing his discussion on the Ten Commandments, Ingram claims to demonstrate that the American legal system is founded on scripture. This book is an earlier example of the argument that socialists and humanists want to change the legal system according to their own religious beliefs.

Johnson, Phillip. *Darwin on Trial.* Washington, DC: Regnery, 1991.

This book offers an interesting analysis of Darwin's theory of evolution conducted by a legal expert. Johnson charges that scientists inappropriately accept Darwin's theory and have unsuccessfully attempted to establish supporting evidence. The author examines the problem of fossils and other topics relevant to a creationist response to evolution.

Jordan, James B., ed. *Christianity and Civilization: Failure of the American Baptist Culture.* Tyler, TX: Geneva Divinity School, 1982.

Selections in this work deal with the role Christians can play in politics. The contributors criticize any attempt to adapt Christianity to humanism in order to gain greater influence in the secular world. Political issues should be faced from an undiluted Christian stance.

LaHaye, Tim. *The Race for the 21st Century.* Nashville, TN: Thomas Nelson, 1986.

The race referred to in the title is the competition between Christians and humanists for control of American culture into the next century. The Christian must not only guard his family against humanist pressures, but also work to defeat the humanistic forces that are distorting society. Although LaHaye accepts political pluralism among religious groups, he rejects any legitimate political role for secular humanists.

―――. *The Battle for the Mind.* Old Tappan, NJ: F. H. Revell, 1980.

This book identifies humanism as a major opponent of Christianity. The author traces the roots of this doctrine back to the Greeks and Romans and follows its development through the Renaissance into the twentieth century. LaHaye claims that although humanists represent a small minority of the population, humanist influence dominates the mass media and government. LaHaye claims that, historically, major scientific and technological advances were made by those who believed in God.

―――. *The Beginning of the End.* Wheaton, IL: Tyndale House, 1972.

Relying upon premillennialism, LaHaye describes the imminent approach of Armageddon, a future of catastrophes. Christians ultimately should accept these coming disasters with hope, for these events prepare the way for Christ's return.

LaHaye, Tim, and John D. Morris. *The Ark on Ararat.* Nashville, TN: Thomas Nelson, 1976.

This account of claimed sightings of Noah's Ark on Mount Ararat is primarily of interest because of LaHaye's leadership position in the religious right, as well as the book's reinforcement of the unquestioning faith those on the religious right have in biblical accounts of history.

Lightner, Robert P. *The Last Days Handbook: A Comprehensive Guide to Understanding the Different Views of Prophecy.* Nashville, TN: Thomas Nelson, 1990.

This is a good source for understanding an important issue for those on the religious right. Lightner discusses the premillennial, amillennial, and postmillennial approaches to biblical prophecy. Acknowledging that sharp disagreements sometimes emerge over these various positions, the author encourages evangelical Christians to recognize their basic agreements over biblical prophecy.

Lindsey, Hal. *Planet Earth—2000 A.D.* Palos Verdes, CA: Western Front, 1994.

In his latest work on biblical prophecy, Lindsey discounts any inherent significance in the year 2000 but does suggest that the "seven-year countdown" to Christ's return could begin before that date. Lindsey refers to a variety of occurrences, including political events in Asia and the Middle East, the formation of the European Community, the increased popularity of occultism, an increasing crime rate, the spread of AIDS, and more severe natural disasters such as earthquakes and floods to support his argument that we are in the end times.

————. *The 1980s: Countdown to Armageddon.* New York: Bantam, 1981.

This is an update for the 1980s of the author's commercially successful *The Late Great Planet Earth.* Lindsey observes in certain worldwide political developments, such as the expansion of the European Common Market and the Trilateral Commission, events foretold in the Bible as occurring soon before Christ's return.

Lindsey, Hal, with Carole C. Carlson. *Satan Is Alive and Well on Planet Earth.* Grand Rapids, MI: Zondervan, 1972.

The authors present Satan as not only the biblical character responsible for the original fall, but also as an evil presence in the contemporary world. They see evidence of this presence in such phenomena as the popularity of witchcraft, the use of drugs, demonic possession, violence, and corrupt politics.

————. *The Late Great Planet Earth.* Grand Rapids, MI: Zondervan, 1970.

This bestselling nonfiction book of the 1970s argues that certain contemporary events, such as the establishment of the state of Israel and the formation of a communist regime in China, are predicted in the Bible. These predictions of human events, in addition to natural disasters, foreshadow the end times and the rapture of Christians.

Matrisciana, Carly, and Roger Oakland. *The Evolution Conspiracy.* Eugene, OR: Harvest House, 1991.

Defending the Christian fundamentalist position on creationisn, the authors portray the conflict between creationism and evolution theory as one between two religions. The authors emphasize what they consider the moral consequences of a complete victory for evolution theory.

Moreland, J. P., ed. *The Creation Hypothesis: Scientific Evidence for an Intelligent Designer.* Downers Grove, IL: Inter-Varsity, 1994.

The essays in this volume argue that explanations for the existence of the universe and of life must include God. Contributors deal with the beginnings of life, the source of organic groupings, explanations of language, and the origins of the universe, with emphasis placed on the "Big Bang" theory.

Morris, Henry M. *The Biblical Basis for Modern Science.* Grand Rapids, MI: Baker Books, 1984.

This book investigates the connections between modern science and the Bible. Biblical understandings are considered relevant to the conduct of the natural sciences.

North, Gary. *Is the World Running Down?: Crisis in the Christian Worldview.* Tyler, TX: Institute for Christian Economics, 1988.

North argues for the religious right acceptance of pluralism. Those in the religious right should be willing to strive within the existing governmental structure, a strategy that has already brought some success. Nonetheless, North does not lose sight of conservative Christian values that are ultimately hostile to a pluralist perspective.

Oakland, Roger, with Dan Wooding. *Let There Be Light.* Santa Ana, CA: Oakland Communications, 1993.

This book contrasts the moral and religious effects of evolution and creation theories. The authors contend that the teaching of evolution has been deceitful and has taken God out of people's lives. Creationism, however, restores humankind's relationship with God.

Parks, Jerald. *False Security: Has the New Age Given Us a False Hope?* Lafayette, LA: Huntington House, 1992.

Parks examines the New Age claim that humankind is being transformed into a higher level of civilization and compares it to biblical notions of the Last Days and the collapse of civilization. We may be faced with a time of darkness not seen since the fall of the Roman Empire and the beginning of the Middle Ages.

Pearcy, Nancy, and Charles B. Thaxton. *The Soul of Science: Christian Faith and Natural Philosophy.* Wheaton, IL: Crossway, 1994.

Pearcy and Thaxton distinguish between a period in which scientists and people generally accepted Christianity publicly and more recent times in which science has become hostile to Christian belief. The authors relate the accomplishments of scientists such as Robert Boyle, Isaac Newton, and Carl Linnaeus, whose scientific achievements occurred within the context of the Christian faith.

Pierce, Alfred R. *It Is Finished.* Revised edition. Camden, NJ: Radiant Publications, 1993.

Alfred Pierce, a lawyer, former mayor of Camden, New Jersey, former chairman of the Delaware River Port Authority, and student of the Bible, claims that the United States is the Babylon of the Book of Revelation and will be destroyed. He argues that Satan is now in control of the world.

Pitts, F. E. *The U.S.A. in Bible Prophecy: Two Sermons Preached to the U.S. Congress in 1857.* Baltimore: J. W. Bull, 1862.

These two sermons, "The United States of America Foretold in the Holy Scriptures" and "The Battle of Armageddon," delivered prior to the Civil War, are notable for their inclusion of the United States in biblical prophecy. Pitts identifies the United States and Russia as those powers described in Ezekiel 38 that will be involved in the final battle of Armageddon.

Robertson, Pat. *The New Millennium.* Dallas, TX: Word Publishing, 1990.

Robertson examines the history of Christianity, its present situation in the world, and its prospects after the year 2000. The author claims that the United States is the strongest Christian nation since the fall of the Roman Empire and the "last great expression" of Christianity's victory.

Rushdoony, Rousas John. *God's Plan for Victory: The Meaning of Post Millennialism.* Fairfax, VA: Thoburn Press, 1980.

This publication argues for postmillennialism and a nondispensational view of history. The author, a reconstructionist, claims that God will not return through an imminent holocaust, but gradually through revelation. Whether a postmillennial or premillennial eschatology is accepted affects Christians' views of their present role because those who believe in the rapture fail to act responsibly in the world. Rushdoony calls Christians to political activity in order to reestablish the Christian state.

Schaeffer, Francis A. *A Christian Manifesto.* Westchester, IL: Crossway Books, 1981.

Written by perhaps the foremost conservative Christian political thinker, this work refutes socialism and humanism and calls Christians to organize against the trend toward immorality in our society. Schaeffer bases his argument on the notion of a "form-free balance," an equilibrium between social responsibility and individual rights. With the antiabortion movement in mind, the author justifies civil disobedience when the government demonstrates its tyrannical nature by disobeying the law of God.

————. *How Should We Then Live? The Rise and Decline of Western Thought and Culture.* Old Tappan, NJ: Fleming H. Revell, 1976.

Schaeffer did not mint the term "secular humanism," but in this sweeping assessment of western culture he certainly makes it the bête noire of conservative Christians in much of the English-speaking world. From the Greeks and Romans to the Renaissance to the Enlightenment, he contrasts the "strengths" of Christianity, rooted in God's absolute truth, to the "weaknesses" of human-centered cultures whose moral relativism inevitably led to a cheapening of human life. Schaeffer admires the Reformation, for it represented the restoration of divine absolutes.

————. *No Final Conflict: The Bible without Error in All That It Affirms.* Downers Grove, IL: Inter-Varsity, 1975.

This is a vigorous defense of biblical literalism based upon a rather traditional fundamentalist position. That is, Schaeffer argues that if one questions the historicity of Genesis, such as the actual existence of Adam and Eve, there is no reason to trust any factual statement in the Bible, including the resurrection of Jesus.

————. *The God Who Is There.* Downers Grove, IL: Inter-Varsity, 1968.

Schaeffer emphasizes the nature of human despair in modern times. He investigates the origins of this condition of hopelessness and its evil consequences. Christianity is offered as the only means of combating despair.

————. *Escape from Reason.* Downers Grove, IL: Inter-Varsity, 1968.

In this brief volume, Schaeffer investigates contemporary thought, tracing its origins from Aquinas to the present. The author is highly critical of the present age, especially the "God is dead" movement, the rejection of rationality, and the turn toward nonrational experience. Evangelical Christians are urged not to separate Jesus from the content of scripture.

Schaeffer, Franky. *A Time for Anger: The Myth of Neutrality.* Westchester, IL: Crossway Books, 1982.

Schaeffer attacks secular humanism and the call by that philosophy's adherents for neutrality in education, politics, the mass media, and the arts. The author claims that secular humanism introduces its own morality, or immorality, into these areas. A society claiming neutrality in fact ridicules and rejects the Christian perspective. An appendix deals with the problem of live births during abortions.

Schlossberg, Herbert. *Idols for Destruction: Christian Faith and Its Confrontation with American Society.* Nashville, TN: Thomas Nelson, 1983.

An intellectual historian provides a sophisticated application of the Old Testament to the contemporary world. Western nations, considered to be in a post-Christian era, have yielded to idols such as historicism, humanism, and materialism. Christians must free themselves from both liberal and conservative ideologies and rely instead on independent biblical truths.

Scofield, C. I. *Scofield Study Bible.* New York: Oxford, 1917, 1967.

This King James version of the Bible contains extensive notes that present a fundamentalist perspective on such topics as dispensational premillennialism, scriptual inerrancy, and the distinction between Jews and Christians. This Bible became a major statement of belief for conservative fundamentalist Christians.

Stoner, Peter W. *Science Speaks: Scientific Proof of the Accuracy of Prophecy and the Bible.* Chicago: Moody, 1969.

In providing evidence for the authenticity of the Bible, Stoner examines the scientific accuracy of the Genesis account of creation and the fulfillment of prophecies about geographical events and the coming of Jesus Christ. The book ends with an invitation to sign one of two statements: the first accepting Christ and the second rejecting him.

Terrel, Steve. *The 90's, Decade of the Apocalypse: The European Common Market—The End Has Begun.* South Plainfield, NJ: Bridge Publishing, 1992.

This premillennialist treatment of biblical prophecy shifts attention away from the United States and Russia and focuses on recent developments in the formation of the European Community as signs of the end times. The author identifies the Antichrist as the first president of the United States of Europe. This person supposedly will become the emperor of a new Holy Roman Empire and will begin wars of conquest.

Thompson, Bert. *Creation Compromises.* Montgomery, AL: Apologetics Press, 1995.

Thompson looks at the 200-year development of geology and the view that its discoveries are incompatible with biblical claims of a recent creation and a worldwide flood. Some scientists and theologians, attempting to discover evidence of a much older earth in scripture, are considered to be parties to a compromise.

Torrey, Reuben A., A. C. Dixon, et al. *The Fundamentals: A Testimony to the Truth.* 4 vols. Los Angeles: Bible Institute of Los Angeles, 1917.

A set of 12 pamphlets each about 125 pages in length, these booklets not only assail modernism but also enunciate what came to be, and in essence still are, the key tenets of fundamentalism: the inerrancy of the Bible and the virgin birth, substitutionary atonement, bodily resurrection, and the second coming of Jesus. Along with these most frequently cited five fundamentals, the pamphlets emphasize the deity of Jesus, the sinful nature of humanity, salvation by faith, and the bodily resurrection of believers; they refute evolution and higher criticism; and they denounce Catholicism, Mormonism, Jehovah's Witnesses, Christian Scientists, and Spiritualism.

Van Bebber, Mark, and Paul Taylor. *Creation and Time: A Report on the Progressive Creationist Book by Hugh Ross.* Mesa, AZ: Eden Publications, 1994.

The authors criticize Hugh Ross, president of Reasons to Believe, for his advocacy of a "progressive creation" position. Though agreeing with Ross that life could not have arisen through natural processes, they point to what they consider his erroneous biblical interpretations, such as his claims that the earth is billions of years old, that there was death before Adam's fall, and that the biblical flood was not worldwide.

Walvoord, John F. *Armageddon, Oil and the Middle East Crisis: What the Bible Says about the Future of the Middle East and the End of Western Civilization.* Rev. ed. Grand Rapids, MI: Zondervan, 1990.

This contribution to apocalyptic literature explains why the presence of oil in the Middle East makes that region the focus of biblical prophecies about the final battle of Armageddon. Walvoord establishes a chronology of events he claims will lead to the rapture and Christ's return.

Walton, Rus. *FACS!: Fundamentals for American Christians.* Nyack, NY: Parson, 1979.

Walton portrays an America based on fundamental biblical principles. The American Revolution was influenced by the political thought of John Locke, who is described as a Christian thinker. The conservative Christian objective is to return the United States to its Christian roots, and to reject any attempt to combine Christianity with humanism.

Whitehead, John W. *The End of Man.* Westchester, IL: Crossway Books, 1986.

Although America still publicly expresses religious faith, Whitehead argues that the dissemination of humanist doctrines has become so extensive that discussion of what is right and wrong can no longer occur. The author advises Christians to maintain their values, avoid accommodation, and actively confront humanist beliefs.

————. *The Second American Revolution.* Westchester, IL: Crossway Books, 1982.

Viewing humanism as a doctrine that places faith in human beings rather than God, Whitehead rejects the possibility of coexisting with such beliefs. The Bible must be accepted as the sole source of authority, applying to all people, including rulers. The author rejects toleration in the sense of accepting other belief systems as equally true.

Zacharias, Ravi. *A Shattered Visage: The Real Face of Atheism.* Grand Rapids, MI: Baker Books, 1993.

The author claims that America has proceeded toward atheism, both personally and institutionally. Christian civilization has been decimated by this atheism and citizens suffer the consequences of alienation, loneliness, and guilt. Zacharias claims that violence is a logical result of atheism.

Zimmerman, Dean R. *Evolution: A Golden Calf.* Salt Lake City, UT: Hawkes Publishing, 1976.

Zimmerman argues that evolution can be correctly labeled a faith, a dogma, or a philosophy, but not a science. Claiming that evolutionists have failed to arrive at an appropriate mechanism to explain the process, the theory of evolution is essentially unfounded. The author concludes that Christianity and atheism, both being religions, should be treated equally: either both or neither should be allowed in the public schools.

Political and Economic Issues

Alcorn, Randy C. *Is Rescuing Right? Breaking the Law to Save the Unborn.* Downers Grove, IL: Inter-Varsity, 1990.

Admitting that the rescuing strategy has been controversial within the Christian community, Alcorn nonetheless claims that the willingness of some to "make sacrifices" means "the lives of babies are being saved." The author concludes that Christians should do all they can to prevent abortions. For some this means taking part in civil disobedience.

Barton, Charles D. *Myth of Separation.* Rev. ed. Aledo, TX: Wallbuilders, 1991.

Focusing on his perception of the correct relationship between church and state, Barton takes quotes from the writings of the constitutional founders and from Supreme Court decisions in the period 1795 to 1952 to argue that the separation of church and state is more myth than historical fact.

————. *America: To Pray or Not To Pray.* Rev. ed. Aledo, TX: Wallbuilders, 1989.

This book claims to provide statistical evidence of an American decline ever since 1962, when the Supreme Court instituted the ban on school prayer and, according to the author, began to disallow religious principles generally in public affairs.

Barton, Jon, and John Whitehead. *Schools on Fire.* Wheaton, IL: Tyndale House, 1980.

The authors are concerned with secularism in the public schools and urge Christians to regain control of school systems. They recommend monitoring textbook selection procedures in order to eliminate books that threaten religion, the family, free enterprise, and patriotism.

Beckman, M. J. "Red." *Born Again Republic.* Billings, MT: Freedom Church, 1981.

Beckman claims a second American Revolution has occurred, resulting in the subtle transformation of the republic established in 1787 into an illegal democracy. A major result of this revolution is the "confiscatory taxation" enforced by the Internal Revenue Service, which is labeled a terrorist organization. In returning the nation to its rightful status as a good republic, Americans should reject big government and follow God's law rather than man-made law.

Boys, Don. *Christian Resistance: An Idea Whose Time Has Come—Again.* Indianapolis, IN: Goodhope Press, 1985.

Basing his argument on centuries of tradition, Boys argues that Christians must resist government when obedience to laws would be a violation of a scriptural command. Boys focuses on such examples of government interference with churches as levying taxes, requiring incorporation, licensing pastors, and accrediting church schools and certifying their teachers. The Supreme Court is criticized for misinterpreting the Constitution.

———. *Pilgrims, Puritans, and Patriots: Our Christian Heritage.* Maitland, FL: Freedom University/Freedom Seminary/Freedom Institute Press, 1983.

Boys examines the history and beliefs of the early settlers to the North American continent in order to trace the nation's Christian heritage. He discusses the religious beliefs of Columbus and the Puritans and the motivations of the colonists in coming to the New World. An additional topic is the meaning of the First Amendment and the role Christians have played in defending personal and religious freedom.

———. *Liberalism: A Rope of Sand.* Maitland, FL: Freedom University/Freedom Seminary/Freedom Institute Press, 1979.

Holding that conservatives are "right" and liberals are "wrong," Boys argues that arrogant liberals, over the past 40 years of their political dominance, have completely failed the nation. Among the topics discussed are public versus Christian schools, homosexual rights, the Equal Rights Amendment, abortion, pornography, church-state conflict, and reverse discrimination.

Brown, Harold O. J. *The Reconstruction of the Republic.* Milford, MI: Mott Media, 1981.

Brown argues that American institutions are essentially biblical in origin and that the Bible has served as the fundamental source of societal values. However, especially since World War II, the government has assumed much of the role of transmitting values. According to Brown, Christians must reassert the dominance of biblical authority, which requires making the churches true Christian communities.

Chilton, David. *Productive Christians in an Age of Guilt-Manipulation: A Biblical Response to Ronald J. Sider.* Tyler, TX: Institute of Christian Economics, 1981.

A critique of Ronald Sider's liberal Christian positions on economic and social problems, this volume vigorously defends a biblically sanctioned relationship between Christianity and capitalism. The Bible demonstrates that the abolition of poverty must originate in the private sphere where wealth is truly produced. In contrast, socialism is viewed as an unproductive system.

Clouse, Robert G., ed. *War: Four Christian Views.* Downers Grove, IL: Inter-Varsity, 1981.

This work surveys the variety of evangelical perspectives on warfare. The contributing authors, writing from evangelical positions, present four views of war: nonresistance, pacifism, just-war tradition, and the crusade.

Colson, Chuck, and Jack Eckerd. *Why America Doesn't Work: How the Decline of the Work Ethic Is Hurting Your Family and Future—and What You Can Do.* Dallas: Word Publishing, 1991.

Colson, chairman of Prison Fellowship, and Eckerd, former head of the Eckerd drugstore chain, identify the loss of a spiritual foundation for the work ethic as the cause of many of the problems now facing the United States, including the decline of American competition in the world market, the deterioration of American schools, and the millions of unproductive people in prison and on welfare. The churches are given a major role in restoring the work ethic.

Colson, Chuck, with Ellen Santilli Vaughn. *Kingdoms in Conflict.* Grand Rapids, MI: William Morrow/Zondervan, 1987.

Colson, a former member of Richard Nixon's administration, was "born again" while serving time in prison for Watergate misdeeds. This volume presents his views on the relationship between the Christian church and politics.

Culver, Robert Duncan. *Toward a Biblical View of Civil Government.* Chicago: Moody, 1974.

Culver examines the notion of civil government from a Christian perspective. The author analyzes scriptural passages from the Old and New Testaments.

DeMar, Gary. *God and Government: A Biblical and Historical Study.* 3 vols. Atlanta, GA: American Vision, 1982, 1984.

These volumes, intended for use by individuals or in church and school, provide a biblically oriented approach to the study of American government. DeMar places the American political process firmly within the Christian tradition and argues that the Constitution reflects scriptural principles in place during the colonial period. Among the topics are the appropriate activities of government (such as maintaining a police force), biblical economics, and the causes of and biblical solutions to poverty.

DeVos, Richard M., with Charles Paul Conn. *Believe!* Old Tappan, NJ: Spire Books, 1976.

DeVos, president of Amway Corporation, makes his contribution to the literature of Christianity and capitalism. The book, in part a tale of the author's own business success, emphasizes the need for individual accountability, the first example of which he finds in the Garden of Eden when Adam and Eve suffer the consequences of disobeying God. DeVos stresses the need for sacrifice in order to succeed.

Dobson, Ed, and Ed Hindson. *The Seduction of Power.* Old Tappan, NJ: H. Revell, 1988.

The authors, each of whom formerly worked with Jerry Falwell, reflect on the flurry of religious right activity in the 1980s. The authors appear less optimistic about the results of this political activity, but recognize the need for continued, but possibly more subdued, involvement.

Doner, Colonel V. *The Samaritan Strategy: A New Agenda for Christian Activism.* Brentwood, TN: Wolgemuth and Hyatt, 1988.

Doner, a lobbyist for Christian Voice in the 1980s, evaluates religious right strategies in retrospect and concludes that the movement was far too negative in its objectives. The religious right was concerned primarily with blocking the objectives of more liberal groups. He suggests an overall change in tactics that includes the positive goal of helping the deserving poor as an alternative to the welfare state.

Duncan, Homer. *Humanism: In the Light of Holy Scripture.* Lubbock, TX: Christian Focus on Government, 1981.

Duncan deals with topics relevant to the relationship between Christianity and American politics. Viewing the Constitution to be a document written by Christians for a Christian society, the author advocates the election of public officials who are dedicated to a Christian morality.

Eidsmoe, John. *Columbus and Cortez: Conquerors for Christ.* Green Forest, AR: New Leaf, 1992.

Admitting that Indians suffered abuses at the hands of Columbus and other explorers, Eidsmoe nonetheless defends Christian intervention in the New World by arguing that many Native Americans who endured oppression under Native American traditions joined the explorers as liberators.

————. *Gays and Guns: The Case against Homosexuals in the Military.* Lafayette, LA: Huntington House, 1991.

Eidsmoe, proponent of a strong relationship between Christianity and the American political system, argues that admitting homosexuals openly into the military weakens combat effectiveness, creates risks to national security, and ends the traditional notion of the military as a rite of passage for young men. The author recommends reversing the existing policy.

————. *God and Caesar: Biblical Faith and Political Action.* Westchester, IL: Crossways Books, 1984.

The author focuses on a conservative economic interpretation of the Bible. He identifies the existence of private property in scripture extending from pre-Mosaic times to the millennium of Revelation. Eidsmore highlights examples of private enterprise in several of Jesus's parables. Aspects of the Constitution, such as separation of powers, are viewed as rooted in the Christian tradition.

Falwell, Jerry. *The Fundamentalist Phenomenon: The Resurgence of Conservative Christianity.* New York: Doubleday, 1981.

This is Falwell's explanation for the Moral Majority, as well as his attempt to interpret the reemergence of conservative Protestantism. Falwell places the foundation of the organization in the fundamentalist Christian tradition, despite his disclaimer elsewhere that the movement is not basically religious.

————. *Listen, America!* Garden City, NY: Doubleday, 1980.

Published during the early years of Falwell's leadership in the Moral Majority, this book encourages political activism among fundamentalists. The author focuses on five issues: abortion, homosexuality, pornography, secular humanism, and the threat to family values.

Feder, Don. *A Jewish Conservative Looks at Pagan America.* Lafayette, LA: Huntington House, 1993.

Journalist Feder claims abortion is not a right because it lacks any moral foundation. He traces America's problems to a lack of sexual inhibitions that leads to the excessive display of other human passions. Suggestions for remedying the situation are offered.

Foreman, Joseph L. *Shattering the Darkness: The Crisis of the Cross in the Church Today.* Montreat, NC: Cooling Spring, 1992.

Foreman provides a biblical defense for Christians conducting "abortion rescues." The book includes a letter written from prison by antiabortion leader Randall Terry in which he justifies his actions.

Fries, Michael, and C. Holland Taylor. *A Christian Guide to Prosperity.* Oakland, CA: Communications Research, 1984.

This book provides investment and savings advice for Christians. The authors criticize the present system that allows people to prosper without working. They recommend a return to the gold standard in order to rectify this situation and suggest keeping assets in gold and Swiss francs.

Geisler, Norman L., A. F. Brooke II, and Mark I. Keough. *The Creator in the Classroom: "Scopes II," the 1981 Arkansas Creation-Evolution Trial.* Milford, MI: Mott Media, 1982.

This book examines the *McLean v. Arkansas* trial dealing with the constitutionality of an Arkansas law that allowed public schools to teach creation science along with evolution in the public schools. The authors provide an account of the proceedings and the final ruling against the Creation-Evolution Act. Extensive documentation is provided in several appendices.

Gentry, Kenneth L., Jr. *God's Law in the Modern World.* Phillipsburg, NJ: Presbyterian and Reformed Publishing, 1993.

This book focuses on "theonomy," which is the claim that Old Testament moral and civil laws remain applicable for Christians and society generally. The author discusses the role of law not only in preaching the gospel and personal Christian conduct, but also in the formation of national public policy.

Grant, George. *Bringing in the Sheaves: Transforming Poverty into Productivity.* Brentwood, TN: Wolgemuth and Hyatt, 1988.

In this treatment of poverty, Grant identifies the return to productivity and independence as the goals of assistance to the poor. The author claims the poor are often responsible for their poverty, especially because of lack of faith in God and the resulting sinfulness.

————. *The Changing of the Guard: Biblical Blueprints for Political Action.* Fort Worth, TX: Dominion Press, 1987.

Grant argues that the successes of the Christian right result from a refusal to compromise religious principles. In order to return America to the theocratic status the founders intended, he recommends a strategy of local, grass-roots politics that includes activities beyond conventional participation. Churches should offer political education as well as opportunities for worship.

————. *In the Shadow of Plenty: The Biblical Blueprint for Welfare.* Fort Worth, TX: Dominion, 1986.

Grant describes government welfare programs as wicked, biblically heretical, and administered by sinful people who have no genuine concern for the poor. Although the church has responsibility for charity, Grant argues that this is a limited role. The ultimate purpose of charity should be to make the poor more responsible and productive.

————. *The Dispossessed: Homelessness in America.* Fort Worth, TX: Dominion, 1986.

Grant analyzes poverty from a conservative Christian perspective. Poverty and homelessness, resulting from the sinfulness of Adam and Eve, can be thought of as punishment. Christians can, through diligence, obedience to God, and the inspiration of the Holy Spirit, achieve prosperity. The responsibility for helping the poor and homeless falls not on government, but the church, a responsibility that includes the need to admonish the idle.

Hall, Verna M., and Rosalie J. Slater, eds. *The Bible and the Constitution of the United States of America.* Chesapeake, VA: Foundation for American Christian Education, 1983.

The authors have compiled a large number of historical documents, including sermons and public proclamations, they claim demonstrate that the Bible was a fundamental influence in the American founding.

Hargis, Billy James. *The Federal Reserve Scandal.* Tulsa, OK: Christian Crusade Books, 1995.

Hargis, leader of the Christian Crusade, argues that "liberals" are the cause of inflation, that the American economy is out of control, and that the value of money still continues to fall. The author suggests ways for Christians to oppose these trends.

————. *Day of Deception.* Tulsa, OK: Christian Crusade Books, 1991.

Hargis focuses on the many ways in which Christians can be deceived. Marxists, "one-worlders," the New Age movement, religious liberals, supporters of theological heresies, and "enemies of the Christian home," such as the entertainment industry and amoral schools, are targeted for attack.

————. *Forwarned: "Fore-Warned Fore-Armed."* Tulsa, OK: Christian Crusade Books, 1988.

Writing prior to the disintegration of the Soviet Union, Hargis warns against the intentions of that country to attain world domination. He points to a continuing arms buildup and communist acts of subversion and terrorism around the world. Yet, western countries foolishly continue to assist the Soviet Union economically.

————. *Communist America: Must It Be? Mid-Eighties Update.* Green Forest, AR: New Leaf Press, 1986.

In this "update" of a book written in the 1950s, Hargis observes that American morality and patriotism continue to deteriorate. The author claims that communism has encircled America and infiltrated its institutions, including the churches, where liberals have challenged such fundamentalist beliefs as the inerrancy of the Bible and the virgin birth of Christ.

Hargis, Billy James, and Bill Sampson. *The Cross and the Sickle: Superchurch—The World-National Councils of Churches' Infamous Story.* Tulsa, OK: Crusader Books, 1982.

This book is a fierce attack on the World Council of Churches and the National Council of Churches, organizations that represent mainline Christian denominations. The authors charge that these organizations have compromised fundamentalist doctrines such as the deity and virgin birth of Christ, have made a "pact" with "Satanic communism," are humanistic in their orientation, and favor a "world supergovernment."

Hargis, Billy James, and Jose Hernandez. *Disaster File.* Tulsa, OK: Crusader Books, 1978.

This conservative Christian expression of anticommunism is divided into three sections, or "books." The first, "Unilateral Disarmament," criticizes the Strategic Arms Limitation Treaty with the Soviet Union; the second, "Suicidal Foreign Policy," attacks American diplomacy for being too compromising toward communism; and the third, "Our Biased National Media," claims liberals dominate the American press and broadcast media to the extent that they constitute a part of the "international Marxist conspiracy."

Heath, Charles C. *The Blessings of Liberty: Restoring the City on the Hill.* Lafayette, LA: Huntington House, 1991.

Heath reviews 200 years of American history during which he believes God has blessed Americans with liberty. Now we are in danger of losing this liberty, so Heath encourages the reader to return to Christianity and choose honest national leaders who will follow a conservative policy agenda that includes providing work for those on welfare, cutting federal spending, and instituting term limits. The author considers this agenda the way to reestablish "God's city on the hill."

Hefley, James C. *America: One Nation under God.* Wheaton, IL: Victor Books, 1975.

This book investigates the biblical principles Hefley believes were influential in forming the American nation. Hefley describes how America has recently deviated from those principles.

Helms, Jesse. *When Free Men Shall Stand.* Grand Rapids, MI: Zondervan, 1976.

Helms, conservative senator from North Carolina and presently the chairman of the Senate Foreign Relations Committee, defends American capitalism and a strong national defense from a Christian right perspective. In his opposition to government welfare programs, the author states that Christ never mentioned or advocated a welfare system. Profitable businesses are considered the best antipoverty programs.

Hunter, Paul. *The Many Faces of Babylon: The Babylonian Influences upon Our Churches.* New York: Revelation Books, 1994.

Contrasting human and biblical systems of organization, Hunter claims that God's plan as presented in the Bible must be followed. The New Age movement comes under attack, as do television, motion pictures, the recording industry, and the government, each of which is charged with deceiving and manipulating Christians.

Kah, Gary. *En Route to Global Occupation.* Lafayette, LA: Huntington House, 1991.

Kah, a trade representative for the state of Indiana, claims to have exposed a frightening secret plan to unite the nations of the planet into a godless New World Order.

LaHaye, Beverly. *Who But a Woman?* Nashville, TN: Thomas Nelson, 1984.

Founder of Concerned Women for America, LaHaye describes the recent activities of the organization. The author provides arguments opposing such proposals as homosexual rights and the Equal Rights Amendment.

LaHaye, Tim. *Faith of Our Founding Fathers.* Brentwood, TN: Wolgemuth and Hyatt, 1987.

A leading figure in the Christian right provides his perceptions of the constitutional framers' religious beliefs. LaHaye stresses, in some cases beyond credibility, what he considers the Christian beliefs of the framers, and concludes that the nation was founded on a general agreement regarding Christian principles.

————. *The Hidden Censors.* Old Tappan, NJ: Fleming H. Revell, 1984.

Christian right leader LaHaye reverses the traditional liberal charge by claiming that the political left is censoring expressions of religious values and patriotism in the mass media. LaHaye gives examples of secular humanist propaganda that allegedly threaten the Christian values supposedly embraced by most Americans.

————. *The Coming Peace in the Middle East.* Grand Rapids, MI: Zondervan, 1984.

LaHaye interprets recent events in the Middle East as a fulfillment of biblical prophecy. The book expresses the religious right's support for an American foreign policy that champions the cause of Israel against its enemies, including the former Soviet Union.

Israel is seen as a major participant in the Battle of Armageddon, which will precede Christ's return.

————. *The Battle for the Family.* Old Tappan, NJ: Fleming H. Revell, 1982.

LaHaye presents a program for preserving a religious right vision of the family and reestablishing a moral nation. Blaming secular humanists for the failure of the family, the author recommends political activism in such areas as abortion, pornography, and television programming.

————. *The Bible's Influence on American History.* San Diego, CA: Master Books, 1976.

LaHaye argues for the importance of Christianity in the establishment and development of America. The author claims that a major role of Christian ministers was educating colonists in political thinking and that preachers served as recruiters of troops at the outbreak of the Revolutionary War. LaHaye impresses on the reader that a contemporary Christian should extend his private Christian life into public spheres, including education and politics.

Lindsell, Harold. *Free Enterprise.* Wheaton, IL: Tyndale House, 1982.

Lindsell argues for the contemporary relevance of a biblical notion of private property. Socialism fails to meet biblical requirements and therefore represents a violation of God's law, regardless of the support it may receive from actual governments.

Marshall, Peter, and David Manuel. *From Sea to Shining Sea.* Old Tappan, NJ: Fleming H. Revell, 1986.

The authors offer a history of the United States from the writing of the Constitution to the Civil War from a conservative Christian perspective. Although many non-Christians took part in developing America, God is seen as guiding the entire nation according to his own plan.

————. *The Light and the Glory.* Old Tappan, NJ: Fleming H. Revell, 1977.

The authors relate their view of the American founding. In a survey of American historical events from Christopher Columbus's landing to the writing of the Constitution, the authors perceive God's benevolent intervention. The Puritans are given much of the credit for establishing a Christian nation. Ultimately, however, God's divine guidance is responsible for the successful Revolutionary War and the Constitution. The authors argue that America is now suffering the consequences of straying from the spiritual path.

McGuire, Paul. *Who Will Rule the Future? A Resistance to the New World Order.* Lafayette, LA: Huntington House, 1991.

McGuire argues that Christians must be willing to take a political stand in order to combat the political and spiritual forces confronting the United States. Christians must oppose the "New Age conspiracy," the move toward socialism, and the globalism of the United Nations.

McIlhenny, Chuck, Donna McIlhenny, and Frank York. *When the Wicked Seize a City: A Grim Look at the Future and a Warning to the Church.* Lafayette, LA: Huntington House, 1993.

When a father takes a biblical stand against homosexual rights, he and his family face a violent reaction. According to the authors, homosexuality is a threat to children, schools, and the Christian way of life.

McKeever, James. *The Almighty and the Dollar.* Medford, OR: Omega, 1981.

McKeever, a millennialist who believes that Christ will return in this generation and therefore that this world is about to end, nonetheless argues that wise Christian investments and profit making are still important. Christians should act as though Christ's return will not occur for at least 50 years, since he might actually delay his coming.

McLellan, Vern. *Christians in the Political Arena: Positive Strategies for Concerned Twentieth Century Patriots!* Charlotte, NC: Associates Press, 1986.

While recognizing America's Christian heritage, the author believes that current difficulties in such areas as education, abortion, child abuse, pornography, and drug abuse point to the need for change, especially in the political realm. McLellan recommends such strategies as teaching children about government and authority and recognizing the importance of patriotic observances.

Nash, Ronald H. *Social Justice and the Christian Church.* Milford, MI: Mott Media, 1983.

This defense of capitalism as the system most compatible with Christian beliefs warns against government involvement in economic affairs. Nash portrays socialism as contrary to both Christianity and basic economic principles. Latin American liberation theology comes under attack.

North, Gary. *Inherit the Earth: Biblical Blueprints for Economics.* Fort Worth, TX: Dominion Press, 1987.

North recommends a religious right emphasis on local politics. Opting for a more long-term strategy, the author sees the importance of political struggles not at the national but at the local governmental levels.

————. *Honest Money: The Biblical Blueprint for Money and Banking.* Forth Worth, TX: Dominion Press, 1986.

North observes that the reconstruction of an economy based on capitalism and Christian values may first require a total collapse of the economy. The author recommends that Christians prepare for hard times by purchasing gold and silver and storing basic supplies.

————. *The Sinai Strategy: Economics and the Ten Commandments.* Tyler, TX: Institute for Christian Economics, 1986.

North argues for the compatibility of Christianity and capitalism, finding a basis for a free enterprise system beginning in Old Testament references. The Ten Commandments provide the religious, legal, and economic preconditions to the development of a free market.

————. *Unconditional Surrender: God's Program for Victory.* Tyler, TX: Geneva Press, 1981.

Referring to the biblical fall, North emphasizes scarcity as a consequence of human sinfulness. True Christians can serve others by profiting from economic enterprise. The poverty in economically undeveloped parts of the world is regarded as the result of sinfulness and a commitment to socialism. Therefore, those nations do not deserve assistance.

Nuttall, Clayton L. *The Conflict: The Separation of Church and State.* Schaumberg, IL: Regular Baptist Press, 1980.

Nuttall bases his analysis on the position that the Bible demands the separation of church and state. Presently, however, the state is attempting to separate the church from the state while at the same time attaching itself more closely to the church. Of particular concern is the attempted licensing and taxation of churches and church activities, which the author believes should be resisted.

Opitz, Edmund A. *Religion and Capitalism: Allies, Not Enemies.* Irvington-on-Hudson, NY: Foundation for Economic Education, 1992.

This book, originally published in 1970, examines differing forms of governing. Opitz concludes that a liberal ideology is conducive to strong government, whereas Christianity and capitalism mutually support one another.

Peters, Peter J. *America the Conquered.* LaPorte, CO: Scriptures of America Ministries, 1991.

Pastor Pete Peters argues that anti-Christian elements in our society have conquered America. Evidence that America has been subdued are found in the Supreme Court's decisions on flag burning, the decline of sexual morality, the harassment of churches, an extensive increase in police powers, the secularization of schools, and the legalization of abortion. Peters advises Americans to turn to God in order to regain their freedom.

Reed, Ralph. *Politically Incorrect: The Emerging Faith Factor in American Politics.* Nashville, TN: Word, 1994.

Reed, executive director of Pat Robertson's Christian Coalition, details the current strategy of the religious right. Broadening the group's range of concerns, the author discusses health care, crime, taxes, school choice, the economy, and the importance of local politics. In an effort to broaden the basis of support for the religious right, Reed tackles the question of past racism in the evangelical movement.

Remnant Resolves. LaPorte, CO: Scriptures for America Ministries, 1988.

The series of resolutions agreed to by "a remnant of God's people," meeting at the Rocky Mountain Family Bible Camp in Cederedge, Colorado, July 1988, calls for self-government under God both in the family and the nation. The resolves promote the God-given right to defend life, liberty, property, and the family, and condemn abortion as murder and homosexuality as a sin against God.

Robertson, Pat. *The Turning Tide: The Fall of Liberalism and the Rise of Common Sense.* Nashville, TN: Word, 1993.

Robertson discusses the end of liberal dominance in America. He claims that President Clinton and his wife Hillary are committed to an unacceptable radical and unbiblical political agenda.

————. *America's Dates with Destiny.* Nashville, TN: Thomas Nelson, 1986.

Robertson presents various episodes in American history, emphasizing the importance of religious belief. The author attributes the nation's current problems to a turn to liberalism at the beginning of this century. A return to conservatism and evangelical Christianity represents the hope of reestablishing traditional values.

Robertson, Pat, with Bob Slosser. *The Plan.* Nashville, TN: Thomas Nelson, 1989.

This book, published after Robertson's unsuccessful bid for the Republican presidential nomination, deals with the campaign and the reasons for Robertson's failure. God has a plan for everyone, and Robertson claims that despite his lack of success, the plan for him was to involve more Christians in politics and to spread the conservative Christian message.

————. *The Secret Kingdom: A Promise of Hope and Freedom in a World of Turmoil.* Nashville, TN: Thomas Nelson, 1982.

Presenting a contemporary interpretation of St. Augustine's distinction between the City of God and the Earthly City, this book contrasts the scarcity of the world and the abundance of God's kingdom. The Christian can gain prosperity in this world through wise investment. A modern interpretation is given to Christ's parable of the talents: to those who have, more will be given.

Rose, Tom, with Robert Metcalf. *The Coming Victory.* Memphis, TN: Christian Studies Center, 1980.

Basing his analysis on scripture, Rose provides guidelines for action in the political, economic, and educational arenas. The author is optimistic about the prospect for greater Christian influence.

Rowe, H. Edward. *Save America!* Old Tappan, NJ: Fleming H. Revell, 1976.

As a prelude to increased political activity of the religious right in the 1980s, Rowe discusses the strategies Christian voters can follow in order to counter what is considered the trend toward godlessness in the United States.

Rushdoony, Rousas John. *The Roots of Inflation.* Vallecito, CA: Ross House Books, 1982.

A defense of both capitalism and Christianity, this book praises hard work, which the author claims existed even in the Garden of Eden. The author criticizes the environmental movement, liberation theology, and welfare programs for the poor as well as the rich. Government assistance threatens capitalism and democracy and encourages class conflict. Citizens are blamed for inflation because of their willingness to become indebted.

————. *Law and Society.* Vallecito, CA: Ross House Books, 1982.

Rushdoony claims that God's law is relevant to each individual and to the world in general. Obedience to God's law brings blessings; disobedience results in evil. Awareness of the consequences of obedience and disobedience allows for a better understanding of history.

————. *Institutes of Biblical Law.* Nutley, NJ: Craig Press, 1972.

This book examines the Ten Commandments and other biblical laws. Rushdoony believes these laws provide a course of action when Christians follow the biblical command to achieve dominion over this world.

————. *The Nature of the American System.* Nutley, NJ: Craig, 1965.

Rushdoony argues that the notion of limited government can be traced to biblical standards of ruling. Contemporary liberalism, however, is seen as attempting to substitute for this limited government a centralized government with essentially unlimited powers.

————. *Politics of Guilt and Pity.* Fairfax, VA: Thoburn, 1978.

Rushdoony rejects the portrayal of American history as a series of events for which Americans should feel guilty. For instance, the author claims that slavery in the United States was far more benign than the slavery of Africa. Welfare programs are described as a modern form of slavery, with the federal government as the slave owner.

————. *This Independent Republic: Studies in the Nature and Meaning of American History.* Nutley, NJ: Craig Press, 1964.

This earlier statement of a common theme within postmillennialist thought holds that Europeans were chosen by God to inhabit America. The author views the Constitution as an essentially Christian document based upon a higher law originating with God.

Schaeffer, Francis A., Vladimir Bukovsky, and James Hitchock. *Who Is for Peace?* Nashville, TN: Thomas Nelson, 1983.

Each author contributes an essay presenting a conservative Christian position on military affairs. Schaeffer argues in favor of the need for a strong military; Bukovsky (a Russian) criticizes the Soviet Union's military policy; and Hitchcock (a Roman Catholic) criticizes the 1983 Catholic bishops' letter on nuclear armaments.

Schaeffer, Francis A., and C. Everett Koop. *Whatever Happened to the Human Race?* Old Tappan, NJ: Fleming H. Revell, 1979.

The authors investigate the effects of secular humanism on the law. They focus on the issues of abortion, infanticide, and euthanasia.

Schaeffer, Franky. *Bad News for Modern Man: An Agenda for Christian Activism.* Westchester, IL: Crossway Books, 1984.

Schaeffer disavows any intention of creating a theocracy in America. However, he calls for avid Christian right involvement in politics. Although he recognizes the primacy of Christian principle, the author admits the importance of achieving political power.

Schaeffer, Franky, and Harold Fickett. *A Modest Proposal for Peace, Prosperity, and Happiness.* Nashville, TN: Thomas Nelson, 1985.

The "modest proposal" in the title refers to a fictional person's suggestion for eliminating unwanted or unneeded people. The book's target is abortion, as the postscript, "Deciphering the Code," makes clear. The authors want to end the alleged "holocaust" of abortion.

Scheidler, Joseph M. *Closed: 99 Ways to Stop Abortion.* Westchester, IL: Crossway, 1988.

Scheidler, who heads the Pro-Life Action League, presents practical advice about stopping abortions, including fund-raising techniques, ways of coping with police during demonstrations, finding alternatives to abortion for women, and strategies for debate. The author recommends nonviolence.

Schenck, Paul, with Robert L. Schenck. *The Extermination of Christianity: A Tyranny of Consensus.* Lafayette, LA: Huntington House, 1993.

The authors contend that radical liberals are attempting to eliminate Christianity in America. American Christians are being subjected to slander and ridicule that represents the prelude to an oppression rivaled only by the persecution of early Christians. To back their claim, the authors refer to what they consider the unfavorable depiction of the clergy in movies, on television, and in popular music and to the perceived bias against Christians in the public schools.

Schwarz, Fred. *You Can Trust the Communists (To Be Communists).* Englewood Cliffs, NJ: Prentice-Hall, 1960.

This classic work from the leader of the Christian Anti-Communism Crusade presents a view of communism as an internally logical doctrine that allows for a high degree of predictability of communist actions. A physician, Schwarz portrays the fight against communism in terms similar to fighting an illness.

Sileven, Everett. *The Christian and the Income Tax.* Louisville, NE: Council for Religious Education, 1986.

Sileven holds that the Constitution limits public officials, not the people, who are subject only to God's law. Rules and regulations over the people, particularly the income tax, are unconstitutional, unscriptural, and contrary to the intentions of the Founding Fathers. Americans should refuse to go into debt, avoid credit cards, refuse to use FDIC banks, and, when on a jury, vote "not guilty" in cases concerning taxes. Sileven claims that anyone who supports such government programs as mass transit, public highways, and the public school system is a "practicing Communist."

Sproul, R. C. *Money Matters: Making Sense of Economic Issues That Affect You.* Wheaton, IL: Tyndale House, 1985.

This conservative evangelical look at economics praises the value of laboring, claiming that God even expected Adam and Eve to work in the Garden of Eden. God has called us to be constructive managers of his creation, to subdue the earth and to make it fruitful.

Terry, Randall A. *Operation Rescue.* Springdale, PA: Whitaker House, 1988.

Terry, organizer of sit-ins at abortion clinics, advocates the coerced closing of these clinics as a means of creating sufficient unrest to force government to outlaw abortion through passage of a Human Rights Amendment.

Thoburn, Robert L. *The Christian and Politics.* Tyler, TX: Thoburn Press, 1984.

Thoburn notes that as Christians retreated from the political realm, secular humanists captured the playing field, to the disadvantage of Christians. The author develops a biblical view of government, analyzes a number of issues—including education, welfare, taxation, and foreign policy—from a biblical stance, and discusses how Christians can involve themselves in politics more effectively.

Vernon, Robert. *L.A. Justice: Lessons from the Firestorm.* Colorado Springs, CO: Focus on the Family, 1993.

The author, a former assistant police chief in Los Angeles, discusses satanic influences in southern California that are responsible for such things as mob violence, racial conflict, and earthquakes. Vernon explains how the present situation developed and discusses whether there is a way to "save" Los Angeles.

Walton, Rus. *Biblical Solutions to Contemporary Problems: A Handbook.* Brentwood, TN: Wolgemuth and Hyatt, 1988.

Walton looks to the Bible for solutions to a variety of political questions, including taxation, welfare, and economic growth. The author advocates a strong national defense as crucial to maintaining a Christian nation and cautions that the United Nations is a major humanist institution. Major aspects of the American constitutional order are claimed to be found in Old Testament accounts of the Hebrew people.

———. *One Nation under God.* Nashville, TN: Thomas Nelson, 1987.

This work advocates an active political role for Christians, especially at the local level, in order to reestablish God's place in American government. Socialism and humanism are seen as destructive of biblical principles regarding government, economics, and education. The author supports a strong national defense, including nuclear deterrence. He expresses opposition to the United Nations, pointing to that organization's anti-American position and support of communism.

Whitehead, John W. *An American Dream.* Westchester, IL: Crossway Books, 1987.

Whitehead, a legal scholar, is wary of the connection between religion and the state, noting that, except for Massachusetts, theocratic systems were rejected in colonial times. However, the author recognizes the importance of the clergy historically in establishing those rights and liberties so important to the "American dream." John Locke is portrayed as important to the transmission of Reformation thought into the era of revolution, including the American Revolution.

————. *The Stealing of America.* Westchester, IL: Crossway Books, 1983.

Whitehead establishes the historical development of freedom and individualism in conjunction with responsibility that originates in Martin Luther's writings during the Reformation. This individualism, Whitehead argues, has been increasingly threatened in recent years by a growing governmental structure. The spread of collectivist influences originating in European thinkers is given some of the blame for the contemporary trend of limiting religious freedoms.

————. *The Separation Illusion.* Melford, MI: Mott Media, 1977.

Whitehead argues that God cannot be separated from civil government and therefore rejects the current interpretation of separation of church and state. In this context, the author presents what he considers the actual intent of the First Amendment regarding freedom of religion.

Whitemarsh, Darylann, and Bill Reisman. *Subtle Serpent: New Age in the Classroom.* Lafayette, LA: Huntington House, 1993.

The authors argue that the public school systems have allowed such evils as suicide, rape, drug use, violence, teen pregnancy, and a general disregard for authority. They identify the cause of these evils in attempts to introduce new moral codes without the permission or knowledge of parents.

Ziglar, Zig. *Confessions of a Happy Christian.* Gretna, LA: Pelican, 1978.

Ziglar, a businessman and consultant, claims that God wants Christians to prosper materially as well as spiritually. He argues that the Bible provides lessons and examples for business success.

Such biblical figures as Abraham, Jacob, Joseph, Moses, and Solomon are mentioned as models of financial achievement.

Personal and Family

Bakker, Jim. *Survival: Unite to Live.* Harrison, AR: New Leaf, 1981.

Jim Bakker presents a premillennialist view of contemporary events from a personal perspective and calls for Christians to unite so that the church might prevail in the coming apocalyptic times.

Bakker, Jim, with Robert Paul Lamb. *Move That Mountain!* Plainfield, NJ: Logos International, 1976.

This autobiography provides a revealing look at the personality of the former PTL leader, beginning with Bakker's younger years and including an account of his conversion experience at the age of 18. Of special interest is Bakker's belief that one must give in order to get, as well as his assurance that God will satisfy requests.

Bakker, Tammy, with Cliff Dudley. *Run to the Roar.* Harrison, AR: New Leaf Press, 1980.

Tammy Bakker gives a personal account of how she overcame anxiety. The book is revealing in describing the fears that could develop in children in the early Cold War years—both fear of God as well as of the perceived communist threat.

———. *I Gotta Be Me.* Harrison, AR: New Leaf Press, 1978.

This autobiography relates Tammy Bakker's life from childhood to the better days of the PTL Club. The book contains interesting material about her upbringing, including her relationship with her mother and stepfather and her early beliefs and fears. Bakker provides insight into her and her husband's theology of giving in order to receive.

Bryant, Anita. *The Anita Bryant Story: The Survival of Our Nation's Families and the Threat of Militant Homosexuality.* Old Tappan, NJ: Fleming H. Revell, 1977.

Bryant recounts her campaign against a homosexual rights ordinance in Dade County, Florida. Portraying herself as similar to Deborah of the Old Testament Book of Judges, she interprets the campaign in terms of bringing the nation back to God. Bryant faults conservative men for failing to support the campaign.

————. *Bless This House.* Old Tappan, NJ: Fleming H. Revell, 1972

In light of their ultimate divorce, this book provides an interesting account of the Anita Bryant–Bob Green marriage. Especially revealing is the couple's attempt to establish a marriage based on the fundamentalist belief that the wife should submit to the authority of the husband. Bryant claims there can still be opportunities for good even in very bad home environments.

————. *Amazing Grace.* Old Tappan, NJ: Fleming H. Revell, 1971.

This is another account of Bryant's personal life, which began in poverty. She discusses her conversion to Christianity, her show business career, and the decision made with her husband and manager, Bob Green, to introduce religious themes in her nightclub act.

————. *Mine Eyes Have Seen the Glory.* Old Tappan, NJ: Fleming H. Revell, 1970.

Bryant, runner-up in the 1958 Miss America contest, popular singer, and, in the 1970s, leading opponent of gay rights in Florida, discusses her life from early childhood. She relates her experiences in the context of submitting to God's will and plan for her life.

Dobson, James. *Dare To Discipline.* New York: Bantam Books, 1977.

An explicit alternative to what are considered Benjamin Spock's liberal child-rearing methods, this book urges early punishment as a means of establishing parental authority and gaining control of children. Dobson attributes contemporary challenges to authority to permissive child-rearing practices.

Falwell, Jerry. *Strength for the Journey: An Autobiography.* New York: Simon and Schuster, 1987.

Falwell begins his autobiography with an account of family heritage and ends in the late 1980s after his stormy experience in the public sphere as leader of the Moral Majority. Of special note are accounts of his alcoholic father, his conversion experience in his mother's kitchen, subsequent preparation for the ministry, and his early days at Thomas Road Baptist Church.

Jeremiah, David. *Before It's Too Late.* Nashville, TN: Thomas Nelson, 1982.

The author addresses a number of moral issues from a conservative Christian viewpoint, relying on biblical authority to argue for the importance of the family. He asserts that homosexuality is the result of a society that has failed to follow God, and pornography contributes to a variety of social problems, including rape and child abuse.

LaHaye, Beverly. *The Restless Woman.* Grand Rapids, MI: Zondervan, 1984.

LaHaye warns of the dangers women face in contemporary society, where even the Christian woman may unintentionally be drawn into destructive competition with her husband. The appropriate domestic role for women is presented through negative examples from the women's liberation movement and positive models of Christian self-sacrifice.

———. *A Woman by God's Design.* Old Tappan, NJ: Fleming H. Revell, 1980.

The traditional sexual roles that many contemporary social scientists regard as culturally established LaHaye treats as biologically based and God-ordained, with a woman's highest expression of femininity being motherhood. To supplement these roles, the author recommends distinct role models for girls and boys. Authority and submissiveness in the home and the church are discussed.

———. *How To Develop Your Child's Temperament.* Eugene, OR: Harvest House, 1977.

Recommending a position somewhere between permissiveness and excessive strictness, this book on child rearing presents a religious right view of the subject. LaHaye assumes the sinful nature of all human beings, including children, who are by nature selfish and desire what is evil. The author discusses strategies for early training and discipline so that the child may be brought under parental control.

————. *The Spirit-Controlled Woman.* Eugene, OR: Harvest House, 1976.

Recognizing the problems the traditional family faces in contemporary society, LaHaye advises that the wife remain submissive to her husband, making his happiness her major objective. Although Christian women ought to marry Christian men, even unsaved husbands should be obeyed. LaHaye advises that even the worst marriages are capable of being saved.

LaHaye, Tim. *If Ministers Fall, Can They Be Restored?* Grand Rapids, MI: Zondervan, 1991.

Christian right leader LaHaye approaches the contemporary problem of ministers who have strayed sexually. He offers a formula for evading temptation and gives advice to churches that must deal with a minister who has fallen.

————. *Sex Education Is for the Family.* Grand Rapids, MI: Zondervan, 1985.

This is a conservative Christian view of sexuality. LaHaye identifies basic God-determined, biological differences between men and women, claiming that men are more capable of leadership and women are more passive. LaHaye denies any biological origin to homosexuality, attributing its development to the faults in child rearing of one or both parents. Advice is given to parents regarding the control of children, especially as they approach puberty.

LaHaye, Tim, and Beverly LaHaye. *The Act of Marriage: The Beauty of Sexual Love.* Grand Rapids, MI: Zondervan, 1976.

This sex manual for married Christians written by religious right activists Tim and Beverly LaHaye provides explicit advice about sexual intercourse. The authors claim that Christians can experience greater sexual satisfaction than non-Christians.

Morgan, Marabel. *Total Joy.* Old Tappan, NJ: Fleming H. Revell, 1976.

Filled with testimonials from women who have followed Morgan's strategies, wives are advised to make their husbands happy and hence less prone to temptation outside of marriage. Although the wife should recognize the husband's authority, she can have her way by looking after her husband's needs.

————. *The Total Woman.* Old Tappan, NJ: Fleming H. Revell, 1973.

This book contains advice about how the Christian woman can satisfy her husband to achieve a better marriage. Morgan follows the biblical notion of the submissive wife, recommending that the woman try not to change her husband, but rather modify herself. If there are problems in the marriage, Morgan advises the woman to take the responsibility.

Robertson, Pat, with Jamie Buckingham. *Shout It from the Housetops.* Plainfield, NJ: Logos International, 1972.

This autobiography of Robertson, the religious right leader and 1988 presidential candidate, describes his privileged pre-conversion life as the son of a U.S. senator, his early successes in school and athletics, and his tenure as a Marine officer. Robertson recounts his experiences leading up to his conversion and his subsequent decision to become a minister.

Robison, James. *Thank God, I'm Free: The James Robison Story.* Nashville, TN: Thomas Nelson, 1988.

In this autobiography, Christian right leader Robison tells of his turn to Christianity after a difficult early life. Robison's mother, a single woman who was a victim of rape, took Robison from a foster home when he was five years old to live a fatherless and impoverished childhood. It was his foster mother, however, who was with him when he committed his life to God.

Schaeffer, Francis A. *Letters of Francis Schaeffer.* Westchester, IL: Crossway, 1985.

Schaeffer, the noted evangelical theologian, deals with a number of topics in this volume, including homosexuality, divorce, spirituality, sinfulness, and the role of the Holy Spirit in a Christian's life.

Schaffer, James, and Colleen Todd. *Christian Wives: Women behind the Evangelists Reveal Their Faith in Modern Marriage.* Garden City, NY: Doubleday and Company, 1987.

Schaffer and Todd portray the wives of the following television evangelists: Jim Bakker, Jerry Falwell, Billy Graham, Rex Humbard, Oral Roberts, Robert Schuller, and Jimmy Swaggart. The authors relate how each couple deals with the pressures of the evangelist's profession.

Schlafly, Phyllis. *The Power of the Christian Woman.* Cincinnatti, OH: Standard Publishing, 1981.

Schlafly emphasizes different roles of men and women from a conservative Christian perspective. Although women are advised not to compete with men and not to abandon motherhood as a fundamental role, Schlafly admires strong women who use their femininity to advantage. The author targets feminists for attack, claiming they are selfish, psychologically unstable, and haters of men.

————. *The Power of the Positive Woman.* New Rochelle, NY: Arlington House, 1977.

Schlafly, leading opponent of the Equal Rights Amendment, presents her views on the American family and related public policy issues. She presents her model for the ideal family and the woman's role in it.

Strober, Gerald, and Ruth Tomczak. *Jerry Falwell: Aflame for God.* Nashville, TN: Thomas Nelson, 1979.

This biography of Falwell was produced by his own organization (co-author Tomczak is creative coordinator of the Jerry Falwell ministries, and copies include a personal message from Falwell himself). The book enthusiastically portrays Falwell as a good student in earlier years, a devoted pastor at Thomas Road Baptist Church, a committed television evangelist and Christian leader, and a family man.

Welch, Robert. *The Life of John Birch.* Appleton, WI: Western Islands, 1960.

Welch, the founder of the John Birch Society, examines the life of the young missionary who inspired the formation of the organization that carries his name. Birch was reportedly killed by Chinese Communists in 1945. Welch calls him the first casualty of World War III, a struggle in which "Christian-style civilization" must triumph completely over communism or be totally destroyed.

Periodicals

The following periodicals and journals present the varied positions of and examine questions relevant to the religious right. Many of these publications are not available through libraries or the more popular distribution channels, but must be acquired directly from the association.

Action Line
Care Net, A Ministry of the Christian Action Council
101 W. Broad Street, Suite 500
Falls Church, VA 22046
Three issues per year. $.20 per copy.

This newsletter provides commentary and analysis of public policy questions regarding abortion. The publication has as its objective "to protect and proclaim the sanctity of human life."

Bible-Science News
Bible-Science Association, Inc.
P.O. Box 33220
Minneapolis, MN 55433-0220
Nine issues per year. $25.

This magazine claims an audience of college-educated Christians, particularly those interested in the natural sciences. Articles investigate arguments about the origin of the world and support a creationist viewpoint.

Chalcedon Report
Chalcedon Foundation
P.O. Box 158
Vallecito, CA 95251-0158
Monthly. Donation requested.

This newsletter deals with issues involving the reconstruction movement and includes articles on the application of Christian principles to contemporary society and culture.

Christian Anti-Communism Crusade Newsletter
P.O. Box 890
Long Beach, CA 90801-0890
Monthly. Free on request.

This publication continues to present information about communist activities around the world (referring to "lively communist corpses") and the efforts of Fred Schwarz's Christian Anti-Communism Crusade organization to counteract those activities. The newsletter also includes commentary on such issues as abortion, homosexuality, and AIDS.

Christian Beacon
Christian Beacon, Inc.
756 Haddon Avenue
Collingswood, NJ 08108-3712
Weekly. $12.

This newspaper, edited by Carl McIntire, deals with religious and social issues of concern to conservative fundamentalist Christians.

Christian Book Distributors Catalog
P.O. Box 7000
Peabody, MA 01961-7000
Bimonthly. Free on request.

This catalog of Christian reading, listening, and viewing resources often contains materials with themes that are of concern to the religious right.

Christian Century
Christian Century Foundation
407 South Dearborn Street
Chicago, IL 60605
Weekly. $30.

This comparatively moderate Christian publication comments extensively on religious right activities and personalities.

Christian Crusade Newspaper
P.O. Box 977
Tulsa, OK 74102-9979
Monthly. Free on request.

This publication of Billy James Hargis's Christian Crusade organization provides critical commentary on current political and economic issues, including American foreign policy. The newspaper still presents a strong anticommunist position.

Christian News
3277 Boeuf Lutheran Road
New Haven, MO 63068-9568
Weekly. $20.

Formerly *Lutheran News,* this newspaper provides a conservative perspective on events relevant to Christians, especially within, but not limited to, the Missouri Synod Lutheran Church, and national and international happenings of interest to conservative Christians.

Christian Reconstruction
Institute for Christian Economics
P.O. Box 6116
Tyler, TX 75711
Bimonthly. Free on request.

This newsletter, published in alternate months with *Biblical Economics Today,* provides scriptural discussions relevant to the biblical reconstruction viewpoint.

Christian Research Book and Tape Catalog
Christian Research
P.O. Box 385
Eureka Springs, Arkansas 72632
Yearly. On request.

This catalog lists a variety of books relevant to the religious right that can be ordered from Christian Research. In addition to Bibles and Bible reference works, many other categories of books are included, such as economics and money, evolution vs. creationism, government, history, law and constitution, and taxes and taxation.

Christian Research Journal
Christian Research Institute
P.O. Box 500
San Juan Capistrano, CA 92693-0500
Quarterly. $16.

This journal contains biblically based articles that deal with such current issues as cults, false doctrine, the New Age movement, and secular humanism. Techniques of evangelizing are presented and current literature on defending the faith is reviewed.

Christian Standard
Standard Publishing Company, Inc.
8121 Hamilton Avenue
Cincinnati, OH 45231-2396
Weekly. $18.

This magazine includes news, commentary, and essays dealing with the revival of the doctrines and rules of Christianity as set out in the New Testament.

The Christian Worldview
American Vision
P.O. Box 720515
Atlanta, GA 30328
Monthly. $20.

This newsletter holds that the Bible should be applied to all aspects of Christian life and provides instruction in the nature of government and the Christian's role in politics. A biblical view is provided for many current issues, such as secular humanism, the New Age Movement, homosexuality, and government intervention in people's lives.

Christianity Today
Christianity Today, Inc.
465 Gunderson Drive
Carol Stream, IL 60188
Eighteen issues per year. $24.95.

This relatively moderate evangelical publication offers commentary on all aspects of the evangelical movement.

The Correspondent
Plymouth Rock Foundation
Fisk Mill, Box 577
Marlborough, NH 03455
Monthly. $25.

This newsletter provides information about local PRF committee activities and reprints articles from these organizations. The prime concern is promoting biblical principles in local government.

Creation Social Science and Humanities Quarterly
Creation Social Science and Humanities Society
1429 N. Holyoke
Wichita, KS 67208
Quarterly. $15.

This quarterly's objective is to further the creation account as found in the book of Genesis, holding to the belief that the Bible is inerrant. The journal publishes articles, book reviews, editorials, letters, and poetry.

Facts & Faith
Reasons to Believe
P.O. Box 5978
Pasadena, CA 91117
Quarterly. $24 donation.

This interdenominational newsletter reports on scientific discoveries that are believed to substantiate the biblical account of creation. The newsletter supports the view that science and religious faith are compatible.

Facts for Action
Christian Research
P.O. Box 385
Eureka Springs, AR 72632
Quarterly. $8.

This newsletter presents a fundamentalist Christian, highly patriotic, and conservative view of current events in American society and politics. The national government and its agencies are the focus of opposition and deep suspicion (for instance, the Internal Revenue Service is referred to as the "Gestapo" and the "Beast").

First Things
Institute of Religion and Public Life
156 Fifth Avenue, Suite 400
New York, NY 10010
Ten issues per year. $24.

Edited by Richard John Neuhaus, this monthly journal of religion and public life includes articles that investigate public policy questions stemming from the intersection of religion and politics.

Focus on the Family
Focus on the Family, Inc.
801 Corporate Center Drive
Pomona, CA 91768
Monthly. Free.

This publication from James Dobson's organization focuses on public policy and issues related to traditional family values. Articles are intended to strengthen families and to support conservative Christian objectives, such as limiting abortion and obscenity.

Fundamental News Service
American Council of Christian Churches
P.O. Box 19
Wallingford, PA 19086
Bimonthly. $15.

This newsletter reports on issues relevant to contemporary fundamentalist churches and comments critically on the National Council of Churches and the National Association of Evangelicals for their compromising attitude toward the faith. The publication also treats social and political issues of interest to conservative Christians.

The Humanist
American Humanist Association
7 Hardwood Drive
Amherst, NY 14226-7188
Bimonthly. $24.95.

This magazine promotes the principles of humanism (the belief that human beings are interdependent and mutually responsible without any help from an acknowledged supreme being) so often considered by the religious right to be in direct opposition to Christian belief.

Journal of Christian Reconstruction
Chalcedon Foundation
P.O. Box 158
Vallecito, CA 95251
Twice annually. $14.

This journal presents articles dealing with the reestablishment of Christian intellectual and cultural standards, as found in the Old and New Testaments.

Lutheran Renewal
International Lutheran Renewal Center
2701 Rice Street
St. Paul, MN 55113-2200
Monthly. Free.

Growing out of the charismatic movement of the 1960s, this newsletter has offered issue positions opposed to those of the mainline Evangelical Lutheran Church in America. In recent issues, this publication has been highly critical of the ELCA for a draft statement on sexuality that attempted to arrive at a compromise position on the issue of homosexuality.

NAE Washington Insight
National Association of Evangelicals
P.O. Box 28
Wheaton, IL 60189
Monthly. $14.95.

This newsletter reports on the various activities of the federal government and political issues at the national level that are of concern to the evangelical leadership.

The New American
The Review of the News Incorporated
P.O. Box 8040
770 Westhill Boulevard
Appleton, WI 54915
Bimonthly. $39.

This John Birch Society publication stands for traditional values, patriotism, independence, and the United States Constitution.

The magazine's stated goal is "to educate and to activate Americans in support of God, family, and country." Articles focus on political science, social opinion, and economic theory and hold to a conspiracy theory regarding the influences on American culture and politics.

Phyllis Schlafly Report
Eagle Forum
P.O. Box 9683
Alton, IL 62002
Monthly. $20.

This newsletter provides reports and commentary in areas of interest to conservative Christians within education, politics, and social and economic policy.

Reason and Revelation
Apologetics Press, Inc.
230 Landmark Drive
Montgomery, AL 36117-2752
Monthly. $5 per copy.

This journal offers defenses of Christianity and presents evidence for its truth. A major emphasis is placed on creationism.

The Religion and Society Report
The Rockford Institute
934 North Main Street
Rockford, IL 61103-7061
Monthly. $24.

This newsletter of religious opinion presents conservative opinion on such topics as homosexuality, school prayer, and church-state relations. Articles in the newsletter have taken an especially strong stand against abortion.

The Rock
Plymouth Rock Foundation
6 McKinley Circle
P.O. Box 425
Marlborough, NH 03455
Quarterly.

This journal focuses on the responses that the Bible provides to secular humanism and to the perceived socialist-inspired alternatives in public policy.

Sanctity of Human Life Update
Care Net
101 W. Broad Street, Suite 500
Falls Church, VA 22046
Bimonthly. $36 per 100 copies for one-year subscription.

Care Net, a ministry of the Christian Action Council, produces this publication as a church bulletin insert. The insert provides information about the antiabortion movement and government action relevant to the abortion issue.

Scoreboard Alert
National Citizens Action Network
P.O. Box 10459
Costa Mesa, CA 92627
Bimonthly. $14.

This periodical, dedicated to activating citizens for the preservation of American values, reports on legislative issues of concern to conservative Christians.

The Servant
Haven Baptist Church
125 South Sherman Street
Denver, CO 80209-1618
Monthly. Free.

This newsletter of the Council of Bible Believing Churches (United States affiliate of the International Council of Christian Churches) presents an extreme religious right perspective on current events in the United States and around the world. The publication opposes what are seen as liberal trends within the Christian church.

Traditional Values Report
Traditional Values Coalition
P.O. Box 940
Anaheim, CA 92815
Occasional. Individual issues provided on request.

This newsletter from the Traditional Values Coalition reports on current issues, such as perceived inroads of homosexuality in the educational system, sex education in the schools, and the relationship between church and state. Traditional family values are supported, and readers are encouraged to promote a constitutional amendment to protect the rights of religious persons.

Voice of Liberty
Voice of Liberty Association
692 Sunnybrook Drive
Decatur, GA 30033-5509
Semiannual. Donation.

This VLA newsletter provides a conservative Christian analysis of current events and focuses on biblical prophecy.

Selected Nonprint Resources 7

This chapter contains a variety of nonprint resources from and about the religious right, including video and audio tapes, radio and television programs, computer software and databases, and electronic mail addresses. The listings include those resources that treat the major concerns of the religious right.

Audio and Video Tapes Presenting Religious Right Positions

This listing includes examples of the religious right's wide range of concerns. The topics include abortion, God's perceived role in American history and the founding of the Republic, creationism and evolution, the end times and the expected millennium, the Clinton presidency, education, environmental issues, secular humanism, homosexuality, biblical inerrancy, American support for the state of Israel, the New Age movement, patriotism, anticommunism, and the political activism of conservative Christians.

Abortion: A Rational Look at an Emotional Issue
Type: ½" videocassette and audiocassette
Length: 180 min.
Cost: $30 for videocassette; $12 for audiocassette
Date: 1994
Source: Ligonier Ministries
P.O. Box 547500
Orlando, FL 32854
(800) 435-4343

R. C. Sproul, head of the Ligonier teaching ministry, discusses what he considers the deepest moral problem in our society. He argues that abortion is against God's law, against the laws of nature, and against reason.

Abortion: The American Holocaust
Type: ½" videocassette and audiocassette
Length: 45 min.
Cost: $20 for videocassette; $6 for audiocassette
Date: 1992
Source: John Hagee Ministries
P.O. Box 1400
San Antonio, TX 78295
(210) 494-3900

John Hagee presents an uncompromising argument against abortion based on the Bible and scientific claims that support the biblical position. He argues that Americans who support the right of abortion are no better than Germans who participated in the Holocaust.

AIDS: What You Haven't Been Told
Type: ½" videocassette
Length: 60 min.
Cost: $19.95
Date: 1989
Source: Jeremiah Films
P.O. Box 1710
Hemet, CA 92343
(714) 652-1006

Fundamentalists provide their perspective on AIDS, assess blame for its spread, and discuss possible protection against the disease.

The American Covenant

Type: ½" videocassette
Length: 52 min.
Cost: $19.95
Date: 1994
Source: American Portrait Films
P.O. Box 19266
Cleveland, OH 44119
(216) 531-8600

Filmed at various historical sites around the nation, this tape examines the formation of the American Republic. Marshall Foster, a Christian historian, narrates ten events in the history of the nation, including the Pilgrims' *Mayflower* voyage and Patrick Henry's "Give me liberty or give me death" oration.

The American Vision: 360 Years Later

Type: audiocassette
Length: 60 min.
Cost: $5.95
Date: 1984
Source: American Vision Press
P.O. Box 720515
Atlanta, GA 30328

This tape provides an overview of the American founding and development from a Christian perspective. From Columbus's search for the New World, seen as a fulfillment of biblical prophecy, to the 1963 Supreme Court school prayer decision, the tape deals with the religious beliefs of noted Americans.

America's Godly Heritage

Type: ½" videocassette
Length: 60 min.
Cost: $20
Date: 1993
Source: Wallbuilders
P.O. Box 397
Aledo, TX 76008
(817) 441-6044

David Barton discusses the Christian beliefs and ideals that he claims have guided America since the founding. Barton cites earlier Supreme Court decisions that affirmed the role of Christian principles in the public realm and criticizes more recent decisions that he considers to be ill conceived because they ignore the intentions of the Christian founders.

Ancient Man: Created or Evolved

Type: ½" videocassette
Length: 58 min.
Cost: $9.95
Date: 1994
Source: Christian Book Distributors
P.O. Box 7000
Peabody, MA 01961-7000
(508) 977-5000

Roger Oakland investigates the creation/evolution debate over the origin of human beings, tests each theory against the evidence, and expresses sympathy for the creationist position.

Apocalypse Planet Earth

Type: ½" videocassette
Length: 45 min.
Cost: $19.95
Date: 1993
Source: Jeremiah Films
P.O. Box 1710
Hemet, California 92546
(800) 828-2290

Hal Lindsey, author of *The Late Great Planet Earth,* once again offers scriptural interpretations of current events. He reaches dramatic conclusions regarding the end of history.

Battle for Our Minds: Worldviews in Collision

Type: ½" videocassette and audiocassette
Length: 90 min.
Cost: $15 for videocassette; $8 for audiocassette
Date: 1994
Source: Ligonier Ministries
P.O. Box 547500
Orlando, FL 32854
(800) 435-4343

R. C. Sproul examines three worldviews in western culture: the classical/biblical perspective, the Enlightenment viewpoint, and post-Christian secularism. Sproul claims that secularism is now dominant and offers Christians advice for an effective defense of the Christian worldview.

Biblical Hermeneutics
Type: ½" videocassette
Length: 30 min.
Cost: $35
Date: 1995
Source: Bible-Science Association, Inc.
           P.O. Box 33220
           Minneapolis, MN 55433-0220
           (800) 422-4253

In this second program on the third video of the *Origins* series, Bob Walsh explains the basics of biblical interpretation from a creationist perspective. He answers charges that the Bible is not relevant to a scientific society. The first program on the tape is *New Age Movement*.

Billy Graham: The Road to Armageddon
Type: ½" videocassette
Length: 47 min.
Cost: $29.95
Date: 1990
Source: Republic Pictures Home Video
           12636 Beatrice Street
           Los Angeles, CA 90036-0930
           (213) 306-4040

In this presentation on contemporary society, the famous evangelist discusses signs of the coming conflagration predicted in the Bible.

Billy James Hargis' 90-Minute Video Tape Alert
Length: 90 min.
Cost: Contribution
Date: 1995
Source: Dr. Billy James Hargis
           Christian Crusade Newspaper
           P.O. Box 279
           Neosho, MO 64850-9987

A new tape under this title is available each month to those who contribute at least $15.00 to the *Christian Crusade Newspaper*. Each tape comments on contemporary national and international events from a religious right perspective.

Christian Crusade Homecoming, 1994
Type: ½" videocassette and audiocassette
Length: 90 min. per tape
Cost: $100 for 12 videocassettes
$80 for 12 audiocassettes
Date: 1994
Source: Christian Crusade
P.O. Box 279
Neosho, MO 64850

These tapes, which can be purchased separately for $15.00 each, provide a record of the Christian Crusade Homecoming event. The tapes include presentations on such topics as world government (Tape 3), evolution (Tape 6), the environmental movement (Tape 8), and "Bill and Hillary's New, False Religion" (Tape 11). Billy James Hargis presents his "State of the Union Address" and speech on the state of communism (Tape 10).

Christians in Action
Type: ½" videocassette
Length: 20 min.
Cost: Distributed free of charge to ministers during the fall 1994 election campaign
Date: 1994
Source: Christians in Action
P.O. Box 590441
Houston, TX 77259-9998

Tim LaHaye presents reasons why Christians should vote in the upcoming election, describing the political landscape over the last two decades. Prominent local ministers offer their encouragement.

Clinton's Circle of Power
Type: ½" videocassette
Length: 120 min.
Cost: $43
Date: 1994
Source: Liberty University
Lynchburg, VA 24506-8001

This controversial tape that Jerry Falwell promoted on his *Old Time Gospel Hour* program includes interviews with Gennifer Flowers, who claimed to have had an affair with President Clinton, and Paula Jones, who has charged President Clinton with sexual harassment. The tape also suggests that the president was involved in killings in Arkansas as well as in the death of White House deputy counsel Vincent Foster.

Creation and Psychology!
Type: ½" videocassette
Length: 30 min.
Cost: $35
Date: 1995
Source: Bible-Science Association
           P.O. Box 33220
           Minneapolis, MN 55433-0220
           (600) 422-4253

In this second program on the second tape of the *Origins* series, Paul Ackerman explains the relationship between creation and psychology, examines the biblical view of the mind, and determines whether a person can be a faithful Christian and also a psychologist. The first program on this tape is *Has the Human Body Been Designed?*

Creation and the Last Days
Type: ½" videocassette
Length: 52 minutes
Cost: $14.95
Date: 1994
Source: Bible-Science Association
           P.O. Box 33220
           Minneapolis, MN 55433-0220
           (800) 422-4253

Ken Ham argues for creationism and against evolution. He indicates that people in the "last days" will deny any evidence of biblical creation and the flood.

Creation and the Supreme Court
Type: audiocassette
Length: 120 min.
Cost: $10.00 for two tapes

Source: Reasons to Believe
P.O. Box 5978
Pasadena, CA 91117
(818) 335-1480

Dr. Hugh Ross discusses the 1987 U.S. Supreme Court decision on the teaching of creationism in public schools, explores the history of creation science, and suggests a way to present creationism appropriately in the classroom.

Darwinism on Trial
Type: ½" videocassette
Length: 120 min.
Cost: $30.00
Source: Reasons to Believe
P.O. Box 5978
Pasadena, CA 91117
(818) 335-1480

This video version of Phillip Johnson's book *Darwin on Trial* calls for rethinking Darwinism because many issues have not been resolved. Johnson suggests the possibility that Darwin's theory may be incorrect.

Dawn's Early Light
Type: ½" videocassette
Length: 28 min.
Cost: $19.95
Date: 1994
Source: American Portrait Films, Inc.
P.O. Box 19266
Cleveland, OH 44119
(216) 531-8600

This tape provides a history of the development of liberty in America and examines the major events leading to the founding of America in order to rediscover the heritage of the nation.

A Distant Thunder
Type: ½" videocassette
Length: 77 min.
Cost: $39.95
Date: 1986

Source: Russ Doughten Films, Inc.
             5907 Meredith Drive
             Des Moines, IA 50322
             (800) 247-3456

This sequel to *A Thief in the Night* continues the dramatization of the end times following the rapture. Evil continues to increase as people are given the choice of receiving "the mark" of the beast prophesied in Revelation or suffering death.

Education and the Founding Fathers

Type: ½" videocassette
Length: 60 min.
Cost: $20
Date: 1993
Source: Wallbuilders
             P.O. Box 397
             Aledo, TX 76008
             (817) 441-6044

Arguing against the "revisionists" who deny the importance of the Christian religion to education, David Barton emphasizes the educational works of founders such as George Washington, Gouverneur Morris, and Fisher Ames, who upheld biblical teaching. Barton refers to the original textbooks and writings of the founders to prove his claim.

Election '94: We Have One Chance Left To Save America's Christian Republic

Type: ½" videocassette
Length: 60 minutes
Cost: $20.00
Date: 1995
Source: Rose of Sharon Tapes
             P.O. Box 279
             Neosho, MO 64850

Billy James Hargis gives a rundown of the November 1994 election results, viewing them as an indication that Christians are becoming more active politically. Hargis, however, warns about future attacks on Christians by socialists and "extreme liberals."

End of the Cold War
Type: ½" videocassette
Length: 30 min.
Cost: $19.95
Date: 1994
Source: American Portrait Films
            P.O. Box 19266
            Cleveland, OH
            (216) 531-8600

Combining elements of scripture and economics, Baptist Pastor Sherman Smith investigates the end of the Cold War and its significance for the church.

End-Times Prophecy
Type: audiocassette
Length: 60 min. per tape
Cost: $36.00 for eight tapes
Source: Reasons to Believe
            P.O. Box 5978
            Pasadena, CA 91117
            (818) 335-1480

The tapes contain lectures by Dr. Hugh Ross on the fulfillment of biblical prophecy in the current world and on prophecies yet to be fulfilled. Each of the four topics are also available separately on two-tape sets for $10.00 each: "Signs of the End," "Israel, A Modern Miracle," "The Rapture Promise," and "Tribulation Dooms."

The Evidence for Creation: Examining the Origin of Planet Earth
Type: ½" videocassette
Length: 60 min.
Cost: $9.95
Date: 1994
Source: Christian Book Distributors
            P.O. Box 7000
            Peabody, MA 01961-7000
            (508) 977-5000

Roger Oakland asserts the logic of creationism, maintaining that evidence derived from observations of the galaxy as well as rock formations on earth support the creationist theory of the origin of the earth.

Environmental Agenda
Type: ½" videocassette and audiocassette
Length: 50 min.
Cost: $20 for videocassette; $6 for audiocassette
Date: 1992
Source: John Hagee Ministries
                  P.O. Box 1400
                  San Antonio, TX 78295-1400
                  (210) 494-3900

After initially stating that he supports action to preserve the environment, John Hagee launches into an attack on the environmental movement, which he describes as dominated by the political left, the occult, the "New World crowd," and the New Age movement. The environmental "crisis" is depicted as a fabrication. God is assumed to have the environment under control without the help of the environmental movement.

The Evolution Conspiracy
Type: ½" videocassette
Length: 48 minutes.
Cost: $19.95
Date: 1989
Source: Bible-Science Association, Inc.
                  P.O. Box 33220
                  Minneapolis, MN 55433-0220
                  (800) 422-4253

This program claims that evolution theory, far from being scientific fact, suffers from many inconsistencies. The ultimate purpose of the tape is to provide scientific facts that support biblical creation and hence to strengthen Christians' belief in a Creator.

Evolution: Fact or Fiction
Type: ½" videocassette
Length: 61 min.
Cost: $9.95
Date: 1994
Source: Christian Book Distributors

P.O. Box 7000
Peabody, MA 01961-7000
(508) 977-5000

Roger Oakland examines the theory of evolution, discounting it as a plausible explanation for the origin of humankind. On the basis of available evidence, Oakland concludes that evolution is subject to serious challenge.

Evolution: Science or Religion?
Type: ½" videocassette
Length: 30 min.
Cost: $35
Date: 1995
Source: Bible-Science Association, Inc.
           P.O. Box 33220
           Minneapolis, MN 55433-0220
           (800) 422-4253

This program appears on the first tape in the *Origins* series, along with *Lessons from a Thunderstorm.* In the evolution program, Luther Sunderland deals with the definition of science, how creation and evolution can be taught in the public schools, Darwin's contributions to science, and the impact of evolution on theology.

Explaining Inerrancy
Type: ½" videocassette
Length: 300 min.
Cost: $129
Date: 1989
Source: Ligonier Ministries
           P.O. Box 7500
           Orlando, FL 32854
           (800) 435-4343

This program presents an extended examination of the doctrine that the Bible is without error.

False Gods of Our Time
Type: ½" videocassette
Length: 100 min.
Date: 1989
Cost: $19.95

Source: Jeremiah Films
            P.O. Box 1710
            Hemet, CA 92343
            (800) 828-2290

The tape offers a fundamentalist view of today's "false gods": the New Age movement, the occult, evolution, humanism, and atheism. Christian theologian Dr. Norman Geisler narrates the presentation.

The Feminist Movement
Type: ½" videocassette and audiocassette
Length: 50 min.
Cost: $20 for videocassette; $6 for audiocassette
Date: 1992
Source: John Hagee Ministries
            P.O. Box 1400
            San Antonio, TX 78295-1400
            (210) 494-3900

Although John Hagee states that he supports such women's issues as equal pay and protection from sexual harassment, he attacks the so-called feminist war on America, asserting that the feminist movement is associated with pagan beliefs. Hagee focuses on the biblical notion that women should be submissive to their husbands.

Fingerprints of Creation
Type: ½" videocassette
Length: 34 min.
Cost: $19.95
Date: 1994
Source: American Portrait Films, Inc.
            P.O. Box 19266
            Cleveland, OH 44119
            (216) 531-8600

Dr. Robert Gantry argues that polonium radio halos are scientific proof that the earth was formed in just a few thousand rather than millions of years. Hence, these halos provide support for creationism.

Foundations of American Government
Type: ½" videocassette

Length: 60 min.
Cost: $20
Date: 1993
Source: Wallbuilders
P.O. Box 397
Aledo, TX 76008
(817) 441-6044

David Barton discusses the biblical principles that once influenced American government and points to contemporary religious right and conservative political leaders who are striving to reintroduce those principles.

Gay Rights/Special Rights
Type: ½" videocassette
Length: 45 min.
Cost: $19.95
Date: 1994
Source: Jeremiah Films
P.O. Box 1710
Hemet, CA 925456
(800) 828-2290

This tape provides a conservative Christian view of what is considered the "homosexual agenda." The observation is made that homosexuals wish to amend the 1964 Civil Rights Act to make sexual preference a right guaranteed under the Constitution.

The Genesis Quandary: Why Two Creation Accounts and Other Puzzles
Type: audiocassette
Length: 40 min.
Cost: $3.50
Date: 1994
Source: Reasons to Believe
P.O. Box 5978
Pasadena, CA 91117
(818) 335-1480

In this tape, Dr. Hugh Ross examines the two creation stories of Genesis, explaining why the book contains two creation accounts. Among the subjects addressed are questions about fossil records and cave men.

Get Out the Vote: 20% More in '94

Type: audiocassette
Length: 25 min.
Cost: Distributed free of charge to pastors
Date: 1994
Source: Family Life Ministries
            370 L'Enfant Promenade SW, Suite 801
            Washington, D.C. 20024
            (409) 246-2885

On this tape, produced for Christian pastors, Tim LaHaye presents a litany of social evils that concern the religious right (school prayer, abortion, sex education, pornography, homosexuality, and organized crime). He calls on pastors to assist in increasing the Christian vote in the November 1994 election in order to throw "liberal secularizers" out of government and to repeal their secularist policies.

God and Government

Type: audiocassette
Length: eight tapes, 60 min. each
Cost: $39.50
Date: 1986
Source: American Vision Press
            P.O. Box 720515
            Atlanta, GA 30328

This tape series provides an excellent view of the conservative Christian position on the purpose of government, the relationship between the church and governments at the national and local levels, and such issues as education, welfare, taxation, and foreign policy.

Gods of the New Age

Type: ½" videocassette
Length: 103 min.
Cost: $19.95
Date: 1988
Source: Jeremiah Films
            P.O. Box 1710
            Hemet, CA 92546
            (800) 828-2290

This Christian fundamentalist examination of the New Age movement points to the dangers of the movement to society. The New Age movement's origins in such sources as eastern mysticism are examined. The tape includes a critical view of the theory of reincarnation.

God's Power and Scripture's Authority
Type: ½" videocassette
Length: 49 minutes
Cost: $24.95
Date: 1994
Source: Bible-Science Association, Inc.
P.O. Box 33220
Minneapolis, MN 55433-0220
(800) 422-4253

Dr. Walter T. Brown, Jr., uses examples from biology, astronomy, and earth science in an attempt to demonstrate that the earth is young and that evolution is impossible. He answers questions about the biblical flood.

God's Providence in History
Type: ½" videocassette
Length: 59 min. Beta, VHS
Cost: $24.95
Date: 1989
Source: Bob Jones University Press
Greenville, SC 29614
(803) 242-5100

Old Testament history is examined in the context of contemporary events. The tape makes the case for the Bible's relevance to modern times.

The Guiding Hand
Type: ½" videocassette
Length: 21 min.
Cost: $19.95
Date: 1994
Source: American Portrait Films, Inc.
P.O. Box 19266
Cleveland, OH 44119
(216) 531-8600

This anti-Clinton film investigates the former Arkansas governor's outcome-based education program in that state. The tape associates President Clinton's education program with homosexuality, abortion, eastern philosophy, socialism, and communism.

The Hard Truth
Type: ½" videocassette
Length: 9.5 min.
Cost: $15
Date: 1992
Source: Christian Research Institute International
             P.O. Box 500
             San Juan Capistrano, CA 92693-0500
             (800) 443-9797

This video is a graphic presentation of arguments against abortion. It is presented as a useful tool against pro-choice opponents by portraying abortion as murder. A study guide accompanies the tape.

Has the Human Body Been Designed?
Type: ½" videocassette
Length: 30 min.
Cost: $35
Date: 1995
Source: Bible-Science Association, Inc.
             P.O. Box 33220
             Minneapolis, MN 55433-0220
             (800) 422-4253

In this first program on the second videotape of the *Origins* series (second program: *Creation and Psychology!*), John Meyer, professor of science at Baptist Bible College, examines the complex structures of the brain and the heart from a creationist perspective.

Homosexuality: Alternative or Abomination
Type: ½" videocassette and audiocassette
Length: 50 min.
Cost: $20 for videocassette; $6 for audiocassette
Date: 1992
Source: John Hagee Ministries
             P.O. Box 1400
             San Antonio, TX 78295-1400
             (210) 494-3900

John Hagee presents a religious right position on homosexuality, arguing that the Bible declares it a sin against God. Much of the presentation focuses on the spread of AIDS.

How Should We Then Live?
Type: ½" audiocassette
Length: 360 min. for three cassettes
Cost: $79.95
Date: 1978
Source: Christian Book Distributors
        P.O. Box 6000
        Peabody, MA 01961-6000
        (508) 977-5000

This series features the conservative Christian thinker Francis Schaeffer. Each of 12 half-hour programs treats a historical era and offers biblical answers to contemporary problems. A study guide accompanies three videotapes.

Image of the Beast
Type: ½" videocassette
Length: 90 min.
Cost: $39.95
Date: 1986
Source: Russ Doughten Films, Inc.
        5907 Meredith Drive
        Des Moines, IA 50322
        (800) 247-3456

In this sequel to *A Thief in the Night* and *A Distant Thunder,* a small group of people is portrayed trying to survive the prophesied end-time events known as the Great Tribulation.

In God They Trusted
Type: ½" videocassette
Length: 30 min.
Cost: $19.95
Date: 1984
Source: American Portrait Films, Inc.
        P.O. Box 19266
        Cleveland, OH 44119
        (216) 531-8600

This tape emphasizes the spiritual aspects of the founding and development of America. Episodes include the Pilgrims, the Declaration of Independence, Washington and Valley Forge, the Constitutional Convention, and Lincoln and the Civil War.

Is Science Religious?

Type: audiocassette
Length: 60 min.
Cost: $5
Date: 1994
Source: Reasons to Believe
            P.O. Box 5978
            Pasadena, CA 91117
            (818) 335-1480

Dr. Hugh Ross discusses the relationship between science and religion with Dr. Dugenie Scott, an anthropologist and head of the National Center for Science Education, an organization opposed to scientific creationism.

Israel: The Apple of God's Eye

Type: ½" videocassette and audiocassette
Length: 60 min.
Cost: $20 for videocassette; $6 audiocassette
Date: 1992
Source: John Hagee Ministries
            P.O. Box 1400
            San Antonio, TX 78295-1400
            (210) 491-5100

In line with the premillennialist interest in Israel and that nation's role in the end-times drama, John Hagee claims God will hold the United States responsible if it fails to defend Israel. Reference is made to Jewish assistance during the American Revolution to indicate that the Gentiles have been blessed through the Jewish people. Hagee uses Old Testament references to illustrate what disasters await those who persecute the Jews.

Keys to Good Government

Type: ½" videocassette
Length: 59 min.
Cost: $20
Date: 1994

Source: American Opinion Book Services
P.O. Box 8040
Appleton, WI 54913
(414) 749-3783

David Barton examines the advice for good government given by such early Americans as William Penn, Benjamin Rush, John Adams, and George Washington. Barton concludes that morality remains the key characteristic of good government.

The Last Days
Type: audiocassette
Length: six tapes, 45 min. per tape
Cost: $18
Date: 1982
Source: Ligonier Ministries
P.O. Box 7500
Orlando, FL 32854
(800) 435-4343

Various aspects of the end times are discussed, including the Rapture, the Millennium, the Antichrist, and Hell.

The Late Great Planet Earth
Type: ½" videocassette
Length: 87 min.
Cost: $9.99
Date: 1987
Source: Video Treasures
1767 Morris Avenue
Union, NJ 07083
(201) 964-5604

Orson Welles narrates this video based on Hal Lindsey's bestseller by the same name. Biblical prophecy is interpreted from a premillennial perspective in predicting future disasters for the planet.

Leadership in the John Birch Society
Type: ½" videocassette
Length: 28 min.
Cost: $15
Date: 1994

Source: American Opinion Book Services
P.O. Box 8040
Appleton, WI 54913
(414) 749-3783

Members of a local chapter of the society are portrayed in action. By describing the operation of local organization in the John Birch Society, this tape provides insight into the advantages of grass-roots political activity that has been the focus recently of many religious right organizations.

Left Behind: Where'd Everybody Go?
Type: ½" videocassette
Length: 100 min.
Cost: $19.95
Date: 1994
Source: This Week in Bible Prophecy
P.O. Box 1440
Niagara Falls, NY 14302-1440
(800) 776-7432

Beginning with a dramatization of the chaos that results after Christians are taken to heaven in the rapture, the remainder of the tape, supposedly "pre-recorded" for those left behind, gives advice for resisting the influence of the Antichrist who will rule during the seven-year period preceding Christ's thousand-year reign on earth. Noted premillennialists such as Hal Lindsey, John Ankerberg, and Zola Levitt explain their interpretation of Bible prophecy.

Liberation Theology
Type: audiocassette
Length: 90 min.
Cost: Free with contribution
Date: 1987
Source: Christian Anti-Communism Crusade
P.O. Box 890
Long Beach, CA 90801-0890
(310) 437-0941

Dr. John Whitehall, vice-president of the Christian Anti-Communism Crusade, discusses the rise of liberation theology in underdeveloped countries and explains its incompatibility with Christian beliefs.

Nations United in the End
Type: audiocassette
Length: 60 min.
Cost: $5
Date: 1994
Source: Reasons to Believe
            P.O. Box 5978
            Pasadena, CA 91117
            (818) 335-1480

On this tape, formerly titled "Iraq Aggression and End-Time Prophecy," Dr. Hugh Ross explains why coalitions among nations in the pursuit of peace are in fact the prelude to Satan's war against Christians. Ross examines the futures of Iraq, Israel, Jordan, and Lebanon on the basis of scripture.

New Age Movement
Type: ½" videocassette
Length: 30 min.
Cost: $35
Date: 1995
Source: Bible-Science Association
            P.O. Box 33220
            Minneapolis, MN 55433-0220
            (800) 422-4253

Ellen Myers, co-founder of the Creation Social Science and Humanities Society, explains that evolution predates Darwin by centuries. She explores the origins of the New Age movement and argues that biological evolution has been used to authenticate "spiritual evolution." This program is the first half of the third video in the *Origins* series, which concludes with *Biblical Hermeneutics.*

Not Mine To Deny
Type: ½" videocassette
Length: 35 min.
Cost: $49
Date: 1989

Source: Broadman
127 Ninth Avenue North
Nashville, TN 37234
(800) 251-3225

This video presents a Christian position in opposition to the right to an abortion.

Our Military under Siege

Type: ½" videocassette
Length: 30 min.
Cost: $19.95
Date: 1994
Source: American Portrait Films, Inc.
P.O. Box 19266
Cleveland, OH 44119
(216) 531-8600

This highly critical presentation of President Clinton's policy on gays in the military provides interviews with military persons who are strongly opposed to changing the policy of homosexuals in the military. The issue is presented as a choice between national security and satisfying the demands of a special interest group.

The Prodigal Planet

Type: ½" videocassette
Length: 134 min.
Cost: $39.95
Date: 1988
Source: Russ Doughten Films, Inc.
5907 Meredith Drive
Des Moines, IA 50322
(800) 247-3456

In this sequel to *A Thief in the Night, A Distant Thunder,* and *Image of the Beast,* the end-times drama continues in a world that has suffered through the devastation of nuclear warfare. A remnant of the faithful battle the Antichrist.

A Program for Responsible Citizenship

Type: ½" videocassette
Length: 30 min.

Cost: $15
Date: 1987
Source: American Opinion Book Services
            P.O. Box 8040
            Appleton, WI 54913
            (414) 749-3783

This tape presents a brief history of the John Birch Society and the policy positions and strategies of the organization. Also discussed are present government policies considered to be harmful to the nation.

A Review of Communist Progress towards the Conquest of the U.S.A.

Type: audiocassette
Length: 55 min.
Cost: Free with contribution
Date: 1985
Source: Christian Anti-Communism Crusade
            P.O. Box 890
            Long Beach, CA 90801-0890
            (310) 437-0941

This lecture by Christian Anti-Communism Crusade founder Dr. Fred C. Schwarz examines communist strategy for the conquest of America, which involves external encirclement, internal demoralization, and nuclear blackmail. The tape provides a view of the world from a conservative Christian perspective.

A Scientist Looks at Creation

Type: ½" videocassette
Length: 80 min.
Cost: $19.95
Date: 1994
Source: American Portrait Films, Inc.
            P.O. Box 19266
            Cleveland, OH 44119
            (216) 531-8600

This two-part program explaining creationism claims to show why many physicists, engineers, and astronomers have changed their minds on the debate between evolution and creation.

Sights & Sounds of Bible Conference '94

Type: ½" videocassette and audiocassette
Length: 90 min. per tape
Cost: $125 for 13 videocassettes; $15.00 per tape
         $100 for 13 audiocassettes; $10 per tape
Date: 1994
Source: Christian Crusade
         P.O. Box 279
         Neosho, MO 64850

Among the lectures included are Keith Wilkerson's "Christians Can Fight Back" (Tape C), Charles Secrest's "America: Turn Back to God" (Tape F), Billy James Hargis's "Russia Talks Peace, Plans War" (Tape H), and Carl Teel's "What the Bible Says about Welfare" (Tape J).

The Silent Scream

Type: ½" videocassette
Length: 30 min.
Cost: $19.95
Date: 1977
Source: American Portrait Films, Inc.
         P.O. Box 19266
         Cleveland, OH 44119
         (216) 531-8600

This early and very emotional antiabortion video claims to provide evidence of the humanity of the fetus. An abortion in the first trimester is depicted, with Dr. Bernard Nathanson narrating.

The Spirit of the American Revolution

Type: ½" videocassette
Length: 55 min.
Cost: $20
Source: Wallbuilders
         P.O. Box 397
         Aledo, TX 76008
         (817) 441-6044

David Barton discusses the importance of the Christian faith to the colonists during the American Revolution. Barton refers to the faith of prominent Americans at the time, such as John Adams, George Washington, Samuel Adams, and Patrick Henry, and focuses on the role they saw God playing in the course of the Revolution. God is portrayed as an unqualified supporter of the American revolutionaries.

The Story of America's Liberty
Type: ½" videocassette
Length: 65 min.
Cost: $19.95
Date: 1994
Source: American Portrait Films, Inc.
             P.O. Box 19266
             Cleveland, OH 44119
             (216) 531-8600

This treatment of America's Christian heritage focuses on the alleged miracles that God performed in assisting the American birth.

Test of Faith
Type: ½" videocassette
Length: 55 min.
Cost: $29.95
Date: 1989
Source: Russ Doughten Films, Inc.
             5907 Meredith Drive
             Des Moines, IA 50322
             (800) 247-3456

A physics professor, claiming that faith is an enemy of science, pressures a young college student to abandon his belief in biblical creation and to concentrate instead on scientific thinking. The tape ultimately points to the errors in the professor's position.

Thief in the Night
Type: ½" videocassette
Length: 69 min.
Cost: $39.95
Date: 1986
Source: Russ Doughten Films, Inc.
             5907 Meredith Drive
             Des Moines, IA 50322
             (800) 247-3456

This first video in a series that presents a premillennial vision of the end times dramatizes the rapture. A wife wakes up one morning to discover that her husband and millions of others have disappeared. The other entries in the series are *A Distant Thunder*, *Image of the Beast*, and *The Prodigal Planet*.

The Universe: Accident or Design?

Type: ½" color videocassette
Length: 60 minutes
Cost: $19.00
Source: Reasons to Believe
            P.O. Box 5978
            Pasadena, CA 91117
            (818) 335-1480

Dr. David Block, director of the religious right organization Reasons to Believe South Africa, presents slides and graphs to demonstrate the wonder of the universe and the awesomeness of its Creator.

Why Communism Kills

Type: audiocassette
Length: 50 min.
Cost: Free with contribution
Date: 1984
Source: Christian Anti-Communism Crusade
            P.O. Box 890
            Long Beach, CA 90801-0890
            (310) 437-0941

In his answer to the title question, Fred Schwarz, founder of the Christian Anti-Communism Crusade, discusses the Marxist rejection of the spirituality of human beings. This rejection leads to the death of the soul as well as the body. Schwarz illustrates his argument with the events in Cambodia under the Khmer Rouge.

Why the Communists Want To Conquer the U.S.A.

Type: audiocassette
Length: 90 min.
Cost: Free with contribution
Date: 1983

Source: Christian Anti-Communism Crusade
P.O. Box 890
Long Beach, CA 90801-0890
(310) 437-0941

Dr. Fred Schwarz, founder of CACC, answers the title question by stating that communists want to remake humankind. He claims that communism is "Satan's substitute for the regeneration of Christ," as evidenced by its three basic characteristics: atheism, materialism, and economic determinism.

Audio and Video Tapes about the Religious Right

This section provides three types of sources on the religious right. The first analyzes the characteristics of religion and the religious right; the second deals with issues of concern to the religious right from an alternative perspective; and the third presents a critical treatment of religious right positions and activities.

Religion and the Religious Right

The Battle for the Bible
Type: ½" videocassette
Length: 60 min.
Cost: $89.95
Date: 1992
Source: Films for the Humanities and Sciences
P.O. Box 2053
Princeton, NJ 08543-2053
(800) 257-5126
FAX (609) 275-3767

This second video in the Bill Moyers series *God and Politics* deals with the liberal-conservative conflict within the Southern Baptist Convention. Fundamentalists have wrested control of the convention from moderates and ultimately want to affect American politics.

In the Name of God
Type: ½" videocassette
Length: 50 min.
Cost: $19.95
Date: 1995
Source: ABC, Inc.
             77 West 66th Street
             New York, NY 10023
             (800) 222-7500

Originally an *ABC News* special presentation narrated by Peter Jennings, this tape investigates examples of growing churches and the techniques they use to attract people. While mainline churches have been losing members, Pentecostal-oriented churches have been flourishing. Some observers voice the concern that these popular churches sacrifice basic Christian beliefs.

The Kingdom Divided
Type: ½" videocassette
Length: 90 min.
Cost: $129
Date: 1992
Source: Films for the Humanities and Sciences
             P.O. Box 2053
             Princeton, NJ 08543-2053
             (800) 257-5126

This tape, the first in the Bill Moyers series *God and Politics,* focuses on the effect that a conflict between two different interpretations of Christianity (liberation theology and evangelicalism) is having on American foreign policy in Central America.

On Earth as It Is in Heaven
Type: ½" videocassette
Length: 60 min.
Cost: $89.95
Date: 1992
Source: Films for the Humanities and Sciences
             P.O. Box 2053
             Princeton, NJ 08543-2053
             (800) 257-5126

Bill Moyers, in this third program in the *God and Politics* series, examines Christian Reconstructionism, a radical religious movement that advocates political activity to achieve a government that adheres to strict biblical standards. Moyers concludes that this movement may prove to be more significant than the religious right of the 1980s.

Praise the Lord
Type: ½" videocassette
Length: 58 min.
Cost: $300.00
Date: 1987
Source: PBS Home Video
       50 North La Cienega Boulevard, Suite 210
       Beverly Hills, CA 90211
       (213) 657-2233

PBS's *Frontline* examines the scandal at the PTL Club and the misdeeds of Jim and Tammy Bakker.

The Religious Right
Type: ½" videocassette
Length: 60 min.
Cost: $89.95
Date: 1992
Source: Films for the Humanities and Sciences
       P.O. Box 2053
       Princeton, NJ 08543-2053

Bill Moyers reports on the "National Affairs Briefing" of religious right members after the 1992 Republican National Convention. Conservative leaders such as Pat Buchanan, Oliver North, Donald Wildmon, and Phyllis Schlafly state positions on homosexuality, feminism, abortion, and the media.

Religious Right Issues

Abortion: The Moral Dilemma
Type: ½" videocassette
Length: 28 min.
Cost: $149
Date: 1995

Source: Films for the Humanities and Sciences
P.O. Box 2053
Princeton, NJ 08543-2053
(800) 257-5126

This program discusses the troubling dilemmas underlying the pro- and antiabortion positions. The Christian parents of one healthy child, having already lost two babies to a fatal inherited disease, but still wanting another child, must face the abortion option.

Faith: Talking with Peggy Noonan

Type: ½" videocassette
Length: 60 min.
Cost: $89.95
Date: 1995
Source: Films for the Humanities and Sciences
P.O. Box 2053
Princeton, NJ 08543-2053
(800) 257-5126

This thoughtful presentation examines the possible effects of expelling religion from public institutions and investigates the role that faith might still play in the public realm. Father Richard John Neuhaus, Michael Lerner, and Bill Moyers are featured.

God and the Constitution

Type: ½" videocassette
Length: 60 min.
Cost: $89.95
Date: 1994
Source: Films for the Humanities and Sciences
P.O. Box 2053
Princeton, NJ 08543-2053
(800) 257-5126

Bill Moyers hosts a discussion about the legality of school prayer with Martin Marty, professor of the history of modern Christianity at the University of Chicago, and Leonard Levy, editor of *The Encyclopedia of the American Constitution*. The participants also discuss the issues of tax exemption for religious institutions and religious symbols on public property.

Liberal Protestantism in the '90s: Forrester Church
Type: ½" videocassette
Length: 30 min.
Date: 1995
Cost: $89.95
Source: Films for the Humanities and Sciences
P.O. Box 2053
Princeton, NJ 08543-2053
(800) 257-5126

Bill Moyers, program host, and Forrester Church, pastor of All Souls Unitarian Church in New York City and son of the late Senator Frank Church, discuss the state of religion in America from a liberal Protestant perspective. Church deals with the ambiguities of his ministry and what can be learned from the variety of religious positions, including the religious right.

Religion, Politics and Our Schools
Type: ½" videocassette
Length: 90 min.
Cost: $69.95
Date: 1988
Source: American Humanist Association
7 Hardwood Drive
P.O. Box 146
Amherst, NY 14226-0146
(716) 839-5080

Seven religious leaders discuss the separation of church and state and its relevance to the public schools.

With a Vengeance: The Fight for Reproductive Freedom
Type: ½" videocassette
Length: 40 min.
Cost: $225
Date: 1990
Source: Women Make Movies
225 Lafayette Street, Suite 212
New York, NY 10012
(212) 925-0606

This video is a reaction to the religious right opposition to abortion, focusing on the reproductive rights of women. The struggles over abortion rights in the 1960s and the 1980s are compared.

Treatments Critical of the Religious Right

Blowing the Whistle on Pat Robertson
Type: ½" videocassette
Length: 60 min.
Date: 1988
Cost: $49.95
Source: American Humanist Association
            7 Hardwood Drive
            P.O. Box 146
            Amherst, NY 14226-0146
            (716) 839-5080

The former producer of Pat Robertson's *700 Club* television program provides an exposé of the televangelist and presidential candidate.

Defending the Rights of Evangelism's Victims
Type: ½" videocassette and audiocassette
Length: 120 min.
Cost: $49.95 for videocassette; $9 for audiocassette
Date: 1988
Source: American Humanist Association
            7 Hardwood Drive, P.O. Box 1188
            Amherst, NY 14226-7188
            (716) 839-5080

Richard Yao and James Luce, founders of Fundamentalists Anonymous, recount cases of religious "indoctrination" and the "deprogramming" of the "victims" of evangelism.

Facing the Fundamentalist/Vatican Challenge
Type: audiocassette
Length: 60 min.
Cost: $9
Date: 1994
Source: American Humanist Association
            7 Hardwood Drive, P.O. Box 1188
            Amherst, NY 14226-7188
            (800) 743-6646

This tape challenges humanists to respond to the religious right attack on fundamental freedoms. Ed Doerr argues that humanists must face the challenge of Vatican opposition to birth control, abortion, and freedom of choice.

Inherit the Wind

Type: ½" black-and-white videocassette
Length: 127 min.
Date: 1960
Cost: $19.99
Source: Movies Unlimited
6736 Castro Ave.
Philadelphia, PA 19149
(800) 523-0823

This fictionalization of the 1925 Scopes trial in Dayton, Tennessee, stars Spencer Tracy and Frederick March, who play roles corresponding respectively to Clarence Darrow and William Jennings Bryan. Fundamentalism is treated in a far from favorable light.

Quality Science Education versus Creationism

Type: ½" videocassette and audiocassette
Length: 60 min.
Cost: $49.95 for videocassette; $9 for audiocassette
Date: 1988
Source: American Humanist Association
7 Hardwood Drive, P.O. Box 1188
Amherst, NY 14226-7188
(800) 743-6646

Laurie Godfrey, John R. Cole, Ronnie Hastings, and Steven Schafersma, Humanist Contributions to Science Award recipients, present scientific evidence in support of evolution and sometimes humorous arguments against creationism.

Sources of Power for the Religious Right

Type: audiocassette
Length: 60 min.
Cost: $9
Date: 1994
Source: American Humanist Association
7 Hardwood Drive, P.O. Box 1188
Amherst, NY 14226-7188
(800) 743-6646

Russ Bellant investigates religious right organizations that attempt to evangelize America through participation in political party politics. In addition, Edd Doerr discusses separation of church and state and describes legal cases won against the religious right.

Today in America, Sex IS Politics
Type: ½" videocassette
Length: 60 min.
Cost: $49.95
Date: 1988
Source: American Humanist Association
              7 Hardwood Drive
              P.O. Box 146
              Amherst, NY 14226-0146
              (716) 839-5080

This video presents a lecture by Dr. Sol Gordon, who focuses on what he considers the absurdity of sex education from the conservative perspective.

Radio and Television Programs

Conservative religious organizations broadcast a wide variety of programs that touch on political and social issues in some way. A selection of such programs is included here. Usually these programs are syndicated and do not appear at a uniform time nationwide. Readers should check local station and cable listings to see if individual programs appear in their area.

Bible Answer Man

Hank Hanegraaf, president of the Christian Research Institute, hosts this radio program that is heard daily on over 60 radio outlets in the United States and Canada, with a claimed audience of up to 120 million listeners. Hanegraaf provides answers to listeners' questions about the Bible, presenting an orthodox Christian perspective on current issues.

Biblical Economics

John Avanzini, who hosts this brief program on Trinity Broadcasting Network on Thursdays at 8:15 p.m. (ET), offers biblical lessons for personal prosperity. Avanzini, a proponent of faith religion, argues that major biblical figures, including Jesus and the apostles, were wealthy and that Christians today should use biblical lessons to gain riches. He recommends that church members submit personal financial statements to their pastors and allow their pastors to travel first class.

Billy James Hargis Television Program

Billy James Hargis hosts this program, which appears on World Harvest and National Christian Networks, Saturday and Sunday nights. It provides a forum for Hargis and his traditional conservative Christian style of political commentary. Although not as well known nationally as he was in the 1960s, Hargis still represents a politically vocal element in the religious right.

Cornerstone with John Hagee

This fundamentalist program is telecast from John Hagee's Cornerstone Church in San Antonio, Texas, and can be seen on Trinity Broadcasting Network at 8:00 a.m. ET Sunday mornings. While not as explicitly political as other broadcasts, such as Billy James Hargis's television program and Jerry Falwell's *Old Time Gospel Hour*, Hagee often offers, with passion and without apology, the religious right position on such social issues as homosexual rights, abortion, and the women's movement. He is highly critical of the Clinton administration and the "atheists in Washington." Hagee often presents evidence from scientific authorities for his positions on social issues, but the Bible is his ultimate authority.

Creation Moments

This radio program, produced by the Bible-Science Association, Inc., is heard on 700 radio outlets in the United States and around the world. The program presents a creationist understanding of science. It presents facts about nature and demonstrates their connection to a Creator. Among the networks carrying *Creation Moments* each weekday are Moody Broadcasting System (1:40 p.m. ET) and Family Radio Network (12:30 p.m. ET). Call (800) 422-4253 for local station information.

Focus on the Family

This daily radio program hosted by Dr. James Dobson is broadcast over 1,450 stations across the country. Although not an explicitly religious program, Dobson and his guests deal with topics related to Christian family values.

Jack Van Impe Presents

Jack Van Impe and his wife Rexella host this program on Bible prophecy that appears on the Trinity Broadcasting Network on Wednesday evenings at 8:30 (CT). Employing a news and commentary format, the Van Impes highlight the biblical significance of natural disasters such as tornadoes and earthquakes and report examples of social disintegration such as increasing crime and violence, which they believe support their premillennialist beliefs.

John Ankerberg Show

Headquartered in Chattanooga, Tennessee, this syndicated evangelical Christian television program appears on the cable Family Channel (10:30 p.m. CT Sunday evenings). Hosted by John Ankerberg, the program presents defenses of orthodox evangelical Christianity against various cults and perceived heresies. Representatives of heretical groups are invited to take part in debate. The program presents conservative Christian positions on such issues as abortion and pornography.

Old-Time Gospel Hour

This program, which is seen on nearly 400 television stations and heard on 500 radio stations, features former leader of the Moral Majority, Jerry Falwell. Falwell presents his fundamentalist beliefs and offers his views in opposition to abortion, homosexual rights, pornography, and crime. He often expresses strong criticism of liberals in government.

Reasons to Believe

This television program appears on Trinity Broadcasting Network and deals with evidence for the existence of God. The basic theme of the program is that science and Christianity can be allied in the fight against secularism.

700 Club

Produced and syndicated by the Christian Broadcasting Network and hosted by Pat Robertson, this television program follows a talk and variety show format and offers news analysis from a conservative Christian perspective. Viewers are invited to call for counseling and prayer.

This Week in Bible Prophecy

This program appears on the Trinity Broadcasting Network on Thursday evenings at 7:30 (CT). Hosts Peter and Paul Lalonde discuss recent world events and scientific developments they believe are fulfillments of biblical prophecies of the end times.

CD-ROMs

Although these products do not focus directly on the religious right, they can serve as a source of information relevant to the movement.

The system requirements for the following products are an IBM PC Class 486 or compatible with at least 400 MB hard disk, floppy drive, at least 4 MB of RAM, WINDOWS 3.1 or higher, and CD-ROM. If the system includes audio and/or video capabilities, then a sound card and video card must be added to the preceding requirements. It is also recommended that there be at least 8 MB of RAM.

ALTA Religion Database on CD-ROM
Publisher: American Theological Library Association
Distributor: American Theological Library Association
820 Church St., Suite 300
Evanston, IL 60201
(708) 869-7788
Price: $1,475–$1,575
Updates: Annual

This bibliographic source includes 800,000 citations of articles from over 500 journals on such subjects as church history, history of religions, war and religion, religion and politics, religion and science, and cults and sects.

Multimedia Family Bible for Windows
Publisher: Infobases, Inc.
Distributor: Infobases, Inc.
                 1875 S. State Street, No. 3100
                 Orem, UT 84058
                 (800) 537-7823
Price: $79.95

An example of the type of biblical sources available, this Bible reference contains 44 dramatizations of stories from the King James version of the Bible. The product also contains color maps of the Mediterranean area and the Holy Land and Bible study helps, including Hebrew and Greek definitions.

Religion Indexes: RIO/RIT/IBRR CD-ROM
Publisher: American Theological Library Association
Distributor: American Theological Library Association
                 820 Church Street, Suite 300
                 Evanston, IL 60201-5603
                 (708) 869-7788
Price: $1,100

This CD-ROM contains 400,000 citations and abstracts from 1975 through 1985 for articles and other works published on the major world religions, including Christianity. Among the topics covered are war and religion, science and religion, politics and religion, and religious education.

REX (Religious Index)
Publisher: FABS International, Inc.
Distributor: FABS International, Inc.
                 120 Parkwood Drive
                 Niceville, FL 32578
                 (904) 897-1430
Price: $895 (annual subscription)
Updates: Quarterly

This bibliographic database contains abstracts for approximately 200 primarily scholarly journals that deal with subjects in religion and theology.

Diskette

Religions in America, pre-1900
Publisher: Advanced Resources, Inc.
Distributor: Advanced Resources, Inc.
144 Parish Square, Suite 144
Centerville, UT 84014
(801) 773-3238
System: IBM PC or compatible; floppy drive; MS-DOS
Price: $9.95

This product covers the history of religion in the United States up to 1900. It includes the names, brief descriptions, founders, historical growth, and interrelationship of religious organizations.

Databases

These databases, although not specifically religious right sources, can yield information relevant to the movement.

ChurchNews International
Resources for Communication (RFC)
341 Mark West Station Road
Windsor, CA 95492-9620
(707) 542-7819
Online Availability: NewsNet, Inc.
Price: $60 per connect hour for *ChurchNews Digest* subscribers; $108 per connect hour for nonsubscribers

Corresponding in part to *ChurchNews Digest* magazine, this database covers Christian church events around the world. This comparatively liberal news source covers such subjects as justice, human rights, women's issues, and corporate responsibility.

RNS Daily News Reports
Religious News Service, Inc.
Radio City Station
475 Riverside Drive, Suite 1902
New York, NY 10115
(212) 870-3440
Online Availability: NewsNet, Inc.
Price: $60 per connect hour for subscribers to
RNS Daily News Reports, $132 per connect
hour for nonsubscribers.

This news service contains the full text of news stories covering religious personalities and events worldwide from 1984 to the present. Included are analyses and reports on economic, political, and social subjects.

Electronic Mail

These discussion lists and electronic newsletters, though not all directly related to the religious right, can provide information relevant to conservative Christian positions on social and political issues.

BIBLE
Mail address: majordomo@virginia.edu
To subscribe: SUB BIBLE

This electronic conference provides a forum for those interested in Bible study and who recognize the authority of the Bible; it is not designed for professional scholars.

BIBLE STUDY GROUP (BSG)
Mail address: jim@hsf.uab.edu
To subscribe: Send a note to Jim Hill at the above address.

Assuming that participants are Christians, this discussion list deals with evidence that God exists and that Jesus Christ is the Son of God.

BSTUDY-L
Mail address: listserv@admin.humberc.on.ca
To subscribe: SUB BSTUDY-L, first and last names

This list, for those who believe that the Bible is God's word, is intended to assist members in dealing with contemporary problems.

CONCHR-L (Conservative Christian Discussion List)
Mail address: listserv@vm.temple.edu (Internet)
  listserv@templevm (Bitnet)
To subscribe: SUB CONCHR-L, first and last names

This list engages in the discussion of a variety of contemporary issues among born-again Christians.

FAMILY RESEARCH COUNCIL
Mail address: listserv@family.netcentral.net
To subscribe: SUBSCRIBE frc-list, first and last names

This list distributes Family Research Council's newsletter.

FOCUS ON THE FAMILY
Mail address: listserv@family.netcentral.net
To subscribe: SUBSCRIBE fof-list, first and last names.

This list distributes the monthly newsletter and other materials from James Dobson's Focus on the Family.

HISTEC-2
Mail address: mailserv@baylor.edu
To subscribe: SUB HISTEC-2 first and last names

This rather scholarly oriented list, for students and scholars, allows the opportunity to distribute and acquire information about evangelical Christianity and its history.

MAILJC
Mail address: mailjc@grian.cps.altadena.ca.us
To subscribe: SUB MAILJC first and last names

This list provides the opportunity for discussion among believing Christians.

THE PROLIFE INFONET MAILING LIST
Mail address: listserve@prolife.netcentral.net
To subscribe: SUBSCRIBE infonet-list, first and last names

This list distributes information from pro-life organizations at all levels and includes newsletters, announcements, and reports of legislative activity.

THE PROLIFE NEWS
Mail address: listserv@prolife.netcentral.net
To subscribe: SUBSCRIBE plnews-list, first and last names

This bimonthly newsletter is intended to inform people about the pro-life position.

THEONOMY
Mail address: server@dlhpfm.uucp
To subscribe: SUBSCRIBE THEONOMY-L, first and last names

This list promotes the relevance of biblical law to all aspects of human life.

Glossary

Antichrist A beguiling satanic figure who supposedly will wreak havoc on the earth, particularly upon Israel and the Jews, until his ultimate destruction by Jesus. At various times the Antichrist has been identified with everyone from the Catholic popes, Charles I, and George III to Napoleon, Hitler, and Saddam Hussein.

apocalypse Derived from a Greek word, apocalypse means to uncover or reveal the future, specifically regarding the Second Coming of Christ. Apocalyptic literature not only points toward the deliverance of God's people from earthly travail, but also looks beyond the end of time. For examples of such writing, see Mark 13:3–31, II Thessalonians 2:3–12, Revelation, and Daniel.

baptism of the Holy Spirit See **pentecostalism.**

born again In John 3:3–7 Jesus tells Nicodemus that he "must be born over again" in order to "see the kingdom of God." Accordingly, in contemporary parlance, a "born-again Christian" is one who allegedly has had a personal, emotional encounter with God through Jesus.

Cane Ridge Revival This was an enormous camp meeting near Lexington, Kentucky, in August 1801. Noted for its emotional excesses, such as the "jerks" and the "barks," this revival fueled the Second Awakening in the American West and gave momentum to such evangelicals as Methodists, Baptists, Cumberland Presbyterians, and, later, Disciples and Christians.

charismatic movement Characterized by emotional, ecstatic forms of worship in which speaking in tongues and faith healing are encouraged, this is a twentieth-century phenomenon. Protestants and Catholics, especially since the 1960s, have been influenced by this movement.

chiliasm See **millennialism.**

Christian reconstructionism Drawing primarily upon Genesis 1:26–28 and Matthew 28: 16–20, this movement, which apparently evolved from teachings at J. Gresham Machen's Westminster Theological Seminary, attempts to reconstruct society in accordance with God's law. Guided by the example of the seventeenth-century Puritans, who had sought to build the Massachusetts Commonwealth on biblical principles, Christian reconstructionists want to subordinate all aspects of life to God's authority. Accordingly, they encourage Christian schooling, certain that public education has been corrupted by secular humanism; condemn the modern state, convinced it has usurped the authority of God; and embrace an optimistic eschatology, persuaded of the possibility of constructive change. In pursuit of their objectives, however, Christian reconstructionists do not advocate civil disobedience.

civil religion Broadly, the term refers to the usage of transcendent religious symbols to explain national purpose and destiny. On one hand, civil religion provides a unifying set of values for Americans of all persuasions, values that inspire the pursuit of justice and equality of treatment for all people; on the other hand, when suffused with an intense nationalism where God and country become one, civil religion easily gives support to aggression abroad and intolerance at home.

creationism (scientific creationism) First enunciated in *What is Darwinism?* (1874) by Charles Hodge, a noted Presbyterian theologian at Princeton Theological Seminary, creationism is the belief that the Genesis account of the world's origin is historically true and accurate. Promoted today primarily by conservative Christians, creationism is an alternative explanation to Darwinian evolution for human origins. Although all creationists attribute creation to God, as described in the early chapters of Genesis, they differ among themselves on critical points. Those who tend to be biblical literalists insist that God created the various species, each of which reproduces its own kind, in a short span of time. Those who interpret Genesis allegorically are inclined to agree with conventional geologists regarding the earth's ancient origins. Although creationists are divided over geology, they are usually united in their opposition to Darwinian biology.

death of God theology Based upon *The Death of God* by Gabriel Vahanian, this movement gained attention in the 1960s. Arguing that many educated Americans no longer relied on God to explain phenomena once attributed to the divine, such as natural disasters and sickness, Vahanian labored to recast Christian theology without a doctrine of God.

Many conservative Christians saw this movement as just another indication of the nation's growing godlessness.

dispensational premillennialism   A theory popularized by C. I. Scofield of Dallas, Texas, in 1909. Scofield divided history into seven dispensations, or eras, each beginning with a divine covenant and ending with God's judgment. He believed humanity was nearing the end of the sixth dispensation, which would culminate in the Second Coming of Jesus, who then would preside over the world for a millennium.

dominion (kingdom) theology   Used by politically involved evangelicals, this term lends biblical sanction to efforts to Christianize the nation's political, economic, legal, educational, military, and communications institutions. Dominion theology undergirds much of Christian reconstructionism.

election (predestination)   The belief that certain people and groups have been foreordained to fulfill God's divine purposes. This view undergirds Israel's position as God's chosen people, as well as the New Testament belief of humanity's undeserved grace. Given the influence of such conservative Presbyterians as Charles Hodge, Benjamin Warfield, J. Gresham Machen, and Carl McIntire, this sentiment runs deep among many American fundamentalists.

eschatology   Derived from two Greek words, eschatology means "end" or "final." Central to eschatology, therefore, are beliefs about death, resurrection, the Second Coming, judgment, and the Kingdom of God. In both the Old and New Testaments, eschatological writers were concerned with the ultimate triumph of God over evil.

evangelical   Derived from a Greek word meaning "good news," evangelical refers to those Christians who emphasize a personal relationship to Jesus ("born again"), biblical authority in matters of faith and practice, and the necessity of sharing the gospel with others (witnessing). Since the late 1940s many conservative Christians, such as Billy Graham, have preferred to be known as evangelicals rather than fundamentalists.

faith movement   Characterized by a frank equation between godliness and materialism, the faith movement looks upon religion primarily as a means to a prosperous and healthy future. This is not startling, for traces of such sentiment are evident in the seventeenth-century Puritans. And in the late nineteenth century the Baptist minister Russell Conwell made a career of one sermon, "Acres of Diamonds," which he preached approximately 6,000 times and which was essentially an exhortation to get rich. Perhaps the only thing that sets such contemporary televangelists as Oral Roberts, Robert Tilton, Kenneth Copeland, Benny Hinn, and Frederick Price apart from a Conwell is the degree of blatancy. With slogans like "name it, claim it," "success-n-life," and "have a need, plant a seed," many of today's prominent evangelists assure listeners that prosperity goes hand in hand with faith. One has only to give (plant a seed) to receive (wealth).

fundamentalism By the 1920s the terms "fundamentalist," "evangelical," and "conservative Christian" were more or less synonymous, each referring broadly to those Christians who subscribed to the five or six basic fundamentals set forth at the Niagara Bible Conference of 1895 and in *The Fundamentals: A Testimony to the Truth* (1910–1915). But the term "fundamentalism," coined in 1920, increasingly became identified with an aggressively strident and exclusionist variety of conservative Christianity, and critics increasingly applied the term pejoratively and indiscriminately to all conservative Christians. As a result, conservative Christians such as those who founded the National Association of Evangelicals in 1942 preferred the term evangelical to fundamentalist. The difference today between a fundamentalist and an evangelical is more a matter of temperament than theology.

glossolalia (speaking in tongues) Apparently coined in the nineteenth century, glossolalia refers to the New Testament practice of "speaking in tongues." Acts 2:4 reports that on the day of Pentecost the Apostles "were all filled with the Holy Ghost and began to speak with other tongues as the Spirit gave them utterance." Christians have never been of one mind regarding this practice. Today, for instance, Pentecostal bodies, such as the Assemblies of God, encourage tongues, but the Baptist fundamentalist Jerry Falwell disapproves.

Gog, Magog Various biblical passages—Daniel 11:15, Jeremiah 1:14, Ezekiel 38, and Revelation 20:8—allude to an evil ruler, Gog, from the northern land of Magog. In the Cold War aftermath of World War II many American fundamentalists identified Russia as Magog and interpreted conflicting American and Russian interests in Israel and elsewhere in the Middle East in light of biblical prophecy. Such views influenced former President Ronald Reagan.

heterodoxy (heresy) Departure from established beliefs and traditions. For fundamentalists, for instance, the denial of such things as the virgin birth and resurrection of Jesus would be heterodoxy.

higher criticism This is a scientific examination of biblical texts, attempting to determine authorship, date of composition, and place of origin. Higher critics study such questions as, Did Moses write all of the Pentateuch? and Was there a second Isaiah? To many conservative Christians from the nineteenth century to the present, this kind of scrutiny undermines the veracity of the scriptures.

Identity Christianity Based upon the belief that white Anglo-Saxons are God's chosen people and that Jews and all other nonwhites are a subspecies of humanity, Identity Christianity unites such white-supremacist groups as the Ku Klux Klan and Aryan Nations.

imminency The belief that the Second Coming could occur at any moment. This idea fuels much of the millennial speculation regarding the end of time.

inerrancy A belief common among many Protestants since the latter nineteenth century that the Bible is without error in its "original autographs" with regard to history, science, and accounts of its literary origins. A remarkable similarity exists between Presbyterian inerrantists Charles Hodge and Benjamin Warfield of the 1880s and Southern Baptist inerrantists of the 1980s. For both, the Bible would be an unreliable guide on matters of salvation and humanity's relationship to God if it were known to be in error on matters of history and science. Inerrantists do concede that scribal errors have over time slipped into existing biblical texts.

lower criticism A scientific examination of biblical texts, lower criticism seeks to ascertain the actual words of a manuscript as it was originally written by the author; or, slightly differently, to determine how accurately existing translations reflect what was said or written. This kind of study poses no serious problem for conservative Christians, for they too are concerned about the accuracy of existing biblical texts and translations. Insisting that the Bible is inerrant in its "original autographs," conservative Christians concede that scribal errors and discrepancies have slipped into the texts over time.

mark of the beast Quite similar to Daniel 7:2–8, Revelation 13:1–18 describes a beast, or an Antichrist, that rivals Jesus in the final days and ascribes to it the number "666." The followers of the beast were to be branded on either the right hand or the forehead with the triple six.

millennialism This refers to a 1,000-year period in which the kingdom of God will prevail. Christians are usually divided over whether the Second Coming of Jesus will occur before (premillennialists) or after (postmillennialists) the 1,000-year reign. Millennial expectations are fueled by the apocalyptic portion of the Bible, especially Revelation, and groups such as the Seventh-Day Adventists and Jehovah's Witnesses reflect the influence of millennial ideas.

modernism Although many conservative Christians by the 1920s used modernism loosely to cover a multitude of alleged "sins," scholars usually use the term more precisely to mean the adjustment of religious ideas to contemporary culture, the immanence of God in human development, and the belief that history is evolving toward the Kingdom of God. As this suggests, modernism is an optimistic view, one at sharp odds with the conservative Christian emphasis upon original sin and human depravity.

natural theology Broadly, the belief that God can be fathomed by reason alone without the need of scripture or revelation. For instance, subscribers to this view would argue that the order of nature, as well as purposeful human existence, afford rational evidence of an intelligent Creator. This attempt at human self-sufficiency disturbs many Christian thinkers who believe that God is more than can be grasped by reason alone. To many Christians, the God of natural theology is little more than a projected image of humanity, a God limited by the human senses.

New Age Movement Drawing upon both eastern and western religious traditions, this phenomenon gained momentum in the 1980s. Its adherents subscribe to an eclectic assortment of beliefs and practices, such as reincarnation, astral projection, astrology, extraterrestrial life, astrology, immortality of the soul, miracles, angels, and yoga.

original autographs This refers to the original biblical manuscripts that were untainted by scribal errors. Although these texts do not exist, inerrantists in the tradition of Charles Hodge, Benjamin Warfield, and J. Gresham Machen contend the Bible cannot be proven to be in error unless the discrepancy exists in the original autographs, which, of course, are unavailable for scrutiny.

original sin Based primarily upon the creation story and the fall of Adam and Eve from grace in the opening chapters of Genesis, this is the Christian doctrine of flawed humanity.

orthodoxy Derived from the Greek words *orthos*, "correct," and *doxa*, "opinion," orthodoxy refers to "correct" or "right" beliefs.

pentecostalism Drawing upon Acts 1:1–5 and 2:4–21, modern pentecostalism stresses those gifts resulting from "baptism in the Holy Spirit," such as glossolalia, prophecy, healing, and exorcism. Historically, contemporary pentecostalism emerged from the Holiness tradition within Methodism and the Asuza Street revival in Los Angeles, California, in 1906. Whereas its early adherents were largely poor and disinherited, Pentecostals have become increasingly middle class. The Assemblies of God, Jimmy Swaggart's denomination, is the largest Pentecostal body in the United States today.

postmillennialism The belief that steadily improving world conditions will culminate in the Second Coming. By this interpretation, Jesus will return after a millennium of human progress. This optimistic viewpoint not only reinforced the reform efforts of liberal social gospel ministers in the late nineteenth and early twentieth centuries, but also undergirds the labors of contemporary Christian reconstructionists.

premillennialism The belief that steadily deteriorating world conditions (wars and rumors of wars) will precede the Second Coming, at which time Jesus will establish a 1,000-year reign. Thus, Jesus will return before the millennium. This viewpoint is generally more harmonious with a conservative, pessimistic assessment of contemporary world conditions.

pro-life (right to life) movement Originating among Roman Catholics, this movement today embraces Catholics, Protestants, and other groups opposed to abortion. The Supreme Court's decision in *Roe v. Wade* (1973), which legalized abortion during the first two trimesters of pregnancy, gave impetus to the movement.

prophecy Derived from a Greek word meaning one who speaks for another, prophecy supposedly is an expression of divine will. Unlike apocalyptic literature, however, which forecasts the end of time, prophetic literature is present-minded, predicting dire consequences in this life if "God's people" persist in their wicked ways. Examples of the prophetic tradition among the ancient Hebrews are Amos, Joel, Isaiah, Jeremiah, Ezekiel, and Elijah.

rapture Refers to that moment when Christ supposedly will come to resurrect the righteous who have already died and to remove, or harvest, the righteous who are still alive. This action will leave the forces of evil in complete control of the earth for seven years, the period of the "great tribulation." In both literature and art, many contemporary Christians portray a world in chaos after the rapture.

revivalism Refers to a reawakening or quickening of the divine spirit, an awakening sometimes accompanied by emotional fervor. Scholars usually trace the phenomenon from Solomon Stoddard, Jonathan Edwards, and George Whitefield to James McGready, Barton Stone, and Charles G. Finney. The Great Awakening (1720s–1740s) swept the eastern seaboard, while the Second Awakening (1790s–1830s) carried the gospel via emotional camp meetings across the western frontier. Methodists, Baptists, Cumberland Presbyterians, and Disciples prospered during this second wave of revivalism. Of particular interest to scholars have been the techniques of revivalism, with debate sometimes centering on whether revivals are "sent down" by God or "worked up" by more human methods.

schism Refers to a factious division, or split, of a religious body. Although sometimes used synonymously, schism and heresy are not the same. Heresy always involves doctrinal matters, whereas schism results primarily from disputes over authority and organizational structure.

Scofield Reference Bible Published in 1909 by Oxford University Press, this perhaps has been the most influential source of dispensational premillennial teachings for American Protestants. Annotated by Cyrus I. Scofield, a lawyer-turned-Congregational preacher, it was originally meant to be a portable reference for missionaries. Since Scofield's commentaries appeared on the same page as the biblical text, it was easy for readers to forget whether a particular idea came from Scofield or the Bible. By 1967, when a revision was released, at least five million copies had been sold.

secular humanism The belief that humans, relying upon reason and acting independently of God, are sufficient unto themselves. Some intellectual spokesmen for the religious right, such as Francis Schaeffer, trace this human-centered view from the Greeks through the Renaissance to the Enlightenment. An alleged consequence of this outlook is the replacement of God-centered absolutes with moral relativism. Much like "modernism" in the 1920s, secular humanism today has become for the religious right a popular catchall for practically all social ills.

situation ethics Coined in 1959 by Joseph Fletcher, situation ethics was a pragmatic and relativistic method for making moral judgments. It aroused the ire of many conservative Christians, implying as it did an abandonment of absolute standards of morality.

social gospel A movement that emerged among more liberal Protestants in the late nineteenth century and reached its peak in the optimistic years preceding World War I. Convinced that the gospel message was social as well as personal, ministers such as Washington Gladden and Walter Rauschenbusch sought to focus the attention of the churches on social ills spawned by industrialization and urbanization. Many conservative Christians objected to the social gospel, believing its social emphasis detracted from the primary responsiblity to individuals.

theonomy Coined by Cornelius Van Til of Westminster Theological Seminary, theonomy, derived from two Greek words, *theos* (God) and *nomos* (law), is submission to God's law. As such, it is an argument for Christian reconstructionism, one steeped in Calvinistic influences. To Van Til, God's elect could grasp divine laws and live accordingly, while those who relied on human judgment, or autonomy, lived in darkness. Broadly, theonomy holds that Old Testament law differentiates between right and wrong and, therefore, should be the basis for modern society.

Index

Glenn H. Utter, professor and chair of the Political Science Department at Lamar University, was educated at Binghamton University, the University of Buffalo, and the University of London. Utter specializes in modern political theory and American political thought. He co-edited *American Political Scientists: A Dictionary* (1993) and has written a number of articles for political science journals.

John W. Storey, educated at Lamar University, Baylor University, and the University of Kentucky, is a specialist in southern religious history. His writings have appeared in numerous scholarly publications, and his study of Texas Baptists and social Christianity won the Texas Baptist Historical Society's Church History Award (1987). He is currently professor and chair of the History Department at Lamar University.